# NO ADVANTAGE GIVEN

## THE INCOMPLETE HISTORY OF U.S. WOMEN'S RUGBY, 1972-2026

20 *Years* USWRF
Growing Women's Rugby

**No Advantage Given: The Incomplete History of U.S. Women's Rugby, 1972-2026**
Copyright © 2026 United States Women's Rugby Foundation

Produced and printed by Stillwater River Publications.
Visit our website at www.StillwaterPress.com for more information.

First Stillwater River Publications Edition

ISBN: 978-1-968548-19-3

Library of Congress Control Number: 2025927166

1 2 3 4 5 6 7 8 9 10
Written by Kerri Heffernan.
Photographs provided by the United States Women's Rugby Foundation.
Cover photograph by Bill English.
Cover design by Elisha Gillette.
Interior book design by Elisha Gillette and Matthew St. Jean.
Published by Stillwater River Publications, West Warwick, RI, USA.

Publisher's Cataloging-in-Publication
(Provided by Cassidy Cataloguing Services, Inc.)
Names: Heffernan, Kerrissa, author. | United States Women's Rugby Foundation,
sponsoring body.
Title: No advantage given : the incomplete history of U.S. women's rugby, 1972-
2026 / written by Kerri Heffernan.
Description: First Stillwater River Publications edition. | West Warwick, RI, USA :
Stillwater River Publications, [2026] | "20 years, USWRF: growing women's rugby."
Identifiers: LCCN 2025927166 | ISBN 9781968548193 (paperback)
Subjects: LCSH: Rugby football for women—United States—History. | Sports for
women—United States—History.
Classification: LCC: GV944.85 .H44 2026 | DDC: 796.333082—dc23

# CONTENTS

# INTRODUCTION

———

**T**HE U.S. NATIONAL RUGBY TEAM IS KNOWN as the Eagles. Every player who takes the field in an international match earns a "cap" and a number marking their place in the long line of those who have represented our country. I was on the first women's national team in 1987 and am proud to be Eagle #7. I didn't think much about that designation at the time—and for many years afterward.

Then, just weeks before the 2025 World Cup, I found myself in Washington, D.C., watching the U.S. women's team face Fiji. I didn't know, Talia Brody—Eagle #307—personally, but as I watched them play, I felt a deep kinship. Decades may separate us, yet I felt invisible rugby threads that connected us across generations.

The founders of women's rugby were young—mostly college students—without a roadmap for building a sporting movement. So, they did what rugby players do: they forged ahead, making the road as they walked. The incredible play and packed stands at the 2025 World Cup in England show just how far that road has taken us. This book seeks to tell the story of that journey—the hills, valleys, and potholes along the way.

In 2018, with the support of the United States Women's Rugby Foundation, I launched the Women's Rugby History Project. Since then, I've gathered enough material to fill a storage unit: original jerseys and Olympic uniforms, photos, films, trophies, newsletters, signed balls, and boxes of meeting notes and memorabilia. My Google Drive "runneth over" with digitized photos, magazines, videos, and documents.

With the USWRF Board's support, we built a pop-up history museum and took it on the road to rugby tournaments for three years. The collection has grown so large that now it's exhibited just once a year—at our annual USWRF conference. Touring the museum can be an emotional experience, especially for young players. I've seen many moved to tears when they realize they are part of a storied, decades-long legacy. They walk away inspired—proud to know they belong to a bold, vibrant community of women and men who love this game.

This book is a collection of those stories—individual narratives that together tell the larger history of women's rugby and its ongoing growth. Among the countless images and memories, a few stand out to me: the 1972 photo of the first two front rows staring each other down; a black-and-white shot of an anonymous Midwest runner surrounded by defenders; the bloodied Penn State player rising to her feet in the 2011 national championship; a Raleigh Venom player breaking through a wall of Life University jerseys; exhausted forwards locking in for a scrum in the rain at the 2009 U.S.-Canada match. Each image, each story, captures resilience, courage, audacity—and above all, love for the game.

This book is a labor of love—from #7 to all current and future players. It is also a thank-you to the generations of women who have played with heart, tenacity, and grace, building and sustaining this extraordinary community. Whether it's Eagle #307 bursting through contact or an anonymous club player lacing up for her first match, we are all part of the same lineage—a shared and wonderful legacy.

*—Kerri Heffernan*

# 1970s

'72 — First Women's Game CU-CSU
'73 — 29 Women's Teams
'77 — Chicago Women's Rugby Club hosts the First National Invitational Championship. Portland Maine women win the title
'78 — 210 Women's Teams

Passage of Title IX — '72
7 Women's Teams
'74 — Alissa Augello forms the first Women's Committee
'77 — Women's March on Washington
'79

**T**HE FOUNDERS OF WOMEN'S RUGBY CAME of age in turbulent and transformative times. The 1960s and 1970s were marked by sweeping social movements—civil rights, feminism, labor activism, and gay liberation—that reshaped American society. The Vietnam War raged overseas while, at home, university students filled the streets and campuses with massive protests. The government's response turned deadly at Kent State and Jackson State, where National Guard soldiers opened fire on students, shattering any illusion of safety on campus. Trust in political institutions eroded further with the Watergate scandal, exposing corruption at the highest levels of power. Meanwhile, universities shifted from acting in *loco parentis*—the campus as parent—to adopting a hands-off approach, granting students unprecedented freedom. Out of this upheaval emerged a generation of young Americans who were skeptical of authority, fiercely independent, and driven by creativity and community. *It was a new world for women. "All of a sudden, it seemed like, 'Yeah, we can do anything'. There was a popular song, 'I Am Woman'—we were all singing that at the top of our lungs when we started the Tufts women's team. We were very inspired by the Equal Rights Amendment, the 1978 March on Washington, and emerging women leaders like Gloria Steinem."* (Mary Money, Tufts University, Beantown and an 'original' 1987 USWNT player)

The chance for women to play rugby emerged with the passage of Title IX in 1972. Before this landmark legislation, opportunities for women to participate in team sports were scarce. Sports programs lived mostly within schools, and schools had little incentive to fund girls' or women's athletics. Team sports were seen as arenas for building strength, aggression, perseverance, and leadership—traits society reserved for men.

Women, by contrast, were socialized to be compliant, dependent, and ever aware of the male gaze and male judgment. But Title IX changed the landscape. By mandating equal opportunity, it flung open doors that had long been bolted shut. And when given the power to choose, women didn't tiptoe through—they

*1972 CSU and UC Scrum*

charged forward. They claimed space on the field, embraced the grit, and rewrote the rules. They chose rugby, not because it was easy, but because it was fierce. Because it demanded everything they were told they could never be.

—

## IT ALL BEGINS: THE VERY FIRST WOMEN'S RUGBY MATCH

**IN THE FALL OF 1972, ON A COLD, DRIZZLY DAY,** the first women's rugby game in the U.S. was played between the University of Colorado (Boulder) and Colorado State University. The CU women wore the black and gold men's jerseys, which had not been washed since the men's last match. *That first game is just a blur,* recalls player Trudi Foreman. *But I had the most amazing time. It was incredible to be on a field, tackling and playing a full-contact team sport.*

The idea to start women's rugby at the University of Colorado Boulder and Colorado State University was born in an unexpected moment—at the Aspen Ruggerfest in 1971. Trudi Foreman, a CU student, sat in the stands with a handful of other women, watching a men's match between CU and the Aspen Rugby Club.

When the game ended, someone organized what they called a "Powder Puff" match—a mock version of rugby meant to entertain the crowd.

*"We were irritated by the Powder Puff match,"* Trudi remembered. *"It was an offensive display of bad rugby. So we started talking about women playing the game correctly."*

That conversation became a turning point. The CU and CSU women who watched that day left Aspen with a shared mission: to build real women's rugby teams at their schools. By the spring of 1971, both groups were out on the field, practicing hard and proving they belonged. *"We had a good number of people at the first few practices,"* Trudi said. *"The core group was very organized."*

Momentum grew quickly. In 1973, the Scarlet Harlots formed in Colorado, followed soon after by the Denver Blues. By 1974, nearly 30 women's teams had sprung up across the United States—most unaware that others were out there doing the same thing.

There had been isolated games before—a single match in 1968 at the Monterey Rugby Tournament stands out—but those were one-offs, fleeting moments. What began in Colorado was different. It wasn't a stunt or a spectacle. It was a movement. It was the beginning of women's rugby in America.

First Women's Rugby Match in St. Louis
Pink Ramblers v. North St. Louis Women
Sunday April 22, 1973

**Top left:** *1972 Colorado State University*
**Top right:** *1972 Julie Marley, UC Colorado*
**Bottom row:** *April 22, 1972. The St. Louis Pink Ramblers and the North St. Louis Women played their first match*

Beyond Colorado, women's rugby was beginning to take root across the country. By 1975—just three years after that first game—there were already fifty-eight women's teams in the United States. One of the earliest was the Eleanors of Pasadena, California, founded in 1973 by Jeanie Salisbury. The Eleanors were the first recorded women's rugby team in California and among the first five in the nation, a bold testament to how quickly the movement was spreading.

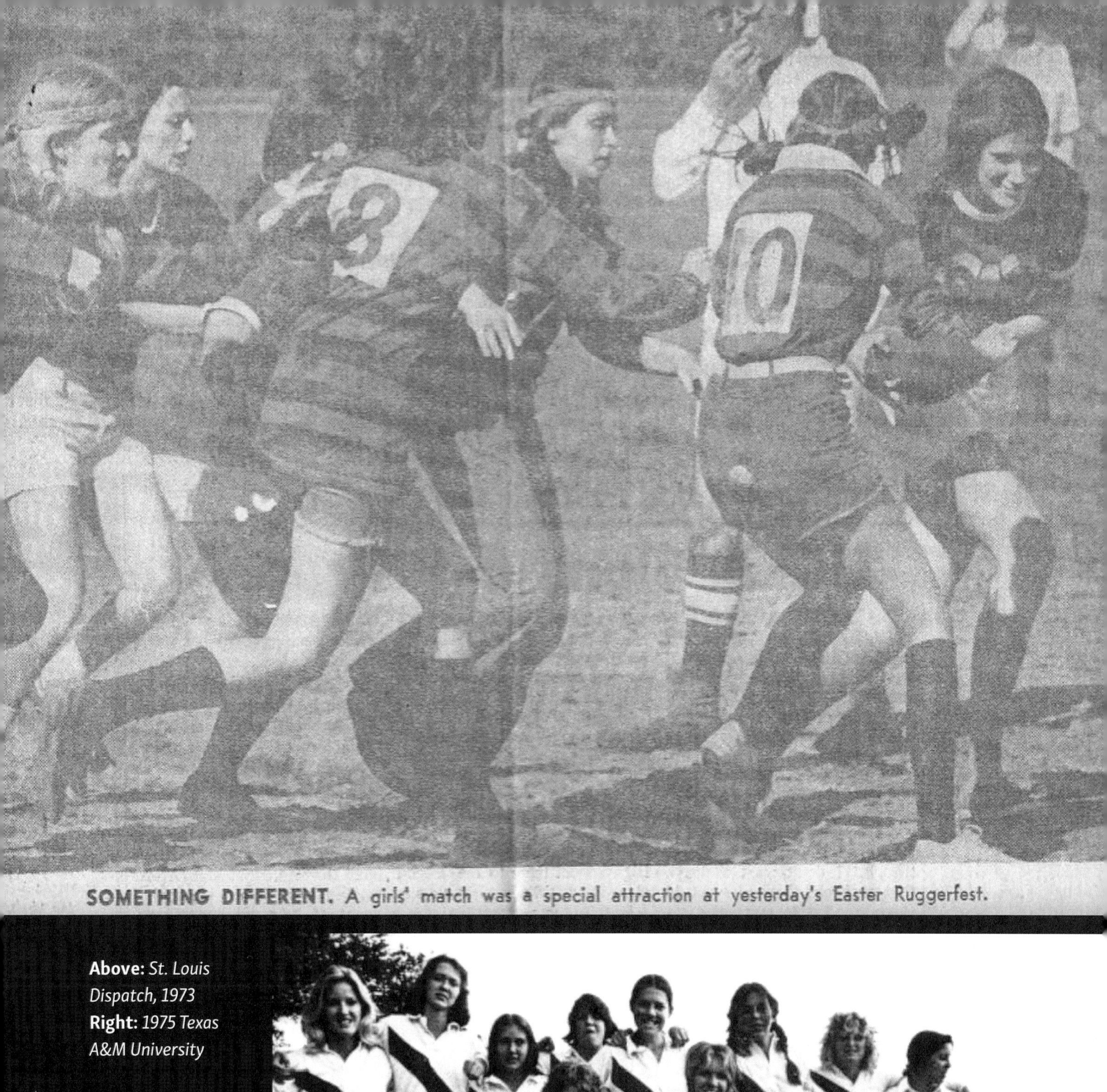

**SOMETHING DIFFERENT.** A girls' match was a special attraction at yesterday's Easter Ruggerfest.

**Above:** *St. Louis Dispatch, 1973*
**Right:** *1975 Texas A&M University*

1975 University of San Diego

1974 Santa Barbara Women

1976 Florida State University

Phoenix Squash Blossoms

1977 Phoenix, AZ Squash Blossoms

1977 Dusty Lentils of Moscow, ID

**RUGBY CLUB**

Front row: Chris Vetter. Second row: Dusty Hess, Beth Wilson, Melody Youtz. Third row: Nancy Olson, Lenora Mobley, Cindy Landers, Sus Williams. Fourth row: Jenny Kleffner, Colleen McEntee, Nola Sorenson, Bidget Sewell, Mary Beth Downing, Marie Dillon, Julie Kinchlo, Sandi Stacki, Margi Georgins, Rosemary McGerkin.

1975 Dallas Reds

1975 University of Wisconsin Women

1977 Louisiana State University

1976 UC Davis

1977 Chicago Women

1979 FSU practice

1979 Washington Furies

1977 Spodedoes of Colorado

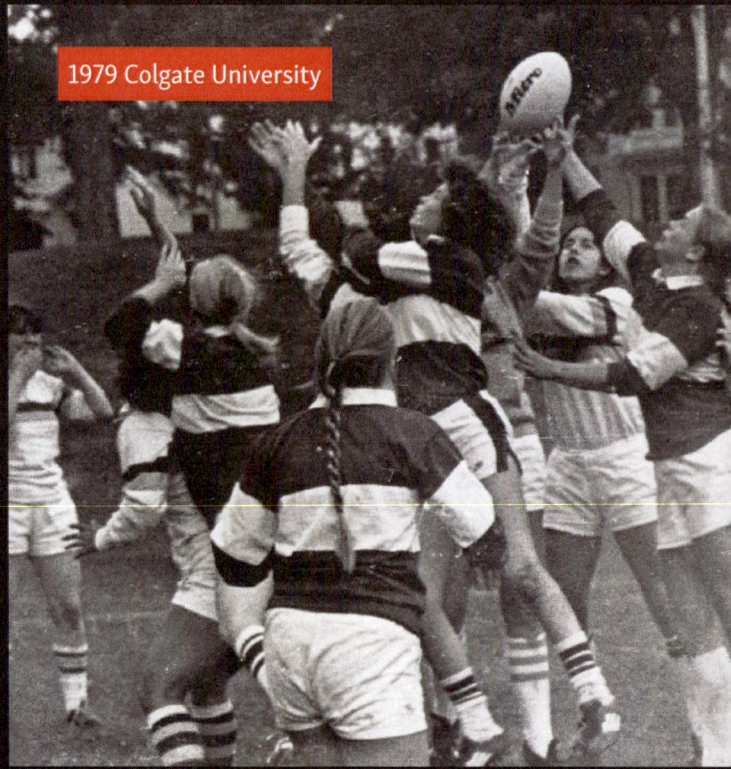
1979 Colgate University

1978 UCLA and Stanford

**Top left:** *1975 Michigan State v Chicago Alewives*
**Top right:** *1975 Wichita WRFC*
**Right:** *1976 tournament rosters*

Sacramento Women's RC

| | |
|---|---|
| Liz Gillis | Kathy Rust |
| Carol Gullion | Lori Ritter |
| Peg Kern | Nola Swan |
| Martha Colbert | Mickey Schuld |
| Dotti Derry | Terri Miller |

Berkeley Women

| | |
|---|---|
| Karen Penhaligon | Michale Parish |
| Diana Davis | Chris Scherick |
| Betsy Gleckler | Janet Fink |
| Sharon Desmond | Lori Shia |
| Danette Parish | Vicki Lippincott |

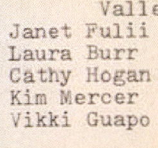

Valley Vagrants

| | |
|---|---|
| Janet Fulii | Julie Hardin |
| Laura Burr | Betsy Hill |
| Cathy Hogan | Miriam Roberts |
| Kim Mercer | Terri Brown |
| Vikki Guapo | Gail Moser |

Lantern Photo by Karen Wallbermfechiel

## Sex play

Bridget Mahoney, a sophomore from Youngstown, displays the official shirt of the Ohio State Women's Rugby Club. "The guys say they have to have leather balls to play rugby," Mahoney said. "So we say we have to have iron ovaries."

Sally Ride

In 1977 Sally Ride joined the inaugural Stanford University Women's Rugby Team. In 1982 she became the first American woman to fly in space as a member of NASA Astronaut Group 8, the first class of NASA astronauts to include women. She served as the ground-based capsule communicator for the second and third Space Shuttle flights, and helped develop the Space Shuttle's robotic arm. In June 1983, she flew in space on the Space Shuttle Challenger. Her second space flight was in 1984, also on board *Challenger*. She spent a total of more than 343 hours in space.

# Beantown RFC

### *New Club takes N.Y. Woman's 7's*

by Alison L. Smith

When Beantown R.F.C. started recruiting a Boston women's rugby team in September, who would have guessed that they'd be champions by December? That's just what happened as the Beantown women won the N.Y. Women's "Sevens Tournament" on November 28, 1976. The tourney was held on Randall's Island in New York City.

Victory was sweet for the seven women who represented Beantown – Peggy Aggenssa, Rita Brown, Kathy Frazer, Nancy Kavanaugh, Ann Lewis, Karen Onufry, and Mary Staid. They played three matches to win the championship. The first match pitted Beantowners against a combined Brockport (New York) and Philadelphia team, resulting in a Beantown shutout, 24-0. The semi-final match was closer. Cortland (New York) fought hard, but lost to Beantown by a score of 12-4. In the finals, Beantown trounced Bethlehem (Pennsylvania) 16-4.

The Sevens Tournament marked the climax of Beantowns first season. Their first game was played in October against the Boston R.F.C. After sweeping Boston, Beantowners packed their bags for a chilly autumn weekend in Concord, New Hampshire, where they met a

Beantown RFC in a set scrum against the Montreal Irish. Not bad form.

women's team from Canada, the Montreal Irish. "A" and "B" games were played during the weekend. Montreal won both games by close margins. Beantown received some consolation from the fact that the Irish, playing for two seasons, and training which includes lifting barbells and scrumming with the Canadian men's team. A rematch is scheduled for April.

The Beantown Club was started primarily by two players, Kathy Frazer and Madeline Mackles. To spark interest, they wore rugby uniforms to Boston men's games and the "drink-up's" afterward. They applied for and got a city permit for a home field, ordered the red, white, and blue jerseys and socks, and white shorts, and arranged a game schedule. The results showed, as

forty-odd women turned out for the twice-weekly three hour practice sessions. The players' ages range from 18 to forty one, and they come from as far away as Concord, N.H. and Portland, Maine.

Continuous and invaluable coaching came from several members of what has come to be Beantown's "brother" team, Beacon Hill R.F.C. Steve Durant

and Wally McGuire of the Hill's "A" team deserve much of the credit for Beantown's ability and enthusiasm – not to mention their just as hearty introduction to off-the-field aspects of the game. Beantown, like any other rugby club, has come to realize that what happens before and after the game is as much a part of the sport as the game itself. As one Beantowner puts it, "There's a spirit of togetherness as the team moves down the field. The idea is to have fun, not necessarily to win. And it's a great chance to be aggressive."

Beantown R.F.C. suffered only one injury this season. Andrea Porter, a seasoned rugger who'd previously played in Colorado, fractured her clavicle early this fall. While still in the emergency ward at Mass. General, she showed her spirit by announcing that she'd be back with the team in time for the nationals in New Orleans. Claiming that "her heart rather than her clavicle" was broken, Andrea continued to follow the games while in a brace and it's looks like she will be ready for the nationals in February. After the nationals Beantown plans to make rugby history by playing an exhibition game in Bermuda – where women's rugby is unheard of.

*SUBSCRIBE*

3rd Annual

## Rocky Mountain Spring Classic

APRIL 30 - MAY 1  1977  DENVER, COLORADO

Page 20, Section 3 ★★★★ Houston Chronicle                   Sunday, October 21, 1979

Photo by Mike Robinson, Chronicle Staff

### Heathen Hearts score

A Heathen Hearts player of Houston dashes with the ball to score as an Austin Rugby Club player misses a tackle during the First | Mini Rugby tournament for women at Bay-land Park. The tourney continues at 10 p.m today.

**Top left:** *1977 cover of the* Rocky Mountain Women's Spring Classic. *Ann Adams Wankner of CSU fights for the ball from Scarlet Harlots player Jill Leitner Jappe*
**Bottom left:** *1979 Houston Heathen Hearts*

By 1977, there were one hundred and nine women's rugby teams across the United States. Because those teams were scattered across wide distances, travel became a way of life for players. On Friday afternoons, they'd pile into cars, packed shoulder to shoulder, and drive for hours just to make kickoff. Over a single weekend, they might play multiple matches—sometimes even suiting up for teams that weren't their own.

They slept on living room floors or in borrowed spaces, fueled by junk food, beer, and adrenaline, before climbing back into their cars on Sunday to make the long drive home. But the miles were more than just travel—they were the threads that stitched the early women's rugby community together. On those weekends, players met each other, shared stories, traded information, started new clubs, and grew the game they loved.

File Photo

A member of the University of Idaho Black Widows women's rugby club runs the ball down the field during a game against Gonzaga University's Sisters of Mercy Oct. 11 at Targhee Field.

## 1978 WOMEN'S RUGBY CHAMPIONSHIPS

February 18-19, 1978
Hosted by the
Belmont Shore Rugby Clubs
Long Beach, California

Photography by
Tom Hoag

# 1ST ANNUAL PABST WOMEN'S RUGBY FEST 1978 MILWAUKEE

## FAR WESTERN
## U.S. WOMEN'S RUGBY CLASSIC
### Bakersfield, California

February 19-20, 1977

*Official Program*
*$1.00*

1976 Ohio State

## THE FIRST NATIONAL CUP CHAMPIONSHIPS

**IN 1978, THE CHICAGO WOMEN'S RUGBY CLUB** organized the National Invitational Championship, inviting teams from the four territories with successful tournament records to Chicago for a championship event. Portland Maine, a team formed in 1977 won, defeating Wisconsin in the final. *"It's hard to imagine we played four games in two days in those days. Chicago 3-0; Houston 18-0; Denver Blues 4-0 (tries were only worth 4), and the finals was 22-0 vs Madison WI."* (Marybeth Mathews)

**Above:** *1978 Portland, Maine, winners of the National Invitational Championship*

### CHICAGO WOMEN'S RUGBY FOOTBALL CLUB

CHICAGO NATIONAL WINNERS TOURNAMENT

September 2 & 3, 1978

Chicago, Illinois

You are cordially invited to compete in the First National Women's Rugby Tournament. Invitations have been sent to the following tournament winners:

| | | |
|---|---|---|
| 1. Ohio State | Mardi Gras 1978 | First |
| 2. Portland, Maine | New England 1978 | First |
| 3. Madison, Wisconsin | Big Ten 1978 | First |
| 4. Chicago, Illinois | Midwest Champions 1977 | First |
| 5. Denver Blues | Rocky Mountain 1977-78 | Second |
| 6. Texas A & M | Mardi Gras 1978 | Second |
| 7. Boston Women | New England 1978 | Second |
| 8. Florida State | Southeastern Regional | Second |
| 9. Emory University (Ga.) | | |
| 10. Belmont Shores (Calif.) | | |
| 11. Ombush (Calif.) | Triple Crown | First |
| 12. Kiwis (Calif.) | | |
| 13. San Fernando (Calif.) | Belmont Women's | Second |
| 14. Houston Boars | | |

Please mail $60.00 entry fee, payable to Chicago Women's Football Club, by JUNE 20, 1978 to:

Kathy Korse
839 Beau Drive
Des Plaines, Illinois  60016
312-439-2662

Teams will be accepted in order of response. Rules, roster sheets, accomodation information and maps will be sent upon receipt of your registration fee.

Trophies will be awarded for First, Second and Third Places.

There will be a party with beer and food on Saturday night.

---

by Steve Cohen

**Chicago, Illinois Sept. 1-2, 1979**

Women's rugby came of age at the Women's National Rugby Classic. This event (2nd annual) brought together nine of the best women's clubs to determine a National Champion and when play ended, Florida State had defeated Wisconsin 6-0.

**Well Organized**

The event was well-hosted by the Chicago Women's RFC and sponsored by Michelob beer. Tournament director Kathy Korse, Mary Larkin and the entire Chicago club proved that competent leadership and hard work produces a well-organized and smooth-running tournament.

**Clubs**

The nine clubs, which earned their invitations through local or regional tournament victories, were: defending champion Portland (Me.), Wisconsin, Chicago, Florida State, Denver Blues, Colorado State, Boston, Hoyden (Atlanta) and the Houston Heathen Hearts.

**Referees**

The referees provided high quality officiating and, importantly, all had a positive attitude towards women's rugby. They were: Pat Prosser (Kentucky), Roger Mazzarella (Ohio), Rick Frey (Indiana), Gandolf Burrus (Texas), and this writer (Michigan).

**Prelims**

In preliminary matches Florida State beat Hoyden 8-4, defending champion Portland 4-3, and Denver 8-0. Wisconsin topped Colorado State 4-0, Houston 10-4, and Boston 6-3.

**Final**

The championship was destined to be memorable as a skilled Florida State team took on experienced Wisconsin. The Madison women finished second last year and were ready for another try at the title.

The match began with Wisconsin controlling set play, enabling scrumhalf Lisa Rusek to feed quality ball to her flyhalf Marianne Slack. The Florida forwards, however, were quick to support their backs and provide a tight defense against continued Wisconsin backline attacks. Despite Wisconsins' height advantage, Florida used good technique in winning most first-half lineouts.

The half ended without any scoring as the temperature (which was close to 90 degrees) and humidity were extracting a

(Photo - Mazzarella)

fearful toll on the players.

**Second Half**

As the second half began, Wisconsin's 2nd row, Bev Baker, began to exercise her height and took over lineout control. The Florida State forwards, however, started to win more and more set and loose possession and fly-half Renate Brady's strong foot produced long kicks to touch and effective up 'n' unders. Also her looping in support of her backs drove Florida towards the Wisconsin goal.

At the fifteenth minute of the second half, Florida won a 5 meter scrum. Talented scrum half Mary Holmes passed to Brady who dummied to her inside center and led outside center Candy Orisini on a scissor for a spectacular try. The conversion by Brady gave Florida a 6-0 lead.

Wisconsin went back on attack, but the Florida backs displayed excellent individual tackling and Brady's kicking and running kept Wisconsin away from the Florida goal.

The Florida forwards, led by prop Annette Ruff and 2nd row Jennie Redner, showed increasing determination and (along with the heat) wore down the Wisconsin forwards to preserve the 6-0 lead. The final whistle came as Florida was attacking near the Wisconsin goal line.

**Great Experience**

The Classic was a wonderful experience for everyone involved and it was beautiful to be with players from all over the country sharing the joy of rugby. Though most of them had never met before, it was evident as the weekend drew to a close that they had become family.

**Coming of Age**

As ruggers, women have truly come of age. They've learned that they cannot survive as a singular team or entity. Instead of competing against each other they've learned that they must compete with each other. Since rugby is a supportive sport, women have grown accustomed to the hard n' rugged play, vigorous training, and long trips. Further, through group efforts and team spirit they have grown as individuals. Their maturity and development as players was evidenced by the excellent conditioning and well-coached play this weekend. Women's rugby has developed in what was previously an all male sport, and it has given women the opportunity to prove, to themselves and others, that as athletes they have no limitations.

From 1978 to 1980, the Chicago Women's Rugby Club hosted the National Classic Tournament—the event that laid the groundwork for something bigger. In 1981, they dropped the word "Classic" and launched the first official Women's National Club Championship. It was a bold step forward, signaling that women's rugby in the U.S. wasn't just growing—it was organizing.

The early success of the Chicago-led championships paved the way for the creation of the Women's Territorial Championships. These "Territorials" gave the best teams from each region a chance to compete for a coveted spot at Nationals. They also became an important stage for identifying top players and building the foundation for future national team selections.

At the time, the idea of a women's national team still felt like a distant dream. But with every tournament, every bus ride, and every match played, that dream was quietly taking shape.

## ADMINISTRATION AND ORGANIZING

IN THE SPRING OF 1979, ELISSA "JELLO" AUG-ello took a groundbreaking step by forming the first Women's Committee, bringing together representatives from the four territories—East, Pacific, Midwest, and West. Not long after, Jello published the first issue of In Support, the Women's Committee's own newsletter. On its inaugural cover, the Committee was described as a subcommittee of the USA Rugby Football Union (USARFU)—a description that, as former Women's Committee Chair Jami Jordan later pointed out, wasn't entirely accurate.

While the Women's Committee was technically part of USARFU, in reality, it operated largely on its own. *"We [the Women's Committee] would make decisions and inform USAR after the fact,"* Jordan recalled. *"But at the time, that's how rugby did business. It was*

*more a collection of confederations, regional and local unions, often operating independently of USARFU."*

Women paid dues to both USARFU and local unions, yet they had no formal representation at any level. Whether they were allowed to join regional or local unions often came down to the whims of male administrators. Some unions opened their doors. Others flatly refused. Many male leaders dismissed women's rugby as a novelty. One administrator summed up their attitude bluntly: *"We thought you'd just go away."*

But the women didn't go away.

In those early years, the Women's Committee focused on connection and communication. Jennie Redner, founder of Michigan State Women's Rugby and a future Committee Chair, created the first comprehensive contact list of women's teams in the U.S.—names, phone numbers, and mailing addresses—published through *In Support*. Jennie's list was more than just information; it was infrastructure. It allowed teams

## A TRIBUTE TO OUR BEGINNINGS

In 1975, with a total of five teams, the Southern California Women's Rugby Association was formed. In four years that original number has more than tripled, with sixteen member clubs and two affiliates. At this time SCWRFA would like to pay tribute to those individuals and teams who were instrumental in the beginning stages of the organization.

The Eleanors, UCSD, Belmont Shore, Ombush, and SDSU were our initial members. Susie Stiers of the Eleanors served as the Associations first President. She was followed by Julie Woodruff of Belmont Shore and Jeannie Salisbury of the Eleanors. Our returning President is Kathie Rosie, playing this year for the KIWI's.

A special tribute goes to Jeannie Salisbury. Through her foresight and persistence the Association was admitted to the Southern California Rugby Football Union, making SCWRFA the first women's association to be admitted to a union in the U.S.

to find one another, schedule matches, and build networks. Just as importantly, it helped identify women who were already organizing at the grassroots level.

Many of these women soon took on bigger roles—posting match results, sharing resources, and coordinating regional and national events. Their work, often unpaid and unseen, built the scaffolding of a national women's rugby community. It was through their persistence, creativity, and defiance of low expectations that a movement found its shape.

The story of women's rugby in the U.S. isn't just about games won or championships claimed—it's about a generation of women who refused to disappear, who built something lasting from almost nothing, and in doing so, changed the game forever.

**Above:** *1977 Chicago Women versus Chicago Alewives. Women's Committee founder, Elissa Augello is pictured behind the ball carrier.*

*Can women play first class rugby and remain feminine or must she become a swaggering feminist? (Hatch Turner, 1978 Rugby Magazine)*

## THE RUGBY WORLD RESPONDS TO WOMEN'S RUGBY

WHILE A NUMBER OF MALE PLAYERS AND coaches were supportive of women's rugby, others were deeply opposed to women's rugby and spent considerable energy trying to 'forbid' women from playing. Some of these men held positions of power at regional and national levels and could make it very difficult for women.

Rugby Magazine was the only publication covering rugby in the U.S. Founded by rugby player and sports businessman John Prusmack in 1975, this private-ly-owned U.S. publication chronicled national and international rugby matches as well as rugby's major stars. While the writers for the earliest issues of this magazine detailed the rise of men's rugby in the United States, they rarely mentioned women's rugby, often covering the sport in just a paragraph or two in their tournament roundups. The few longer stories about women debated the seriousness of women in sports. Although a few women managed to secure a small section of the magazine to cover their own matches in 1978, this space was not enough. Women wrote letters to the editor in an effort asking for increased coverage.

Writing about the lack of representation of women, rugby player Betsy Ogburn wondered, *Why is there such a total disregard for women in this sport? Is it the same as*

*all sports in the past—male dominated, therefore women are on the low list of priorities?* She attributed the lack of coverage of women's rugby to sexism in the sporting world, noting that popular publications tended to treat men's sports as more important than women's. With this imbalance of coverage in mind, Ogburn offered to write for Rugby. However, the editors rejected Ogburn's criticism and insulted Ogburn in their response to her

request to write for Rugby, proclaiming, "*Your help is certainly appreciated…We ask that all articles be intelligent, informative, and as well-researched as possible.*"

Ironically the editors openly blamed women for the lack of coverage of women's rugby while refusing to publish women's contributions. *Coverage of women's rugby is up to the initiative of women's players and the administration.* They portrayed women's rugby as a 'women's issue' and framed women as the drivers of their own lack of representation.

Much of the early media coverage of women's rugby focused less on athleticism and more on appearance. Articles often fixated on the "attractiveness" and supposed sexual availability of the players, rather than their skill or accomplishments. Coverage also made frequent references to "raging feminists"—a loaded phrase that was often used as a euphemism for queer women.

In reality, many lesbians did play rugby. The sport's close-knit community, sense of camaraderie, and vibrant social scene offered something rare at the time: a space where queer women could feel safe, be themselves, and find others like them. For many young women coming out, rugby wasn't just a sport—it was a refuge.

# Woman's Rugby:
## Fashion, Fad or Real?

by Dennis McLaughlin

Rugby seems an improbable sport for women, even if more and more barriers between the male and female world are crumbling. Yet it is one of the few team sports in which women can participate without too much difficulty.

The emphasis here is on "team" sport. Except in high school and maybe in college and if a woman has progressed through the very organized structure of softball, there aren't any sports for women, after school days, that offer team competition. Bowling leagues and doubles in tennis aside.

In fact if you mention tennis to Angie Clark, founder, charter member, co-captain and kingpin of the Philadelphia Women's RFC, and one of her teammates, Betsy Tomlinson, the room literally bristles with pique. Tennis itself doesn't heighten their irritation. But there is a stereo-typing accompanying the popularity of tennis today, imply the two women. They are not convinced that women's great migration to the courts, clubs and lessons is a result of the break-down of the Victorian precepts against women and sweat. Rather, it might be the result of extensive marketing and strident promotion by the media trend spotters.

Anyway, the women don't really have any axes to grind. Besides, they'd be more likely to take issue with this reporter's statement that women can participate in rugby without too much difficulty.

For the last year and a half Clark and Tomlinson have been coping with the organization problems of recruiting, practice,

Woman's Rugby Clubs in college are becoming very popular as evidenced by the LSU Woman's side.

club affiliation, scheduling, transportation and the rest of the bag.

The one problem that has been solved is the one of affiliation. Some of the charter members of the Philadelphia Women's RFC had been introduced to rugby by their male friends, most of whom played for or followed the Whitemarsh RFC of the Philadelphia area. When the women began to play and to take the game seriously, the Whitemarsh men offered coaching help and sideline support. It seemed a natural thing that the men's and women's teams might merge. For a while, the women called themselves the Whitemarsh Motleys. But a vote among the men of Whitemarsh mandated no such affiliation; the women decided that they did not want any such affinity either. Principally it would have meant that the women would have been playing ten minute games between starts of the men's fixtures.

Now the Philadelphia Women's RFC faces the ordinary problems of a rugby club. Enthusiasm of the women on the roster, though, is not one of them. "At first," Clark says, "some of the women began playing because rugby was a novelty. But once they were active they discovered they enjoyed the sport and, more importantly, exulted in the team concept. A lot of the girls had never played on a team or as a team except in those sports where performance is individual."

All of the women on the club agreed that they experienced a particularly good feeling from working together as a team. Shari Hersh says: "In one game we scored a try and all seven forwards were there to touch the ball down. Scoring a try is an incredible feeling."

"I like clapping the team off the field, our own and our op-

ponent's," says Betsy Tomlinson, co-captain, "there's a bond made there in team sports that women have had little chance of enjoying."

It requires a lot of work, however, to score those tries As Hersh says the scores are usually low. But the women are learning, in part because they are receiving coaching help from some of the men active in Philadelphia rugby.

"We expect to get a hold of films that will show us some polished rugby techniques to help our training. We have already begun fund raising and we're tapping areas for player recruitment," says Clark. Right now the club has over 20 members whose age range from 15 to 35. However, it may be comforting to those mainstays of male chauvinism that as far as the women of Philadelphia are concerned the men can play their game and the women will play their game."

"Women in general," says Clark, "lack the training in athleticism. We're sorry for that, but we don't concede that there exists a real difference in the inherent athletic ability between men and women."

And there is no loss of femininity once a woman begins developing that ability. No one's lost a boy friend because of rugby.

"We are not developing ourselves into a threat to men," says Clark, although she admits that some men she knows get that feeling. It was no less heightened when one man found himself alone at a party after the women's game and endured some uneasiness as the women went into a repetoire of randy songs.

"Of course we want to raise the standards of our game," says Clark, "but we're not trying to break into the male lineup. We play different styles. Besides I'm not anxious to mark my male opponent. There is quite a size difference."

Woman's rugby is by no means just in college. Here a girl's high school side gets into a real maul.

# Women's Rugby: More Than A Passing Fancy

by Jan Schalle

(Photo - Pat Carr)

The great majority of men and, unfortunately, women don't believe in the ladies game. The general consensus is that it takes leather balls to play rugby, and women don't fit that prerequisite in the least. Those few who do stand as observers generally aren't interested in women's rugby as a sport...it's only an amusement to see whose chest will bounce the highest or how much rear end will show when the scrum comes together.

**Women Are Expected—**

It's accepted - no. I'll even say expected, for women to ride 100 miles, stand in snow, mud, rain, any ambient temperature, and even the gloom of night, just to encourage fifteen fools to knock themselves silly running into fifteen other fools whose women are stalwartly cheering them from the opposite sideline.

**Too Fragile"**

However, let them on the pitch? Let them have a chance to prove they may be as competent as their idols? Let them make a contribution to the advancement of American rugby besides serving chicken and potato salad at tourney dinners? Never. They're too delicate. Besides, God made women to scrub, not scrum.

**As Boring As Some Men's Games**

'It's sort of like real rugby, only in slow motion.'

Admittedly, from the sidelines, some women's games are boring, just like the men's, but the main problem is that the ladies' game is in its adolescence. Teams cannot pick from players with five years experience; we must utilize those few who are willing to labor through its virginal state.

**First Contact Sport**

Perhaps the action isn't as fast, but a greater amount of fitness is required because the hitting doesn't come as naturally. Generally, it's the first time women have encountered a contact sport, and overt physical agression is not mastered easily. But as an often-bruised player, I can bear witness to the fact that women on the field DO mean serious business when they want the ball.

**Dykes and Feminists?**

Popular opinion is not the only aspect to consider. What about the players? Are they all dykes or just frustrated and rowdy feminists? Are they serious about the game? Typical questions are : "Aren't you afraid of what people will think?" "Do you really enjoy getting hurt and beat up?" "Why?"

**Integral Part of an Organised Sport**

...Why not? Women like to stay fit and many enjoy being slightly unladylike on a Saturday afternoon. Any mindless idiot can jog. Anyone who can afford lace panties can play tennis. Rugby's uniqueness is being given the opportunity to be an integral part of an organised sport without having to look cute. Many ungraceful movements can be camouflaged butting into a ruck, and the backline really appreciates some 'beef' in the scrum.

**Men Needn't Answer**

What seems strange is that these are the same questions asked of men when they first begin playing. THEY don't have to answer - a simple shrug of the shoulders and a vacant grin creates enough macho that no response is necessary. Push the issue, ask him 'Why?' a second time. No doubt the answer will deal with personal athletic satisfaction regardless of sideline critique, which is, in general, the real reason most women are on the field.

**Rugby - A Game Everybody Enjoys**

There are no rewards, no gratuities, no peer pressure to conform to what's hip this season - it's simply a matter of conquering a sport that can be enjoyed by all. Besides, we should have a chance to find out for ourselves if all those bumper stickers are true - especially the one about rucking's supremacy being superseded only by one other aspect of life's activities.

**Quality Is Improving**

So, look out, men...valid critics have complimented women's rugby by saying that the ladies' game is closer to 'true' rugby because there are no 'football stigmas to overcome. The overall quality of American rugby is improving. Instead of criticising the women for not adhering to the norm of social standards, perhaps the men should work on the quality, not the speed, of their game, or they may be surpassed by some tough little women who aren't afraid to ruck for their rights.

(Reprinted from the Virginia R.F.U Newsletter)

---

## Big Apple Classic

### October 14-15, 1978

### New York City

Old Blue Women's RFC invites you to participate in the Big Apple Classic to be held the weekend of October 14-15th. The format of the tournament will include 8 teams with each team playing a minimum of 3 games. Although many of the details are still being worked on - we will be sending a future mailing with information on accommodations, entry fees, playing fields, and parties.

We anticipate a large response therefore we will be accepting teams on a first-come, first-served basis. Let us know soon if you are interested.

Old Blue looks forward to hearing from you and having a great tournament. S.Donegan, 88 68th St. Bklyn, NY 11220 212-836-5886.

## Portland Women New England Champs

Providence, R.I., May 13-14, 1978.

The finals of the annual New England Tournament saw Boston RFC facing Portland RFC in the finals of the women's division Portland was the defending champion in the tourney, and retained the crown by defeating Boston 12-6. The match was hard fought with Portland gaining the advantage only in loose play.

Outside center Rita Brown scored both Portland tries, as well as successfully kicking both conversions. Boston forward Christie Somers scored, with Ikie Spears making the conversion.

## Boston Women Win At Portland

Eight teams competed in the women's division of the Portland, (Maine) Tournament, and in the finals Portland, the defending champions lost to Boston (4-0). These same teams reached the finals of the New England Tournament in May and in a hard-fought contest Portland won 12-6.

**Deglon Scores**

Boston's score came when they gained possession from a ruck inside the Portland 25 and Scrumhalf Ellen Kearns whipped a pass weak side to wing Stephanie Julio. Julio surged forward and just as she was about to be tackled at the five, passed to fullback Debbie Deglon who, with perfect timing and fierce determination, dove for the try line. (Deglon got her wrist out of a case just last week.)

Other teams competing in the Portland tournament were Montreal Irish; McGill Mac-Donald (Montreal); Concord (N.H.); Hartford, (Ct.); Beantown (Boston); and Chicago (Il.)

**National Winners Tournament**

Portland RFC and Boston RFC will both be traveling to Chicago in September to compete in the first ever National Winners Tournament. In order to qualify for the tournament, a team must have won a major tournament in the past year. The tournament, to be held on September 2 & 3, will bring together ten of the top women's teams in the country. Portland and Boston will be New England's two representatives.

## National Women's Tournament

Sept. 2nd & 3rd
Chicago, Illinois

The Chicago Womens Rugby Football Club is hosting the First National Womens Tournament in Chicago September 2nd and 3rd. All teams invited have won a major tournament in their area.

For further information, please contact:

Kathy Korse
839 Beau Drive
Des Plaines, Illinois

If you really need shorts...

try Gymphlex®

LEADING MANUFACTURERS OF BRITISH RUGBY SHORTS

Matt Godek Rugby Supply
P.O. Box 565
Merrifield, Va. 22116

Leather Balls Ltd.
P.O. Box 6305
Arlington, Va. 22206

Rugby American
3829 Plyers Mill Rd.
Kensington, Md. 20795

The Rugby Shop
312 Adelaide St.
West Toronto, Ontario M5V 1R2

The Gant Rugger has become an American Tradition. The Gant Rugger 100% cotton brawny knit. Gant Corporation, New York, New York 10022.

THE GANT ATTITUDE

That camaraderie was more than just team spirit; it was a shield. Mixed tournaments that brought together men's and women's teams could be dangerous spaces. Heavy drinking, large numbers of men, and hyper-masculine attitudes sometimes created environments where sexual harassment, assault, and homophobic attacks were real risks. Women relied on one another for protection as much as for support.

This culture also seeped into advertising. Female players were sometimes sexualized to sell products—as in a Gymphlex ad showing women playing without shorts, or beer ads portraying "rugby girls" draped over male players. Another ad even showed a woman positioned between a male player's legs. Instead of celebrating their strength, skill, or grit, these depictions reduced women players to props in someone else's story.

National and local newspapers occasionally ran articles on women's rugby, these posts were rarely in the sports section—rather they were human interest stories- 'how strange it was that women played rugby.' Women's Sports magazine occasionally covered women's rugby matches and twice, Sports Illustrated noted players in their Faces in the Crowd feature.

*WOMEN'S RUGBY*

# Portland Wins National Women's Classic

Portland defends against a Chicago back movement (Photo-Ebright)

by Mary Larkin

The first annual National Women's Rugby Classic was held this Labor Day weekend in Mt. Prospect, Illinois. Eight U.S. teams competed in the tournament which was sponsored by Michelob and hosted by the Chicago Women's Rugby Football Club. Portland, Maine and Boston represented the East; the Houston Boars and Florida State University hailed from the South; Colordo State University and the Denver Blues represented the West; and the Midwest entries were Wisconsin (Madison) and Chicago. In order to qualify for entry into the tournament, each team had to be a tournament winner in its area.

The competition was divided into two divisions in which three preliminary games were played in a round robin tourney. The final featured Madison, Wisconsin and Portland, Maine with the strong Portland side beating Wisconsin 20-0, on 4 tries and 2 conversions. Chicago and Florida State vied for 3rd place with Chicago winning in triple overtime, 4-0.

Chicago Women's Rugby Football Club would appreciate any women's club sending in results of any tournament held so that records will be available for entry into next year's tournament. Please send scores to:

Kathy Korse
839 Beau Drive
Des Plaines, IL 60016

# Women's Rugby Flies High At Air Force Academy

By Alan Osur
Coach, USAFA RFC

Last spring the Air Force Academy women's side completed its first year of competition against other Colorado clubs and became the first Service Academy to field a women's side.

**Started In Sept. '77**

Its beginning last September was somewhat tenuous, as the women had to build on a nucleus of one experienced player. Yet the club held together and during the ERRFU championship in October actually had twenty-two cadets and a 2 and 2 tournament record.

Interestingly enough at least nine of the players had never seen rugby before that weekend. During the fall, around five or six would show up at the Friday practice and nine to twelve for the games. The spring season was very different and the side became well-organized under Cadets Allene Dowden and Sue Slaver. In nine games the women achieved a 3-3-3 record.

**Rugby Takes Hold**

After some initial prodding, women's rugby has taken hold at the Academy. Its success is attributed to the enthusiasm of the women themselves, the support and coaching from the coaches and cadets of the men's side, and the fine support of the Academy.

**Representative Activity**

At the Academy, rugby is a "Representative Activity," halfway between a club and a varsity sport. Significantly the Club can practice every day during the spring, as opposed to just Fridays in the fall. Fifty men and twenty women were "on-season," and by the end of the spring slightly over 10 percent of the women at the Academy were playing rugby – this includes a "side-of-the-hill" gang of three or four.

**Contact - A Problem**

There are a few points that can be made about coaching women's rugby that might help others. First, we started with the wrong premise – that good women athletes will immediately pick up rugby. This premise holds true for the men but for the most part, the women initially had trouble with contact, and over the year we did not work on it enough. Often there was a reluctance to hit hard in practice and during games and as a remedy the women were scrimmaging against the men by the end of the spring. This seemed to give the women more confidence in their abilities and an understanding of what their capabilities are.

**Coach Men and Women Separately**

Another important point is to keep the men and women separated during the actual

(Continued on Page 27)

# Norfolk Breakers, Neptune Champs

## *Capture Ruggerfest With 4-0 Victory Over William & Mary*

by R. Boothly

The Norfolk Breakers battled William and Mary for the championship of the Neptune Ruggerfest marking the fifth time that these two sides have faced each other for a number one tournament spot. Due to the tactical defense applied by both sides the match was forced into sudden death to break a scoreless [illegible]. The Breakers finally tipped the scale [illegible] by inside center Cathy Haskett leading them to a 4-0 victory and bringing the series of championship matches between the two sides to 4-1 in favor of Norfolk.

**Breakers 8, Maryland 0**

The Breakers earned their spot in the finals by defeating the University of Maryland in the first round with two tries by winger Debbie Wickes. The Norfolk scrum dominated the match with excellent rucking and mauling in the second half. This aided by the unmatched speed of Kathy Dugan and Debbie Wickes brought the Breakers to an 8-0 win.

**Breakers 24, Indiana 4**

In the second round the Breakers faced Indiana University, a team of impressive size and strength. The Breakers backfield, known for its speed and quickness, played excellent defense, keeping continuous pressure on the opposing backs for a 24-4 victory. Winger Darby Lister, the leading scorer of the women's division brought in four tries for Norfolk while Kathy Dugan raced to another.

**William and Mary 8, Va. 0**

William and Mary paired with the University of Virginia in the second round after drawing a bye in the first. While UVA's forwards dominated with constant possession, they were unable to score because of William & Mary's excellent defense. This pressure defense led to breakdowns in which Holly Trester and scrumhalf Leigh Cichester scored tries to bring the final score to 8-0.

**Final**

Tension was high as the championship match began and

(Continued on Page 27)

Kathy Dugan of the Breakers on the move vs. William & Mary. Cathy Haskett is in support.

# A ROUGH DAY FOR THE LADIES

HUNTINGTON BEACH — Some might have called it organized mayhem — although, to the uninitiated on the sidelines, there may have been doubt about the organized part.

But the first-ever Women's National Rugby Championship held at Dwyer Junior High School last weekend was still considered a success.

After all, it was that noted rugby authority, Billie Jean King of pro tennis fame, who once called it "a hooligans' game played by ladies."

Despite the chill air and the occasional rainstorm, the ladies pushed, pulled, blocked, kicked and ran with wild abandon Sunday. When they were done, the UC San Diego Sirens had downed the University Women from UCLA, 8-4, for the title.

The consolation game, in which Belmont Shore wiped out the Eleanors of Pasadena, 21-4, was so wild that the 150 or so spectators, many of whom had some unique methods for beating the cold, couldn't even keep up at times.

Actually, as rugby tournaments go, it was a pretty mild event. Out of the eight teams which took part, only one player was knocked out briefly, two others went to the hospital to have cuts stitched and one suffered a mild back strain.

Monday, even as the bruises began to show up, those involved were looking forward to next year when the second national tournament will be held, this time involving teams from out of state.

# The U.S. Rugby Scene . . .

# Rugby Girls Are Having A Ball

**In a note, addressed to the ladies, included in the Hawaii Rugby Football Union's distinctive programme compiled for the 1975 bi-annual Pan Pacific Rugby Tournament it is explained that soccer is a gentleman's game played by hooligans and rugby, by way of contrast is a hooligan's game played by gentlemen.**

One can only conclude that there are an awful lot of female gentlemen in the United States of America.

In the same programme the female reader is told that the game of rugby is difficult to understand unless one has played it — "so you already start at a disadvantage."

One further concludes, from a cursory inspection of the situation there, that an awful lot of ladies of the U.S. are going about the business of overcoming that disadvantage.

And the reason for the expansion of organised women's rugby is simply explained by the kingpin of the Los Angeles University side, Marilyn Glucksman as: "It's a great team sport, it's great exercise and you meet great people."

As a reason for participation, does that reckoning differ so very much from that of the involved New Zealand male?

The first U.S. women's rugby side was arguably formed at the University of Colorado in 1971, but the team lacked for competition. Marilyn was offered a deal in 1972 which involved a free weekend trip to Colorado in return for playing in a short exhibition game there against the university side.

At the time she was an 18-year-old student at the University of New Mexico. She's been hooked ever since.

And today reliable estimates of women's teams across the country put the number at between 70 and 100; a crowd of 4000 watched the finals of the second annual inter-club championships contested by eight teams at Huntington Beach, California, last year — won 4 - 3 by Belmont Shores at the expense of Old Mission Beach; thanks to the motivation of Mona Kelety, an expatriate Florida lass, the first annual National Collegiate Women's Rugby Championship tournament will be hosted at Texas A and M University about the time of this publication's release.

This last is a significant event. It establishes women's rugby at just the level where Jack Gleeson sees it necessary for real progress in U.S. male rugby to emanate from.

## Sound Technique

According to a livewire member of the San Diego State University's Women's Rugby Club, Anne Powis — well met after the West v San Diego County match — the formation of a national union for female ruggers is only perhaps three or four years away.

Coached by the S. D. County coach, Mike Pithy from South Africa, Anne's team claims to be the best in California with a 34 - 4 win recorded last season over University of California Santa Barbara while flank forward Carter Orrison quotes Pithy as regarding the girl's mauling, scrumming and "slipping" (hand to hand passing among the forwards) as at least the equal in technical achievement of the all-star male team he is responsible for.

Three women's teams in San Diego — two college and one club; three in Los Angeles — one college (or university) and two club; one at Huntington Beach, another at a Bakesfield and two in San Francisco make it possible for female ruggers in California to evolve a quite comprehensive series of matches through the season.

The UCSB team, for instance, from mid-January through to late April was able to compile a schedule of three home matches, six away games and participation in three tournaments including the one at Santa Barbara late April.

Other tournaments are held in the Mid-West states, in Colorado, Arizona, Dover and elsewhere but the Santa Barbara one deserves special mention here.

## Presence Felt

At the 9th annual SB tourney the Sirens of San Diego and the Eleanor Rugby Club os Pasadena were matched in a special feature game. A year later, 1975, eight teams formed their own division in one of California's largest tournaments with the number more than doubled to 22 last year and further progress, numerically is expected.

The girls are also making their presence felt in San Diego. Four teams fronted in the January 76 event, 10 or 11 this year with power to add.

And the "disease" is spreading. The San Francisco Women's Rugby Club was admitted to membership of the Northern California RFU in November of last year prompting the question, why?

Miss Glucksman's reasons are, on the surface, pretty acceptable. And the facts to some extent speak for themselves. But are there other causes?

Some would have it that American youth has pretty

*"Come 'hair' you." San Diego's Anne Powis brought to a halt by a fairly (?) obvious means in women's rugby.*

by August R. Demma
Midwest Editor

# Happening in Hammond

## Men in Action

For ten years the annual Mardi Gras exodus of students from Southeastern Louisiana University has meant an influx of rugby players from points all across North America. The 1976 version of the Hammond, Louisiana Mardi Gras Rugby Tournament was staged with nearly sixty teams participating (1200 players), which should have put a strain on a community of only 12,000 residents, but with most of the university's 6000 students away on the Mardi Gras break (that is an official school holiday) the town almost seemed deserted. Hammond was quite able and eager to accommodate the incoming horde.

Warm weather and the Mardi Gras celebration are the attractions which brought clubs from twenty-four states and Canada. Modes of travel were quite varied, as one might expect, ranging from a seemingly decrepit Volvo to Boeing 747's. The Lincoln Park Rugby Club of Chicago arrived via Amtrak, while Atlanta Old White traveled in the more conventional super camper. A contingency of referees from St. Louis flew in privately owned aircraft. At least one chap claimed to have been teleported to Hammond, although this was never confirmed. The others traveled in the usual assortment of sedans, station wagons, vans, sports cars, pick ups, VW's, campers, undergraduate limousines ('69 Chevies), Z's, Cadillacs, etc. Some of which looked respectable, some not. One of the more disreputable looking modes of conveyance was this writer's 12 year old Volvo 544. While it ran like a champion on the way to

Hammond, it did develop trouble once there. Per chance, when it was necessary to look into the matter a rugger from Clemson, SC happened by who was also a foreign car mechanic. While rendering expert assistance, the problem was not detected until a passer by inquired as to why the air cleaner on the rear carburetor was blocking the air intake? With that problem solved we went on to enjoy the rest of the tournament.

The tournament was held at the Hammond Airport (which shut down two runways for two days), at which twelve pitches were created out of interrunway wasteland. Since each team was guaranteed four games, about 120 games were played on the weekend. Two of the more interesting, if not technically pleasing, games were played on Sunday afternoon prior to the tournament final. The championship of the women's division was one of them.

### Women in Action

The University of South Florida met Indiana University in the women's final. As is typical of young rugby clubs, there was very little scoring, so little in fact, the game ended in a scoreless tie. Since a winner had to be determined, an overtime period was played. After sixty more minutes of scoreless play

referee Raymond Cockroft, ended the match and ordered a scrumoff to determine the winner. The action then moved to the center of the pitch were several hundred onlookers surrounded the ladies. The two opposing scrums then got together and each side put in five balls. Indiana won the most hooks, the game and the championship.

Immediately following the women's final an event was staged that may have rocked the very foundation of Twickenham. A side composed entirely of referees challenged the host club (Southeastern Louisiana) to a game of rugby. This unlikely contest was the brainchild of Keith Seaber (USA selector), who both selected and captained the side while apparently in a level headed state. Those who were expecting a flawless performance by the '31st MEN', witnessed a lawless display which resembled the Third Panzer Division rambling over the Russian Steppe. The referees won the game (although the exact score was never made public), not with the usual tactics of strategic kicking and the like, but with such devises as subtrefuge, guerrilla warfare, kamakaze missions and out and out cheating. Also, they did not hurt their cause by using a squad of twenty-five (all at the same time) and providing their own

referee (usually Norman Lambert, although he did take 'two minutes' on several occasions). Any resemblance between the laws inforced during the match and those of rugby union football was purely coincidental. Everyone enjoyed the show, even the referees.

The Schlitz Brewing Company provided beer to all players for two full days plus a generous array of prizes and trophies to the winning teams. Besides the huge trophies presented to five different teams, various types of coolers and jackets were also presented to the players. Even the referees were presented with plaques for their services.

New environments often bring surprises. The hard water of Hammond, Louisiana made it mildly unpleasant to shower since the water was quite incapable of removing soap from the skin. In order to get at least a reasonable amount of the slippery stuff off, it was necessary to remain under the shower until one resembled a prune. You could drink it though.

Combining an awesome forward pack with a shifty back line, the Bloomington Blues, Illinois raced to the championship of the Tenth Annual Hammond Mardi Gras Rugby Tournament held on

the last weekend of February. The Blues defeated a very tough Iowa State University side in the final game, 11 to 0.

To reach the final game the Blues disposed of Brockport State of New York (10-3), Tulsa, (16-0), University of Georgia (21-3), Boston University (21-4) and Ohio State University (19-3) in that order. Iowa State eliminated Atlanta Old White in their semifinal match.

The outcome of the tournament final was never really in doubt as the Bloomington Blues dominated play in every respect. Possession was the key to the Blues' victory as they mounted attack after attack from line-outs and scrummages. Blues' forwards Dick McGuire and Lauren Chouinard made a shambles of the lineouts as they took ball after ball, and hooker Dewey Worsley did his part in the scrums. Former All-Midwest scrumhalf Bob Criscione got the action flowing with his fine all around play. Standoff Steve Rhoads, while not a running threat, was a valuable link in the three-quarter line as both a passer and a kicker.

Marty Zurn opened the Blues scoring after fifteen minutes with a 25-yard penalty goal. At the 25 minute mark winger Bruce Thornton raced 40 yards down the touch line for the games first try. The first half ended with the Blues leading 7 to 0.

The Blues kept Iowa State in their end of the field for the greater part of the game, but superb kicking by the Iowa State standoff and fullback often put the Blues up against their own goal line.

The final score of the contest came on another long run by Bruce Thornton early in the second half.

Defensive pressure by the Blues prevented Iowa State from mounting many serious threats. The Blues pack also controlled the loose play, thus sealing the victory.

The Blues finished second to Old White in the same tournament last year.

Old White took third place with a 4 to 0 victory over Ohio State in the consolation game. In the championship of the consolation bracket Clemson University defeated Topeka, Kansas.

In the women's division Indiana University took the first place trophy after winning a scrummaging contest with South Florida. The special contest was the last resort after a one hour overtime period had no scoring. Now that is endurance.

An unusually fine corps of referees was assembled by the always capable Reagan Malone of Kansas City. Included among them were Keith Seaber (St. Louis), Peter Jones (Memphis), Reg Golledge (Columbus, OH), Jim Russell (Denver), Peter Simpson (New York), and the ever present Norm Lambert (St. Louis). And of course there was guest referee, Ed Lebow, from New York and RUGBY.

The tournament was sponsored by the Southeastern Louisiana Rugby Club, the City of Hammond, the Schlitz Brewing Co. (free beer for two days ain't bad) under the directorship of Dr. David Shepherd. The event was held at the local airport where twelve pitches were mowed out of the vast acreage of flatland.

While the tournament was designed to accommodate 64 teams, the final field, was 55 including three Canadian sides.

## In the South Women Take Rugby Seriously

Women's rugby clubs doing "Their Thing" at Hammond. Photos by Peter Simpson, who refereed The Final.

## INTERNATIONAL TOURS

**IN OCTOBER 1979, A WELL-ORGANIZED MID-**west Women's Select Side embarked on a tour of Great Britain. There was just one catch—there weren't any women's teams in Britain to play against. So the Midwest squad brought two sides and spent the tour playing each other on foreign soil.

This wasn't the first time U.S. women's teams had gone abroad; American sides had been touring internationally as early as 1977. But perhaps the most influential trip came in 1985 with the WIVERN tour. WIVERN, a national invitation side, traveled to England and France to face university and club teams. The British press was caught off guard by the high level of U.S. play, and the lopsided scores turned heads.

The impact went beyond the scoreboard. WIVERN's dominance inspired several British clubs to invest more seriously in coaching and developing their women's sides. What began as a bold experiment became a spark for change on both sides of the Atlantic.

By the end of 1979 there were 210 women's teams in the U.S.

*Back in 1972...*

| | |
|---|---|
| *Yearly tuition at private university (fees, room and board)* | **$3,090** |
| *Yearly tuition at public university (fees, room and board)* | **$1,550** |
| *Monthly rent* | **$165** |
| *Per capita income* | **$4,880** |
| *Adults with a bachelor's degree* | **12.0%** |

**NOW IT TAKES MORE THAN LEATHER BALLS TO PLAY RUGBY**

MIDWEST WOMEN'S RUGBY 1979 GREAT BRITAIN TOUR

Courtesy of CHICAGO WOMEN'S RUGBY FOOTBALL CLUB

WOMEN

**Midwest Women Tour Great Britain**

# 1980s

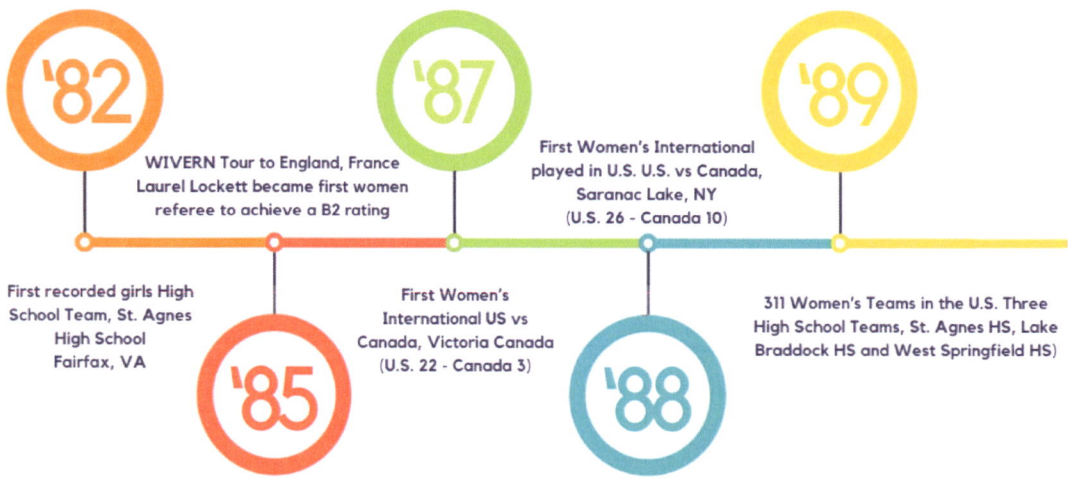

**'82** WIVERN Tour to England, France Laurel Lockett became first women referee to achieve a B2 rating

**'87** First Women's International played in U.S. U.S. vs Canada, Saranac Lake, NY (U.S. 26 - Canada 10)

**'89**

First recorded girls High School Team, St. Agnes High School Fairfax, VA

**'85** First Women's International US vs Canada, Victoria Canada (U.S. 22 - Canada 3)

**'88**

311 Women's Teams in the U.S. Three High School Teams, St. Agnes HS, Lake Braddock HS and West Springfield HS)

**T**HE 1980S MARKED A TURNING POINT FOR women's rugby in the United States—a decade defined by explosive growth, the birth of the women's national team, and the first international matches.

In early 1980, the fledgling Women's Committee was officially folded into USA Rugby, becoming the USARFU Women's Committee. This step signaled the formal inclusion of women's rugby into established governing structures, but it was hardly a smooth process. Most rugby unions were run almost entirely by men, many of whom either refused to admit women's teams or accepted their dues without offering services, resources, or representation in return.

Within the women's game, there was deep debate: should women build their own governing bodies or work to change the existing structures from within? Ultimately, many chose the latter. That strategy not only strengthened the unions over time but also became a training ground for a new generation of women administrators. Most of these pioneers were young—often just out of college, launching careers, still playing the game, and, in many cases, starting clubs simply so they could keep playing. They organized the sport the old-fashioned way: through handwritten letters, long-distance phone calls, and in-person meetings at tournaments and regional gatherings.

Affiliating with existing territorial unions brought short-term benefits. It gave women access to regional select side play and InterTerritorial Tournaments (ITTs), where the competition was fierce and the coaching top-tier. Playing in these settings gave athletes the chance to sharpen their skills and measure themselves against the best. Over time, ITTs became the primary pathway for selecting the U.S. Women's National Team.

Some unions proved to be ahead of their time. In 1980, Karen Dunfey became the first woman president of the New England Rugby Football Union (NERFU). Dana Bateman took on leadership roles as secretary of the Eastern Pennsylvania Rugby Union and director of the Eastern Rugby Union. Leslie Kellenberger served as secretary of the North Carolina Union and as an "at-large" ERU director.

These women—young, determined, and often underestimated—were not just building teams. They were quietly reshaping the power structures of American rugby.

*Back in 1982...*

| | |
|---|---|
| *Yearly tuition at private university (fees, room and board)* | **$7,600** |
| *Yearly tuition at public university (fees, room and board)* | **$3,200** |
| *Monthly rent* | **$320** |
| *Per capita income* | **$11,538** |
| *Adults with a bachelor's degree* | **17.0%** |

# WOMEN PROFILE:

## Jennie Redner

**Name:** Jennie Redner
**Birthplace:** Pontiac, Michigan
**Age:** 24
**Present Residence:** Orchard Lake, Michigan
**Occupation:** Sales Engineer
**University:** Michigan State University

### PLAYING EXPERIENCE

**Years Playing Rugby:** 4
**Positions Played:** All forward positions, but mostly second row
**Favorite Position:** Wing forward
**Present Club:** Detroit
**Previous Clubs:** Michigan State & Ohio State
**Representative Experience:** MWWRFU Select Side 78, 79, 80, 81.
**Most Valuable Teammate:** Tanya Fry, fullback, Ohio State.
**Most Difficult Opponent:** Bev Buhr, No. 8, Madison.
**Favorite Player:** Joe Sauer, second row, Milwaukee. I'd like to be as effective in loose play as Joe is ... someday!
**Toughest Opposing Team:** Chicago
**Favorite Tournament:** Classic City Ruggerfest-Athens, Georgia
**Biggest Disappointment In Rugby:** Peoples' irresponsibility and willingness to let a few do all the work.

### REFEREEING EXPERIENCE

**Years Refereeing:** 1
**Refereeing Highlight:** Detroit vs. Michigan at the 1981 Cherry Pit Tournament
**Referring Ambition:** To be the first female B-level referee

### ADMINISTRATIVE EXPERIENCE

**Administrative Positions Held:**
USARFU Women's Committee:
  Chairperson May 81 - Present
  Secretary/Treasurer Sept. 79 - May 81
Midwest Women's RFU:
  President Jan 80 - Present
  V. President Aug. 78 - Jan 80
Midwest Women's Referee Society:
  Executive Committee Aug 80 - Present
Michigan State University WRC:
  President & Captain Jan 78 - Dec 79
**Administrative Goals:**
(1) To see the four territorial union develop strong and cohesive women's organizations.
(2) To see these four territories work together towards:
  (A) Improved relationships with men's rugby.
  (B) Better communication.
  (C) Improved levels of rugby skills
(3) To achieve the following long term goals:
  (A) National select side competition
  (B) National university championship
  (C) National touring side
**Observations On Women's Rugby:** Women's rugby has grown tremendously in the four years I've been involved, but I don't see that much change in the quality of play. We need coaches and good refereeing to improve the level of play.
**Leisure Interests:** Running, Cross-Country Skiing, Racquetball.
**Favorite Book:** The Fountainhead, Ayn Rand
**Personal Ambition:** To complete my MBA and run a marathon.

## Lockett Opens Door For Women Referees

by John Mellish

The appointment of a woman to referee the ERU Division II Men's Championship (Philadelphia, April 27-28) definitely raised a few eyebrows. But, when the dust has settled, Laurel Lockett had made believers of everyone present. It was obvious to all that it is possible for women to compete with men on an equal basis in at least one area of rugby.

The 29-year-old Lockett was born in New York City, majored in pre-law at Smith College. She was introduced to rugby through the Beantown RFC but retired early in her career to take up refereeing in 1981-82. After joining the New England Society, she rapidly rose through the local grades to C1, showing a great deal of character in the process. She attributed her progress to the coaching and encouragement of Don Morrison and John Hayes, who supported her throughout.

After moving to Florida last year, Lockett joined the Florida Society and soon came under the eye of national evaluator Bob Jones. His recommendation of an immediate advancement to B3 grade resulted in an invitation to Philadelphia.

Her sensational game was watched by four ERU evaluators, whose performance sheets submitted after the game showed two "A" ratings (out of seven categories), an almost unheard of mark for a referee of her grade.

The ERU Referee Society hopes that other women, who have perhaps been doubtful of their reception, will now take the step toward their local referee society, through the door opened by Lockett.

Lockett, an attorney specializing in environmental conservation, resides in Tampa, Florida.

*B-3 referee, Laurel Lockett, is in control of the action in the ERU Second Division Championship match between Severn River and Light Horse.*
*(Photo-Hagerty)*

## Dallas Rocks For Special Olympics

The Dallas Rugby Club and friends are working together to benefit the 2,000 Special Olympians in the Dallas area. Funds raised will provide entry fees and equipment enabling these special athletes to participate in basketball, swimming, track, softball, bowling and other sports. Your contributions will help insure the continuation of these programs.

On Friday, June 7, 1985, the first annual dance, "Rock-It with Rugby," will be held in the Reunion Ballroom of the Hyatt Regency Hotel. Entertainment will be provided by Johnnie D and the Rocket 88's. Tickets for this event are:
  Patron $62.50 per person; $125 per couple/$500 a table
  Regular $30 per person; $60 per couple; $240 a table
  Patron tickets include a black tie affair held prior to June 7th and an invitation to the Dallas 7's Rugby Tournament on June 8th as well as the "Rock-It With Rugby" Dance.
  Please send your tax deductible donations and/or ticket monies (check made payable) to: Dallas Rugby Charity Ball, 2530 Hillsboro, Dallas 75228.

stone Way, Louisville Kentucky 40223. Checks for payment must accompany all orders.

The 1985 MWRFU handbook will be a valuable addition to any rugby player's library.

*Laurel Locket became the first woman referee to achieve a B2 rating and referee men's league play.*

*The Potomac, in blue and white, competes against New England, in green, in regional select side play*

## September 20 & 21, 1980  New York, NY

The Third Annual Big Apple Classic was hosted by Old Blue Women's Rugby Club and sponsored by Miller Beer.  Entrants included defending champions Portland (Maine), Montreal Irish, Beantown, Cornell University, Hartford Wild Rose (Conn.), Rutgers and Cortland State (NY).

In the third place contest, the Wild Rose returned to the pitch after only a thirty minute rest to battle the rested Cortland State.  The younger, faster college players used their possession to produce several long runs and a three try victory over Wild Rose.  Hartford's efforts and spirit earned them the Third Half Award for Sportsmanship.

Portland advanced with victories over Beantown "B" and Hartford to earn a slot in the final match.  Beantown  qualified by defeating Montreal and Cornell University.  The Final started sluggishly with  the Portland forwards dominating and Beantown's backs using their limited possession to better advantage. Weariness seemed to overcome Portland near the end of the first half, and the second phase ball produced by the Beantown backrow nearly resulted in two tries.

Late in the second half, Beantown's number eight, Laurel Lockett, scored from a five meter scrum for the games only score.  Lockett's try gave Beantown gave Beantown the upset victory and the Championship.

---

## WOMEN

# N. England Wins First ERU Select Tourney

**By Widgie Still**

**Washington, D.C.
November 5-6, 1983**

In a weekend of shutouts, the New England Rugby Union women handed the Florida Women's Rugby Union a 10-0 defeat in the first women's select side tournament ever held in the United States. The tournament involved eight Eastern Rugby Union select sides including North Carolina, Potomac, Eastern Penn. Florida, New England, Virginia, Georgia and Met New York. This "first-ever" event took place on a cold, sometimes rainy and windy weekend before thousands of spectators and interested tourists.

"The outcome was not as important as the event," said ERU Women's Chairperson, Judy Tixier. Echoing her thoughts, ERU President Mike Machado called the tournament a "landmark for women's rugby." Machado indicated that the ERU is planning to make this an annual event and ultimately develop a National Select Side Tournament.

**Final**

The final between New England and Florida was hard-fought even though the outcome was rarely in doubt. New England dominated from the opening kick off and a smooth backline movement got the ball to winger Micky McVann. She

Florida scrumhalf Mary Holmes prepares to put the ball in vs New England in Championship.
(Photo L. Lukas)

brought the ball to the one meter line, where a scrum was called. New England scrum half Connie Cepko took the ball from the scrum and dove over for the try and an early 4-0 lead.

New England kept the pressure on for the first 15 minutes, but Florida was able to utilize its kicking game to keep New England at bay. Finally though, the ball went from fly half Karen Onufry to the outside center, who passed back to looping scrum half Cepko. Cepko passed to fullback Sue Yaghgian, who had joined the line and Yaghgian fed the winger for an easy try in the corner. The conversion by Onufry was good giving New England a 10-0 halftime lead.

**2nd Half**

New England started strong in the second half, but penalties and Florida's kicking foiled any scoring threat. In the final 15 minutes, Florida picked up the pace and New England appeared to be waiting for the final whistle.

**Consolation**

In the highest-scoring game of the day, the Potomac Rugby Union took third place with a 26-0 victory over Met N.Y. Met New York's only scoring opportunity came early in the match with a penalty kick and from there on it was all Potomac.

Wing forward Judy Tixier, with two tries had an outstanding game.

The tournaments organizers produced a first class program which included team lineups and letters from senators in the states represented. Also, each participant received a hand calligraphied certificate acknowledging their participation in this historic event.

1983: First Eastern Rugby Union Championship

## CLUB RUGBY

**BY 1980, WOMEN'S RUGBY IN THE UNITED STATES** had grown to 212 teams. All were classified as club teams—there were no college divisions yet, and youth or high school programs didn't exist. Most clubs relied on weekly tournaments to get matches, packing their weekends with as much rugby as they could play.

That same year, Florida State University captured the 1980 Women's National Rugby Classic, the de facto national championship. The tournament brought together eight teams from the East, Midwest, and West. Although Pacific teams were invited, none made the trip.

Throughout the 1980s, the National Championships were defined by an intense rivalry between Florida State and Beantown. The two powerhouses met in four finals and, between them, claimed seven of the nine national titles that decade. Their battles on the pitch set the standard for competition, inspired countless new teams, and carved their names into the early history of women's rugby in America.

**1981:** The Women's Rugby Classic is renamed the Women's National Championship. The *First Annual Women's Rugby National Championship* was held May 23 – 25 in Oakbrook IL. The field included sixteen teams. Teams played four matches over two days. Belmont Shore beat Beantown in a close final. Players from both teams were awarded gift boxes of make-up from Avon along with champagne—not a good combo after a tough rugby weekend.

**1982:** First recorded High School girls team, St Agnes High School, Fairfax VA.

By 1989 there were three high school teams in the U.S.—St Agnes High School, Lake Braddock High School and West Springfield High School. All were in Northern Virginia.

*1980 the California Kiwis become the first U.S. women's team to tour New Zealand*

*1981 Belmont Shore v Beantown*

# Women's Union Formed

The Pacific Northwest RFU was formed July 12th. Rising from the ash of Mt. St. Helens in Yakima, Washington, this new Union serves Washington, Idaho, Montana and Oregon. (possibly SW Canada, someday)

Alice Shepard and Kristine Chatwood were elected to run the Union until officers are elected at the next meeting.
Alice Shepard
13920 Par Place NE
Seattle, WA 98125
Kristine Chatwood
3003 SE Taylor
Portland, OR 97214

## Rugby M.V.P.
### Kathy Cantu
### Belmont Shores

Kathy Cantu prepares for the throw in vs Beantown.
[Photo-Prammack]

---

# Women's Game Is Growing

by Thomas Link

"Women's rugby has come a long way since the first game was played in Colorado in 1972," states Ed Lee, USARFU Historian and Archivist. "The growth of the women's game in America has been tremendous."

### Jennie Redner

Jennie Redner, past chairperson of the USARFU Women's committee, has been one of the main catalysts behind the rapid growth of the sport.

"We've grown from just 75 to over 7500 players in the past ten years, and we continue to grow every year. Now with over 250 clubs, the U.S. is the oldest and largest women's rugby-playing country in the world."

### Athleticism

Lee Chichester, Editor of the Women's Committee national newsletter, In Support, cites the growth of athleticism among American women as a major factor in the rapid progress of the women's game.

"Witness the emergence of women's marathons and bodybuilding as well as the growth of tennis and racquetball for women," says Chichester. "Fitness among all Americans has developed into a national pastime. That female athletes have gravitated toward rugby comes as no real surprise to most. It is rugby's uniqueness and challenge which convert regular athletes into rugby athletes."

### Attractions

"I like the competition", comments Michigan State scrumhalf Marie Wolfe, who played college basketball before turning to rugby. "You're always learning something new on the field."

Prop Liz Seaton never played sports before joining the Michi-

Marcia Borge, new chairperson of the USARFU Women's Committee. (Photo-Link)

gan State team. "I was a member of the marching band in high school. Rugby's biggest attraction for me is the comraderie off the field as well as the physical challenge."

### Professionals

About 75% of the women players nationwide are college graduates in professional or skilled labor positions.

"With women now in jobs so stress-producing, rugby is a great tension reliever," states Chicago's Marcy Borge, USARFU Women's Committee newly elected chairperson.

Even as rugby attracts women from various backgrounds the overall level is improving because better athletes are beginning to come to the game.

### Better Athletes

"Title IX, which gives equal funding to women's sports in high school and college, has been a tremendous boost to rugby," says Borge. "It has created a larger pool of women athletes to draw upon."

Beantown coach Kevin O'Brien is a veteran of 28 years of rugby. "It's only this year that Beantown is getting athletes

from other team sports. In the past we used to get runners or swimmers who wanted competition."

### More Coachable

O'Brien, who coaches two men's teams in Boston as well as perennial women's powerhouse Beantown, feels that women are more coachable than many men.

"In men's rugby in general there are too many egos to contend with because they've grown up playing football. A lot of women are more single-minded in that they want to play winning rugby and understand that in order to do that they've got to play good rugby. They do the things they have to do and so they don't get into the frustrating rubbish (personal battles and fights) that some men do."

Lee Chichester points out that "In some instances, the replacement of finesse for brute strength makes women's rugby a more refined game than the men's."

Coach O'Brien is excited about the progress women's rugby has made on the field. "The overall standard of technique is a lot higher this year, and I expect the level to continue to improve."

### Growth

As the game continues to attract better athletes and the standard of play rises, chairperson Borge has high expectations. "I see women's rugby growing and improving over the next ten years to the point where the U.S. will have established territorial select sides regularly playing each other and even a national team to compete internationally."

Borge's goals for women's rugby are threefold. "We must increase visibility of the game, improve our image, and strive for a higher level of play across the country."

---

# Beantown: National Champs

By Jennie Redner

Oakbrook, Ill.
May 29 & 30, 1982

Suburban Chicago's picturesque Oakbrook Sports Core was the site of the final Annual Women's National Championships. Hosted by the USARFU Women's Committee, the tournament featured the nation's top eight teams vying for the National Championship and beautiful USARFU trophies.

### TEAMS

Each of the eight clubs qualified for the Nationals by competing in regional and then territorial events. The top two teams from each territory earned the right to come to Oakbrook. The Eastern RFU teams fared the best with Beantown finishing 1st and Florida State coming in 4th. The Midwest Union was second overall, with Chicago and Wisconsin placing 2nd and 6th, respectively. Houston and New Orleans, from the Western RFU were next, finishing 3rd and 7th, and the Pacific Coast's representatives, Belmont Shore and She Hawks, took the 5th and 8th slots.

### PRELIMINARIES

The first round pairing saw the Pacific face the East and the Midwest face the West. The tournament's first game Saturday morning was possibly one of the most exciting, as 1979 and the National Champion Florida State upset defending 1981 National Champion, Belmont Shore. Although dominated by FSU's offense, Shore did not allow Florida to score in the first half. Two missed penalty by Belmont in the second half could have made a difference in the match, but FSU scored a try and conversion late in the game to win 6-0.

The other first round matches were more one-sided as Chicago soundly defeated New Orleans 30-4, Beantown ran circles around the She Hawks 64-0 and Houston defeated Wisconsin 20-4 to advance into the championship bracket.

### SEMI-FINALS

The first semi-final, which took place Saturday afternoon, paired FSU against Chicago. In a very close match, both teams scored two tries and one conversion, to level the score (16-16) at the end of regulation play. Tournament rules specified that tied teams play a 10 minute period of 5's and if still tied, sudden death 7's. Chicago put on tremendous pressure to score in the 10's, because the prospect of facing FSU's talented backs in 7's was unpleasant. However, neither team could get near in-goal in the first overtime period. In sudden death 5's, Chicago attacked off the first scrumwage as FSU's defense was out of po-

sition and Connie Bloom scored the game winning try, giving Chicago a sweet 18-16 victory.

Beantown faced Houston in the second semi-final and Houston became a 20-4 victim in Beantown's march to the Championship. Houston held Beantown to four points in the first half, but could not stop the onslaught in the second frame. Anne Fowler scored two tries and two conversions, while Nancy Breen and Karen Onufry contributed one apiece.

Saturday night festivities featured a Hawaiian party on the pool patio of the Hyatt Oakbrook Hotel. Beantown's Salvation Army dressed and partying, although New Orleans deserves an honorable mention.

### THIRD PLACE

Sunday morning's raw bout of Florida State and Houston vying for third place. The Houston Hearts feature several former Florida Hurlers, so a match between these clubs is one of very similar playing styles. FSU's fans however scored a try in the first minute of the match to quickly put FSU into the lead. But Houston came right back with a pushover try by Monica Romagnoli. Later in the half as FSU never gave Chris Harju a penalty goal and Houston lead 7-6. Then in the second half, another Harju goal rounded out the Hearts' scoring.

Both clubs are to be commended for their superb play and the improvement over last year's standings.

### CHAMPIONSHIP

The Championship was played at 1 PM, allowing both teams to get a good night's sleep. However the Mid-western heat and humidity really took it's toll during this game. Bright sunshine, 85 degree heat and 96 percent humidity made it uncomfortable for spectators, much less players. To prevent injury and heat prostration, referee Steve Cohen allowed water to be brought onto the field at all time outs.

Beantown put on an excellent display of 15 person rugby. Both forwards and backs scored in a balanced attack keyed by tailback Nancy Breen, who played an excellent game. Chicago appeared to tire early due to the heat and a very difficult overtime game the day before. They played valiant defense most of the match, but it was clear that Beantown was the stronger team as they rolled to a 25-0 shutout.

### AWARDS

At the awards ceremony following the Beantown victory, USARFU President Dave Chambers noted the tremendous growth and administrative strength of women's rugby and reiterated USARFU's support of the women's game. He then awarded tournament balls to Houston and Florida State for placing 3rd and 4th, and two beautiful miniatures of the National Championship Cup to Beantown and Chicago. The permanent Cup resides in my

Farmington Hills living room, where any rugger is welcome to see this magnificent USARFU tribute to women's rugby.

### ALL TOURNAMENT TEAM

All national long, independent selectors viewed matches to choose the All-Tournament Team. The goal of this selection was to honor players who don't get the recognition they deserve for contributions to their club. The selector's task was difficult, as the competition for each position was fierce, and each player was given an individual certificate as award.

**Props**
Molly Perdue, Chicago
Mary Moynihan, Beantown
**Hooker**
Missy Bowers, Chicago
**Second Row**
Laurel Lockell, Beantown
Marti Barnes, Belmont Shore
**No. 8**
Anne Fowler, Beantown
**Wing Forwards**
Sharon Fields, Houston
Marcia Holtz, Wisconsin
**Flyhalf**
Polly Freeman, Wisconsin
**Scrumhalf**
Kathy Fiore, Florida State

**Inside Center**
Molly Perdue, Chicago
**Outside Center**
Candi Orozo, Florida State
**Wings**
Laura Agostino, Wisconsin
Vanessa Calabrese, Chicago
**Fullback**
Sharon Ammons, Florida State

Congratulations, ladies!

In Summary, I'd like to thank three special people who helped make Nationals happen in a big way: Mary Larkin, Matt Gedek and Roberta Lewis. Thanks!

Beantown's Ann Fowler prepares to pass. (Photo-Prammack)

---

**Top left:** *1980 the Pacific Northwest forms the fourth Women's Union.*

**Bottom right:** *Marcia Borge, one of the early women's committee members and architect of the women's national club championships, was at the forefront of a gifted group of female leaders.*

**Top right:** *1982 Beantown claim their first National Championships*

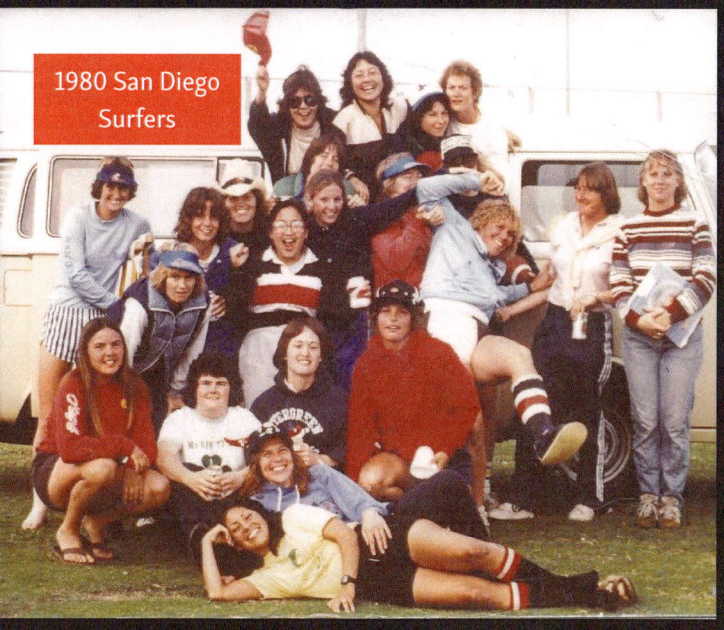

1980 San Diego Surfers

1981 Houston Heathen Hearts

1981 Dusty Lentils (Idaho)

1981 San Diego State University

1982 Dartmouth College

1985 New Orleans Halfmoons

THIS IS THE LIFE!

1984 Hartford Wild Roses

1985 Norwich University

1989 Santa Monica Women

I can't tackle now, dear. I'm off weekends.

2nd ANNUAL

MAID IN THE SHADE

WOMEN'S rugby TOURNAMENT

march 18-19, 1989

TALLAHASSEE FLORIDA

## Women's Referee Society

In what is believed to be a first,
the Midwest Women's Rugby
Union has formed it's own
referee society. The Midwest
Women's Referee Society
(MWRS) is parallel in structure
to the Midwest Men's Society,
and uses the same forms and sys-
tems developed by them
(Except genders were changed!)
    Society Chairperson, Leslie
Jamison's pioneering efforts and
dedication to women's rugby
have made the Society possible.

The 1980-81 Society Secretary i
Sandy Starrett and the Executiv
Officers are Suzy Ankenbrand
Elissa Augello, Kathy Korse an
Jennie Redner. All offices ar
held for a term of one year. Th
next election will be held at th
1981 Annual General Meeting.

    To be a member of the Society
you must have attempted th
referees exam (not necessaril:
pass) and pay Individual Mem
ber Annual Dues of $6.00
However, only members passing
the exam are eligible to vote.

Club Dues are $5.00 per year
and entitle member clubs to have
referees assigned to their games.
At the present time, there are a
limited number of women
referees who are available only
to do tournaments. As the
number of referees increases,
clubs will be able to have refs
assigned to their weekend club
side matches.

    The Society's first Annual
General Meeting will be held
Saturday Night of the MWRFU
Tournament, October 18th, in W
Lafayette at the Holiday Inn. A
cocktail hour (beginning at 6:00)
and dinner (proper dress re-
quired) will precede the meeting.

    If you are interested in more
information about the Society,
please contact Leslie Jamison,
Chairperson, Midwest Women's
Referee Society, 10135 E. South
Shore Dr., Unionville, IN 47468.

One of the great stories in the history of U.S. women's rugby is the **1984** National Championships. The Chicago Women's Rugby Club set a high bar for the National Championships, hosting them at The Polo Grounds. The 1984 Championships were the first to host an awards banquet and to select an All-Tournament Team—which became an early identifier for the 1987 Women's National Team. But how they were able to pull off the Championship is really a story worth hearing.

**Top left:** *1983 Jennie Redner, one of the first women referees to officiate men's matches in action*
**Middle left:** *1982: First recorded High School girls team, Lake Braddock, Fairfax, VA.*
**Bottom left:** *Chicago Women's Rugby Club patch*
**Top right:** *1980 Midwest women form the first Women's Referee Society*

*One million bucks to Steve Cohen*

"*The Chicago Lions RFC had quite a bit of influence in Midwest rugby at that time and convinced the Midwest Referees' Society not to support the Women's Nationals that year. Thankfully we were rescued by the East and West Referees' Societies. In fact a number of referees really stepped up to help us.*" (Mary Larkin, Chicago WRFC) One of those early referee supporters was Steve Cohen who crossed lines to referee at the 1984 Championships. In gratitude the Women's Committee awarded Steve a million dollar check.

*The Eugene Housewives, logo by Jill Chappel*

For much of the 1970s and 1980s, rugby—both men's and women's—lived firmly in the realm of counterculture. A big part of that identity revolved around the sport's drinking culture. It wasn't uncommon to find kegs right on the sidelines at college and club matches, and beer companies frequently sponsored tournaments and events. Tales of legendary drinking sessions and outrageous antics were passed down as proud team lore.

Team socials were rowdy affairs, filled with raunchy songs, irreverent skits, and plenty of alcohol. With few governing bodies or formal structures to police behavior, rugby operated on its own informal code. Women partied just as hard as the men—though, notably, with far less of the sexual violence that plagued some men's spaces.

Amid this irreverence, women's teams found creative ways to subvert and parody the patriarchal culture that surrounded them. One of the most famous examples was the Eugene Housewives—a team that turned the raunchy, male-dominated rugby narrative on its head and made it their own. Their humor was bold, biting, and empowering, proving that women could inhabit the culture of rugby on their own terms.

While men wore shirts with, *it takes leather balls to play rugby,* the Pittsburgh Women's Team countered with t-shirts that read *No Balls at All* and the Ohio State Women wore the infamous *Iron Ovaries* Tee's.

# Women Executives In U.S. Rugby

Compiled by Thomas Link

A recent issue of New Zealand's **Rugby News** contained an article entitled "Woman is Elected Supporters President" and described Margaret Robertson's unprecedented election as the first female president of the Otago Rugby Supporters Club.

The article states, however, that she does not believe that women have a place in rugby administration. "Rugby is very-much a man's game," Robertson said. "Women can help on the social side but I do not think they can administer a man's game."

Ms. Robertson's sentiments are anything but true in America. The United States rugby community has found a valuable source of energy and a wealth of new ideas in their female administrators.

In the accompanying survey, **Rugby** has asked four prominent East Coast administrators to detail their exposure to the game, explain its attraction, and share their views of female administrators in a predominantly male sport.

The respective clubs and unions these women represent are admittedly indebted to their dedicated contribution to the game.

We at **Rugby** encourage the U.S. rugby community at all levels to attract more capable women administrators, a virtually untapped reservoir of energy, hard work, and creative ideas.

## Valley Women Win

by Anne Hoogsteden

April 9-10, 1982

The second annual Rutgers Rugby Classic was won by the Valley Women (Amherst, Mass.), who defeated the Cherry-OH's (South Jersey) in the championship, 14-4.

Valley's powerful scrum overwhelmed the Cherry-OH's. The Valley Women played very consistently; winning nearly every hook and getting the ball out to their wings. Although the game was played mainly in the Cherry-OH's end of the field, their defense allowed Valley only three tries. In the second half, the Cherry-OH's broke through the Valley defense with quick passes to the wing for their only try.

**Prelims**

To reach the semifinals, Valley defeated New York and Franklin & Marshall while the Cherry-OH's defeated the Maulie Maguires (Bethlehem) and the Rutgers B side.

In the semifinals, Valley defeated Rutgers (18-0) and the Cherry-OH's overcame Montclair (10-6).

| Name: | Dana Bateman | Karen Dunfey | Leslie Kellenberger |
|---|---|---|---|
| Age: | 31 | 29 | 30 |
| Marital Status: | Single | Married to Roy | Married to Jim |
| Education: | Northampton Community College, A.A.S. | Boston University- Philosophy major | B.A. in political science, Westhampton College (Univ. of Richmond) |
| Occupation: | Sales Office Coordinator American McGaw | E.R.U. Salaried administrator and mother of 6 mo. daughter | Commercial property management |
| Years Involved in Rugby: | 8 | 8 | 8 |
| Present Position in Rugby: | Secretary, EPRU ERU Director | President, NERFU | Secretary, N.C.RFU At-large ERU Director ERU Tours Chairman |
| Previous Administration Experience: | Bethlehem Hooligan Newsletter Editor | 1976-77 Treasurer, Boston Women; 1978 NERFU Director (first woman on the Board); 1979-80 NERFU Secy. of Tours and Tournaments; 1981-82 President of NERFU. Boston Int'l. Tournament Committee Member 1980, '83. Co-chairman USA v. England Committee (1982). | NCRFU Newsletter Editor Select Side Match Secretary |
| How were you introduced to rugby? | In August 1975, the Newport (Wales) RFC was touring part of the EPRU. The Lehigh Valley All-Stars, a combination of the Bethlehem Holligans and Allentown Blues, had scheduled a game. The night before the game I met several players and they convinced me to come out and watch. | In 1975, a former boyfriend began playing with Boston University. In 1976 he switched to the Boston RFC, the same year a Boston women's RFC was forming. I joined ("It'll be good exercise, and our training is on the same night.") and the friendship of that group of women was a totally new experience — team camaraderie — and I loved it. | Dated a couple of guys in college who played at the University of Richmond, married one who played for N.C. State and then took up refereeing. |
| How did you become involved in the administration of rugby? | I began helping Tim Cassidy do "The Kazoo," Bethlehem's newsletter. When Tim "resigned" I took over as editor. I also began arranging hosting in players' homes when the Hooligans had incoming tours. | In 1978, a woman from rival club Beantown was nominated for Boston-area director. Though I hadn't even thought of a union position, I figured if she could run, so could I, and agreed to let a friend nominate me. | Since I always accompany my husband in his rugby travels, I was in a good position to see what areas needed improving. On the way to the Union AGM in 1978, I mentioned that I thought I'd run for Union Secretary at the next AGM. I knew I could do as good a job as some of the other bozos who were nominated. My husband nominated me that year instead. And I was elected. |
| What is it about your administrative involvement that makes it a worthwhile expenditure of time? | Getting to travel to places I've always wanted to go to, and knowing that I'll have something in common with the new people I'll meet. Being involved with an excellent executive committee in the EPRU. We've organized and run two very successful coaching clinics (over 225 people at this year's!), set up a mini rugby program and are putting together a high school presentation. It's a pleasure to work with people who want to help rugby grow and act responsibly toward that end. | Rugby has enabled me to succeed in a leadership position and my jobs did not (partly due to my rugby involvement, or over involvement). Now, with the ERU Administrative Office opening up, my years of effort will pay off for me. I can run the office from my home, which enables me to look after my daughter as well. | In North Carolina, the strides made in the last few years are remarkable. Part of it is simply the maturing process in rugby but part of it is this: If I haven't done anything else in the last three years I have succeeded in keeping communications open between the clubs and between the Union and the ERU. We have an updated contact list available on each club at all times, we have a newsletter that comes out consistently and our handbook is tops (with thanks to Karen Dunfey and the one she did for New England) |
| Have you encountered problems as a woman administrator in a male-dominated sport? | Generally, no. | Working for a men's rugby organization often results in no credit or appreciation. Some men are willing to let a woman do the work, while the men retain titles of significance, and the club gets the benefit. | Only with Kevin Kitto. Everyone else has praised my work. (His letters always started "Dear Madam"). I do think it's harder for non-Americans to accept women on any level of rugby, administrating or playing. |
| How can we get more capable women involved in the administration of rugby? | Very simply, we must ask them. This can be a problem as men usually don't want to ask women. Face it, one man can't play, coach, select, referee **and** organize; he may need help. They must admit they need help, then try to create a welcome atmosphere for women. | It's time that administrators, selectors and referees, etc. who have been involved solely in men's or women's rugby integrate and eliminate duplication of effort. Women administrators, selectors and referees must insist on their deserved recognition, and work with men for the future of our great sport. | The women now involved are good role models for future women administrators and we all need to give them lots of positive reinforcement. As far as recruiting, it's my experience that, with a vast, untapped pool such as this, many do not serve because they have never been asked. We shouldn't be shy about asking women to participate. |

*1983 feature in Rugby Magazine on women administrators*

# National Club XV Champions

 **1980** Florida State University

 **1981** Belmont Shore

 **1982** Beantown RFC

 **1983** Beantown RFC

 **1984** Florida State University

 **1985** Florida State University

 **1986** Beantown RFC

 **1987** Beantown RFC

 **1988** Minnesota

 **1989** Bary Area SheHawks

Atlanta Hoydens

Beantown RFC

Chicago

Florida State University

Beantown RFC

San Diego Surfers

Florida State University

Florida State University

Florida State University

Florida State University

1986 Bay Area SheHawks (BASH) with Coach Kathi Morrison

**Left:** *In Support, the rugby publication for women's teams*
*Houston Heathen Hearts v Philadelphia at*
*1982 National Championships*

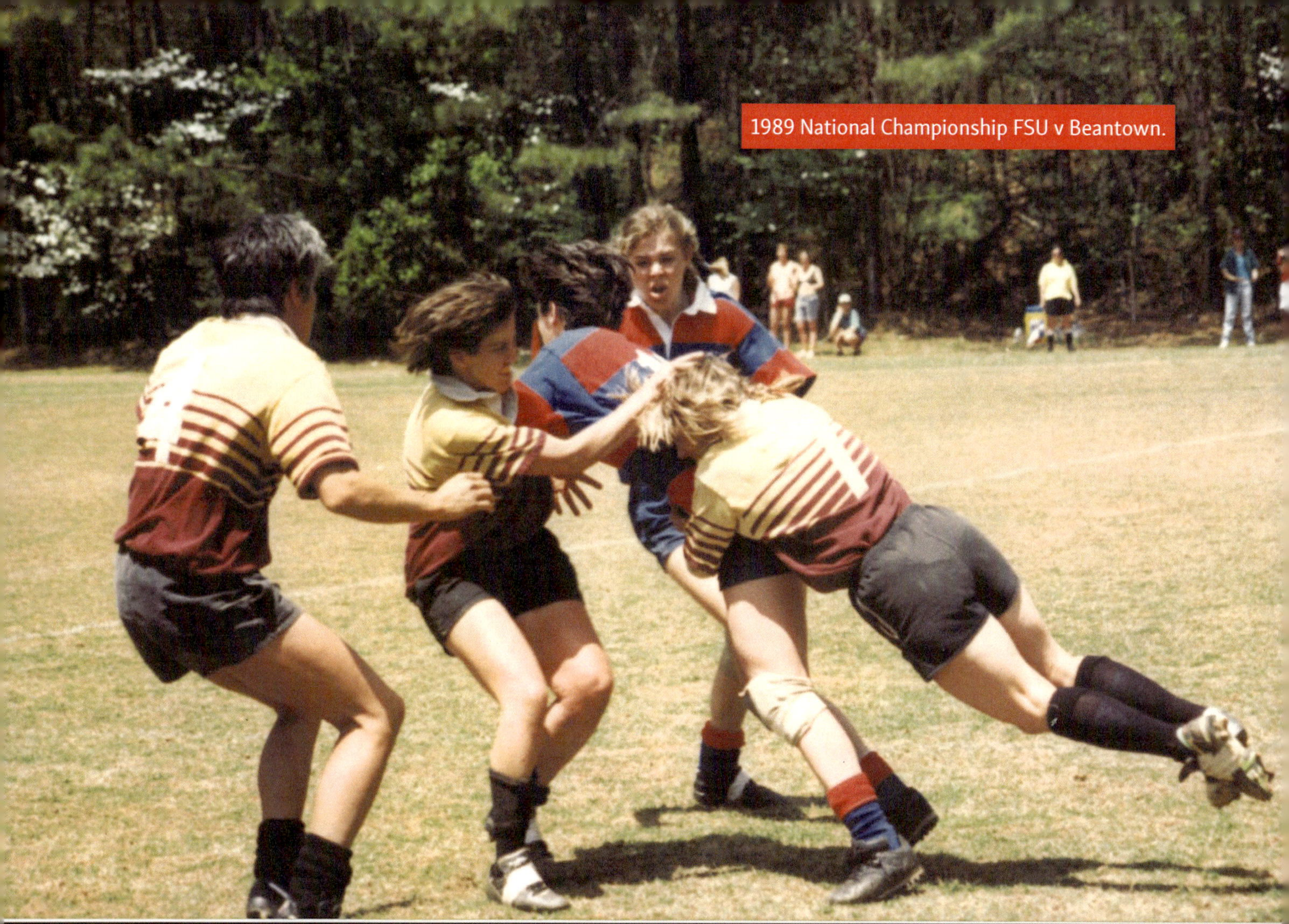

1989 National Championship FSU v Beantown.

# Florida State:Natl. Champs

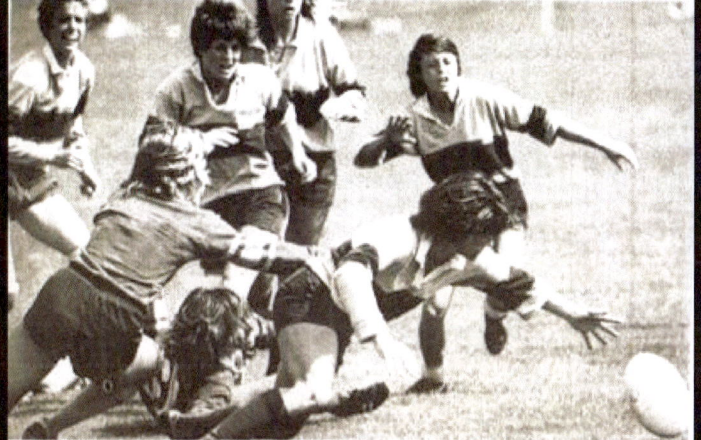

Hoyden players [black band] scramble for the ball in final vs Florida State. Florida State won 14-0. [Photo Hagerty]

1980 MICHELOB ALL-STARS

| Position | Player | Team |
|---|---|---|
| Prop | Mary Ellen Moynahan | Beantown |
| Hooker | Pam Mullins | Beantown |
| Prop | Betsy Kimball | Beantown |
| 2nd Row | Sue Meany | Ohio State |
| 2nd Row | Bev Buhr | Wisconsin |
| No. 8 | Kathy Flores | Florida State |
| Wing Forward | Vicky Bowlen | Florida State |
| Wing Forward | Judy Lee | Wisconsin |
| Scrumhalf | Mary Homes | Florida State |
| Flyhalf | Renata Brady | Florida State |
| Inside Center | Cindy Beebe | Chicago |
| Outside Center | Candi Orsini | Florida State |
| Wing | Linda Lillis | Chicago |
| Wing | Jamie McKallister | Florida State |
| Fullback | Karen Hornsby | Florida State |

**Left:** *1980 FSU Atlanta Hoydens*

**Right:** *1980 All Star National Champion All Star Team*

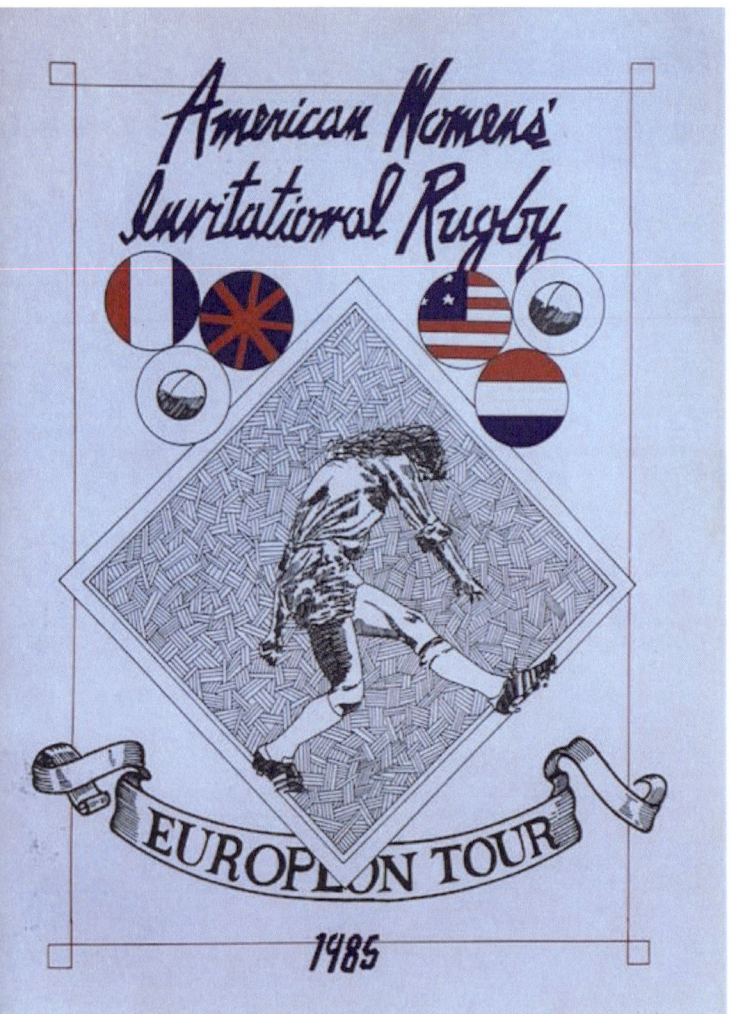

## CREATING THE WOMEN'S NATIONAL TEAM

1985: WOMEN'S INVITATIONAL VAGABONDS, EMISSARIES, AND RUGBY NOMADS (WIVERN)

**THE OPPORTUNITY TO PLAY FOR LOCAL,** regional and territorial championships, a national club championship and to make the 'All-Tournament team' was hugely motivating to many women. Not surprisingly, women's rugby improved, and the blueprint for a women's national team began to take shape. In 1985, Patrick Foley, a coach from the Midwest, invited top players to take part in an invitational touring side, the WIVERNS. The response to his invitation was overwhelming and in the fall of 1985, thirty top players left to play select side and club teams from England and France. The U.S. dominated their opponents, and the British press took notice.

Kathy Flores and Kerri Heffernan

Ruth Bernack, Kathy Flores, Nancy Thorley, Christine Hardju

# Rugger dolls no pushovers

## GEOFFREY NICHOLSON on the growth of women's rugby.

CURIOUS that women should be taking up rugby just when so many men and boys seem to be abandoning the game, put off by its thin vein of brutalism, its cautious repetition, its social and political conservatism. Curious but undeniable; and there is a natural explanation.

On a dank Friday evening at the Wasps ground in north London, Wivern Women's RFC — the 'American Barbarians' — won the third match of their European tour with an attractive briskness and considerable style. Having already beaten a Yorkshire selection at York University and the Midlands at Loughborough, both by 44 – 0, they ran through five tries against the South without any audible reply except heavy breathing.

'That was the hardest game I've ever played,' said Tricia Moore, the South's captain, tugging off her lock's headband and with it several strands of auburn hair. 'But at least we were holding them at the end.'

Today at the University College ground in Shenley there will be another show of strength, when the WRFU (again the W is for Women's not Welsh) put on their first 15-a-side day-long tournament, sponsored by Rugby Travel. Twenty-four teams will take part : two provided by the Americans, the rest from clubs and colleges all over the UK.

Women's rugby is in no way a parody of the men's game, despite the pints on the touchline and the cry of the American coach, (Mr) Pat Foley, 'Let's calm down out there, you guys.'

As any old buffer will tell you, the purest, most enjoyable rugby is played by well-coached schoolboy sides. It is eager, fit and optimistic. It doesn't know that you're not supposed to be able to score direct from set-pieces. Physically undeveloped, it doesn't resort to physical coercion. And that is a more valid comparison with the women's game.

It has the complementary virtues of its vices. Since as a rule women don't trust their kicking (though that may come, and there were a few uncompromising boots to touch), they make their way by running the ball. Since they are not as strong as men, the scrums and mauls (there are scarcely any rucks) are only brief pauses in the flow of the game. The tackling is certainly not faint-hearted, but although one sending-off has been recorded, the play is notably clean.

In the United States women have been playing rugby for 10 years. 'It's much more of a finesse game for us,' said their manager, Darilyn Million, a greenkeeper from Illinois. 'Even the men acknowledge that. They also have the advantage of having probably played basketball, and *not* having played American football, which the men have to unlearn.'

But what's the attraction of rugby, apart from the acknowledgement that women aren't all sugar and spice and also like to get their knees dirty. 'Oh, the first time I played it I just loved it ; I never wanted to play anything else,' said Million, who coaches and referees. 'It's the sociability, the camaraderie. When one of us touches down the ball it's all 15 of us who scored that try.'

They need no longer feel like pioneers. Tomorrow Wivern move on to play two matches in France, where there are around 60 women's clubs. The game is also played in Holland, Sweden, Spain, Italy and, it's rumoured, Russia.

In the UK it grew up in the universities only in the late Seventies, and the WRFU are little more than a year old. They play to the men's rules, but although they are recognised by the RFU — who checked their constitution, put them in touch with their insurance brokers, and provided the services of Don Rutherford and Alan Black for a coaching weekend — they have no plans to apply for affiliation.

There are some 35 clubs at universities or attached to male clubs like Wasps and Finchley and probably 700-800 regular players. Today nearly half of them will be at Shenley, playing 10 minutes each way for a cup or the plate, with the final at 3.20. But if you go there to patronise the little women you might find the smile wiped off your face.

---

## THE AMERICANS ROAR IN AND THE COACH'S CRY IS: EAT 'EM

# Rugby without frills from the deadly women in white

### By SANDRA BARWICK

Crash : U.S. girl catches a Warwick player

Bang : This time it's a Warwick player diving into the tackle

THE tackles came in hard, the injury toll mounted.

There was no quarter asked or given in the first Women's Rugby Football Union tournament yesterday.

Even the Americans were there, fielding two sides that looked fitter and faster than anyone and equipped with a coach who could outshout the opposition.

'C'mon guys,' yelled Darilyn Million to her charges, 'eat 'em.'

On the pitch at Shenley, Hertfordshire, the fourth aid of the day lay waiting for the ambulance. A St John Ambulance man shook his head : 'When they said it was women's rugby I thought it would be a quiet day. This is worse than the men.'

Britain's women's rugby is just seven years old and with only a few sides mainly from universities and colleges. Twenty two were playing yesterday. In America, which has more than 300 clubs, the game has been going for ten years. Yesterday that extra experience showed as the British demonstrated the national virtue of being good losers.

Kathy Flores, from Florida, captain of one of the Wivern (Women's International Vagabonds Emissaries and Rugby Nomads) sides, said : 'We've got a lot of aggression and energy and we really go in to very hard tackles. We hit them real low and throw them up.'

### Chilled

In navy shorts and white shirts, her team had tanned, hard-muscled legs in contrast to the chilled-pink limbs of some Welsh opponents.

Even the most fragile-looking Americans were fiercely fit on a regime of weight training and hard running. Carmen Morrison, a 30-year-old who plays wing three-quarter, showed the scorching pace expected from a former Olympic chase hurdler.

And she disproves the notion that all female rugby players must be 'butch'. She lists her hobbies as dance and fashion and holds down a job with a fashion company.

'Being fit is not unfeminine,' she insisted. 'And I really *enjoy* playing rugby.'

Wallop: Kate Fletcher of Warwick is floored

### Limping

The Wyvern sides have slaughtered all opposition on their British tours.

They reached the semi-finals yesterday but were drawn to play each other and so withdrew, leaving the way open for Wasps, a team from Wembley, to win.

The tournament's final injury count was four in hospital (none hurt seriously) and numerous bumps and bruises.

Warwick University's Kate Fletcher, 21, ended up limping and bandaged to the knee.

'I just ran wrong,' Sue said. 'Rugby girls, you see, don't complain.

PICTURES: BILL CROSS

**1986 Participants in the first women's national team selection camp**

## 1986-1987: THE FIRST WOMEN'S NATIONAL TEAM

**AFTER THE SUCCESS OF THE WIVERN TOUR,** the Women's Committee began to organize a true Women's National Team. USAR administrators accepted an invitation from the Canadian women for the first women's international match yet declined to recognize a U.S. women's national team. The Women's Committee led by Kathi Morrison, Mary Larkin, Judy Tixier, Diane Terwilliger, Marcia Borge and Kitty Keller generated a list of players from Territorial Championships and the National Club Championship and held the first selection camp at Stanford University. Approximately forty-five players were invited to a three-day camp that included physical testing and rotating matches. Twenty-one players were selected—they were the first twenty-one Eagles.

*"The selection camp leading up to the match WAS BRUTAL! The beep test, the mile run, the max lifts and the marathon play for selectors…all in one day with little to no breaks."* (Candi Orsini, Eagle #11)

In a petty move, USAR administrators forbade

**1987: First US Women's National Team**

Bottom row left to right: Vicki Middaugh, Karen Ryan, Kathy Flores, Robin Pace, Deb Dennis, Annie Misko, Christine Hardju, KO Onufry, Barb Bond, Candi Orsini
Top row: Tanya Fry, Cynthia Bystrak, Kerri Heffernan, Mary Money, Mary Sullivan, Lori Reese, Annie Flavin, Dawn Farwick

| | NATIONAL TEAM | 1986 - 1987 |
|---|---|---|

# 1986 – 1987 NATIONAL TEAM

| | | |
|---|---|---|
| 1 | CYNTHIA BYSTRUCK | MIDWEST |
| 2 | DEB DENNIS | PACIFIC |
| 3 | DAWN FARWICK | PACIFIC |
| 4 | ANNIE FLAVIN | EAST |
| 6 | TANYA FRY | MIDWEST |
| 7 | KERRI HEFFERNAN | EAST |
| 8 | ANNIE MISKO | PACIFIC |
| 9 | TRACEY MOENS | WEST |
| 10 | MARY MONEY | EAST |
| 11 | CANDI ORSINI | EAST |
| 12 | ROBYN PACE | EAST |
| 13 | LORI REESE | MIDWEST |
| 14 | KAREN RYAN | MIDWEST |
| 15 | MARY SULLIVAN | EAST |
| 16 | KO ONUFRY | EAST |
| 17 | BARBARA BOND | PACIFIC |
| 18 | TAM BRECKENRIDGE | PACIFIC |
| 19 | JEN CRAWFORD | EAST |
| 20 | POLLY FOUREMAN | MIDWEST |
| 21 | MARGIE MCCLURE | EAST |

**USARFU WOMEN'S COMMITTEE**

*Jami –*
*FYI*

October 16, 1987

Dear National Team Member,

Congratulations on being selected to the National Women's Side! This letter is meant to inform you of some of the things that are going on with efforts to coordinate this event.

The upcoming fixture between the Canadian National Women's Side and the National USARFU Women's Side promises to be both a historic and exciting event. As a member of the first National USARFU Women's Side, and participant of our first sanctioned international match, you will be representing both the United States and women's rugby.

This match will be held in conjunction with the Canadian *"Beavers"* and the United States' *"Eagles"* match. There will be representatives present from the Canadian Rugby Union, United States Rugby Football Union, and national and international sponsors. The impression you make here will determine the viability of our future international matches. With this in mind, We would like to go over a few pertinent and sometimes overlooked points of protocol.

Behavior should be appropriate, both on and off the pitch. Any infraction will be dealt with severely, including possible suspension from the team.

Official tour clothes are: Grey Skirt (or nice grey slacks), White Blouse, Navy Blue Blazer (or navy blue sweater). These tour clothes are to be supplied by you. Official tour clothes should be worn in transit, and at all official functions. No shorts, t-shirts, or sweats, except for official tour sweats (if provided), can be worn in any public areas of the hotel. At this point in time we believe hotels will be paid for all participants, and arrangements will be made by us.

It is expected that you will treat all officials and referees in a respectful manner. Any actions to the contrary will be dealt with severely.

On tour your staff will be: Head Coach - Kevin O'Brien; Assistant Coach - Dave Hooper; Team Manager - Darilyn Million. As official representatives of the women's committee both Dianne Terwilliger, and Mary Larkin will be present to deal with miscellaneous items.

We all are very excited for this match, and are looking forward to a well-played and victorious outcome.

Yours in rugby

*Dianne Terwilliger*

Dianne Terwilliger, Chairperson

*Mary A. Larkin*

Mary Larkin, National Events Coordinator

# IN SUPPORT OF WOMEN'S RUGBY

*Letter that went out to players selected for the first Women's National Team*

Dear Mr. Fleener:

    The behavior of Fred Paoli during the banquet for the USA and Canadian teams on November 14, 1987 must be reprimanded.

    Making statements like, "women have bastardized the sport" and "the only reason women play is to make a political statement", during a speech at an International event is an embarrassment for <u>all</u> rugby in the United States. The damage inflicted to the rugby community, especially women's rugby, will be felt for years to come.

    Mr. Paoli owes a public apology to you, as president of the USARFU, and the president of the Canandian Rugby Football Union. It is imperitive that it is received and published in Rugby Magazine and Strategic Rugby.

    I am sending a copy of this letter to Jerry Gallion, president of the Eastern Rugby Union, and requesting an indication of the territories' support be sent to you.

    I implore you to refer this incident to the USARFU disciplinary committee. Please respond to my request by the USARFU meeting in December.

        Sincerely,

        Jami Jordan, Chairperson
        ERU Women's Committee

the women from calling themselves the Eagles or using any recognizable USAR logos. They were given no resources for the historic match and no USAR administrators attended the women's match. Rugby Imports, a supplier historically supportive of women's rugby, stepped up to provide kit for the first women's national team.

It's telling that letters to female players in the 1980s often included reminders to *"behave."* This wasn't entirely without context—rugby at the time was steeped in a drinking culture, with bawdy songs, late-night socials, and hard-partying traditions. But the Women's Committee understood something crucial: the fledgling U.S. Women's National Team wasn't just playing to win. They were playing to prove to local, regional, and national rugby leadership that women were serious, committed, and responsible ambassadors of the game.

As Women's Committee Chair Jami Jordan recalled,

there was resistance within USA Rugby to the idea of a women's international match. *"I remember reading a letter from Mary Larkin, the National Events Coordinator, to the women's team,"* Jordan said. *"She made it clear that the stakes were high and that the team was expected to present themselves in a professional manner."*

The first U.S. women's test match against Canada took place in 1987 in Victoria, British Columbia, as the curtain-raiser to the U.S. men's game against Canada. Coached by Kevin O'Brien (East) and Dave Hooper (West), the U.S. women were well-matched against a strong Canadian side. The game was fast, physical, and fiercely contested—and in the end, the U.S. women claimed a decisive 22–3 victory.

The U.S. men lost to Canada 20–12. After the match, the Canadian hosts invited all four teams to a joint cocktail hour and banquet. But what should have been a unifying moment quickly unraveled. During the captain's remarks, U.S. men's captain Fred Paoli

# Male chauvinist pigskin!

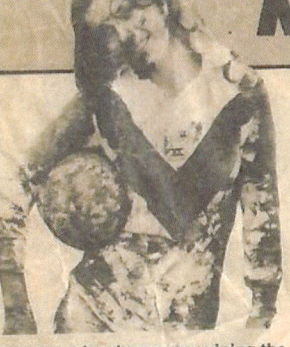

Women rugby players are ruining the game, says the U.S. men's coach.

**By LAURIE MacFAYDEN**
**Staff Writer**

They came, they saw . . . they left in a huff.

The Canadian women's rugby team, bolstered by 10 players from Edmonton's Coven and Rockers clubs, didn't fare well in Saturday's exhibition game against Team USA in Victoria.

But it wasn't the 22-3 loss that left a bitter taste in the players' mouths — it was a direct insult from the U.S. team's captain.

### 'Bastardization'

Though more than 4,000 people turned out to watch the first ever Can Am women's rugby match, Denver lawyer Fred Paoli informed the co-ed post-game banquet crowd that women are ruining the game.

"If women choose to play rugby, that's their right," Paoli said in his after-dinner speech. "But I don't and can't condone their bastardization of our great game.

"Men's rugby is a civilized war for survival and honor, and women can never play as men do," he said.

More than half the audience stormed out.

"To have this idiot American lawyer stand up and tell these women they're *bastardizing* the game, after they worked their butts off out there on the field, was just (bleeping) ridiculous," said Canadian team manager Frank Hunt of Calgary.

"Everyone left. Not just the women, but most of the men, too," said national coach Ian Humphreys, who also coaches the Coven.

"It was really upsetting for the girls. This guy claimed to be a great believer in the American Constitution and the Equal Rights Amendment, then proceeded to tell us that women shouldn't be playing rugby."

Added fullback Shelaine Kozakavich: "It was pathetic. We couldn't believe anyone would stand up and spout crap like that. It ruined the whole tournament."

### 'Aerial ping-pong'

Humphreys maintains the women's rugby game is technically superior to the men's, and said the U.S. situation is no exception.

The American women "don't rely on kicking the ball to gain ground," he said. "Their men just play aerial ping-pong."

## US Women 22, Canada 3

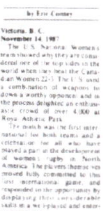

United States National Team

Canadian National Team

**Left:** *Rugby Magazine's write up on the historic 1987 match including the selections—a list of the first fifteen Women's National Team players. The team would not be recognized as Eagles or receive caps for a number of years.*

used his time at the podium not to speak about the match, but to denounce women's rugby and question its legitimacy. As Women's Committee member Mary Larkin later reflected, *"At that time, men frequently let women know what they approved and disapproved of."*

Paoli's comments stunned the room. They offended not only the U.S. and Canadian women's teams but also the Canadian hosts. In a powerful and united act, the U.S. and Canadian women stood up and walked out of the banquet. It was a defining moment in women's rugby history—one that sparked uncomfortable but necessary conversations about entitlement and sexism within the sport.

While USA Rugby remained largely ambivalent, many local unions were outraged—not just by Paoli's remarks, but by the governing body's silence in the face of such blatant disrespect. Letters flew back and forth in *Rugby Magazine*. Paoli refused to admit wrongdoing but eventually issued a limited apology to the Canadians for putting them in a difficult position with their national governing body.

This incident laid bare the deep divide between men's and women's rugby—and between USA Rugby and its own grassroots. Yet, despite the men's disapproval, the Can-Am women's series thrived. For the next ten years, the U.S. women remained undefeated

against Canada, letting their play on the field speak louder than any speech at a banquet ever could.

## 1988: THE FIRST WOMEN'S INTERNATIONAL MATCH IN THE U.S.

BY 1988, THE U.S. WOMEN'S NATIONAL TEAM was making history on the field, but off it, they continued to receive minimal support from USA Rugby (USAR). The team was still denied the title of *Eagles* and forbidden to wear official USAR logos. Every selection camp, training, and match was a *pay-to-play* endeavor for the athletes themselves. Yet despite the lack of institutional backing, public support for the women's program was steadily growing. *(Above: the first USWNT logo)*

As Jami Jordan recalled, Rugby Canada was notably more supportive of its women's program. In the 1988–89 correspondence, the Women's Committee formally requested that USAR Executive Committee members attend national team matches, pointing out that members of Rugby Canada's Executive regularly showed up to support their women. The response

from USAR's leadership was silence—and for the next eight years, not a single USAR Executive Committee member attended a women's national team game.

The second international women's rugby match—and the first ever played on U.S. soil—took place on August 2, 1988, at the Can-Am Tournament in Saranac Lake, New York. Excitement rippled through the crowd as the U.S. Women's National Team took the field under head coach Kevin O'Brien (East) and assistant coach Dave Hooper (West). Both the U.S. and Canadian teams arrived with veteran rosters—strong, disciplined, and eager to make their mark on history.

The U.S. backline boasted two future Hall of Famers at center, Jenn Crawford and Candi Orsini, whose speed and skill became a constant threat. Up front, the forwards dominated the physical contest, securing possession and setting the tempo. Their hard work opened the door for a dynamic attack, and the backs capitalized with precision.

When the final whistle blew, the U.S. women had claimed a 26–10 victory. It wasn't just a win—it was a statement. On home soil, in front of a growing fan base, the team showed the power, and skill that would define a new era of women's rugby in America.

The U.S. women line up before the 1988 game v Canada. Future Hall of Fame players, Candi Orsini, Jenn Crawford and Kathy Flores are pictured at the head of the line. The starting fifteen included six future Hall of Fame players.

# Rugby

"All The News That's Fit"

September

# U.S. Women
# Top Canada 26-10

Canada Fullback Nancy Kouwenhoven advances the ball against the U.S. Women in their recent international in Saranac Lake, NY. The U.S. Women won their second international 26-10. (Photo - Lee)

| UNITED STATES | | | | CANADA | |
|---|---|---|---|---|---|
| **Player** | **Club** | | | **Player** | **Club** |
| Annie Flavin* | Beantown | 1 | | Brenda Treleaven | Winnipeg Wasps |
| Mary Money* | Southeast Harlequins | 2 | | Val Gompf | Winnipeg Wasps |
| Karen Ryan* | University of Minnesota | 3 | | Helen Newsham* | Edmonton Rockers |
| Tam Breckenridge | Belmont Shore | 4 | | Tina Fuchs* | Simon Fraser University |
| Lori Reese* | University of Minnesota | 5 | | Brenda McKenzie | Edmonton Coven |
| Kerri Heffernan* | Beantown | 6 | | Stephanie White | Calgary Renegades |
| Kathy Flores (C)* | Florida State | 7 | | Ruth Hellerud-Brown (C)* | Regina Breakers |
| Barb Bond | Bay Area Shehawks | 8 | | Susan Johnson | Edmonton Rockers |
| Margie McClure | Beantown | 9 | | Corinne Skrobot* | Edmonton Coven |
| Polly Foureman | Madison | 10 | | Karen Richardson* | Ste. Anne de Bellevue |
| Annie Misko* | Bay Area Shehawks | 11 | | Dawn Williams | Regina Breakers |
| Karen Onufry | Beantown | 12 | | Arlette Strashok | Edmonton Rockers |
| Jen Crawford | Berkeley All Blues | 13 | | Shelaine Kozakovich* | Edmonton Coven |
| Candi Orsini* | Florida State | 14 | | Jenny Vincent | Ste. Anne de Bellevue |
| Mary Sullivan* | University of Minnesota | 15 | | Nancy Kouwenhoven* | Pocomo |

**Coach: Kevin O'Brien**
**Assistant Coach: Dave Hooper**

**Coach: Ian Humphreys**
**Assistant Coach: Steve Burgess**

*participated in 1987 Test

**Referee:** Don Morrison (USARFU)
**Touch Judges:** Ed Browder and Mark Binning (ERU)

**The United States Women's National Team (Photo - Lee)**

One of the highlights of the 1988 match was the sponsorship of Lands End who provided jerseys to the U.S. women's team. Lands End sent a crew to the tournament to cover the match and create a spread for the catalog.

**Left:** Lands' End used the match as material for their catalog featuring players and coaches as models and featuring the team.

## IS A U.S. WOMEN'S RUGBY TEAM!

I like the aggressive nature of the sport, that you have to use your whole body. And, the other players are almost like family. If you play rugby, you can move into a new area, and instantly have friends."

Deb Dennis, Scrum Half: "I was always a lockerroom rat. Softball, volleyball, tennis. After four years of field hockey at Southern Illinois, I went for my Master's, and was looking for another sport to play. My roommate happened to be captain of the rugby team.

Rugby helps you rely on people, work with people, trust people. I like that."

And, Jen Crawford, Center: "The best thing I like about rugby is, you play your heart out. It's more challenging physically than any other sport I've played. By the end of regulation, you're dead. Then, you celebrate with the other team. There's lots of camaraderie."

Camaraderie. Challenge. The other women I talked to pretty much echoed those honorable words. And no, not one woman said: "You know, Red, what I like is to really pulverize somebody."

I was impressed by their willingness to sacrifice for their sport. But I wondered, just how well could they play rugby?

### Pretty darn well.

The U.S. team seemed a little nervous, a little disorganized as the CanAm game got underway. (This in spite of the confidence-building powers of their 'tough as the game' Lands' End rugby

*Star "Hooker" Mary Money*

jerseys.) They spent the early part of the first half bottled up at the wrong end of the field.

But then they began to get it going, driving the Canadians back in the scrums, putting the ball in the hands of their speedy backs. Wing Candy Orsini, in "real life" a movie stuntwoman, began running like one, with total shifty abandon, and romped in for the first try at the 11-minute mark, to make it 4-0, USA. Tie kick also was wide.

Canada fought back with a try of its own to tie it at 4, and I realized there's a special thrill to seeing a ponytailed woman speeding down a playing field. (But please, don't analyze that.)

Now, I've seen some classic runs, in football and in rugby, but what came next was one of the best: center Jen Crawford slashed through no less than six tackles for a try, making it 8-4, USA. And, converted the kick too. 10-4!

So ended the first half, a little too close for my liking. I fingered my rabbit's foot nervously.

### Second half runaway.

But I needn't have worried: the second half was strictly nolo contendre, despite a game effort by the Canadian women. First scrum half Margie McClure, then Orsini, then wing Annie Miskio, then McClure again dashed in for tries, while the Canadians could muster only a try and accompanying kick. The U.S. backs ran wild.

Finally, mercifully, the match ended, at 26-10. This win by the women's team completed an unprecedented USA sweep over Canada in 1988, following as it did the men's 20-12 "Sevens" and 28-16 full side wins earlier in the year.

It was as exciting a match as I've seen (and I've seen, uh, eight or nine runs). Even the male ruggers in the crowd seemed impressed, some vociferously, some grudgingly.

And I drew one conclusion, that the women's game is a finesse game, a game of swift running and deft teamwork, not endless running kicks or trying to run over people. Perhaps because women are not brought up in the wham bam "gridiron tradition."

Not that the women's game is for creampuffs: the scrums are fierce, the hitting is hard. Luckily, there were no injuries in this game, but in the 1987 women's CanAm (won 22-3 by the USA), U.S. rugger Dawn "Kiwi" Farwick suffered a broken jaw. And kept playing!

Just as impressive as the game itself was the postgame banquet that night, as the women of the two teams congratulated each other, toasted each other, reaffirmed their common commitment to Rugby.

And, sang to each other too, apparently a rugby tradition. Then, even sang to me, "Red Mulcahy," a lilting rendition of "Teen Angel." Inappropriate for a man of my advanced age, but what the heck. It brought a further blush to my already florid cheeks.

So, if any of you men's ruggers are grumbling, grumble no more. Women's rugby is here to stay. And the U.S. women's national team plays the game in a way to make us all proud.

(And they sure sing better than you guys!)

## YES, VIRGINIA, THERE

*(And they whomp Canada 26-10 for the CanAm crown.)*

by Red Mulcahy
Lands' End Sports Editor
Photos by Chris Mooney

Lake Placid, New York, August 8— Never again will ordinary music sound as sweet to my ears, because...

I have been serenaded by the U.S. Women's Rugby Team!

It was an unlikely conclusion to an August weekend in which I came to Lake Placid on a Friday skeptical of the notion of women even playing rugby, left Lake Placid the following Monday intrigued, charmed, impressed by the dedication, the humor, the undeniable rugby ability displayed by the women of this U.S. national team. A team that whipped Canada 26-10 for the 1988 CanAm championship. And a team that may well be the very best women's rugby team in the world!

But I'm getting ahead of myself...

The first women's rugger I met in Lake Placid was team manager Darlene Connors—"Bubba" to her friends, but still Darlene to her mother—in "real life" a Boston nurse and "Hooker" for perennial rugby club power Beantown. She was apologetic about the hotel we'd all been booked into, a distinctly Dickensian place with sloping floors, brown water, and employees who seemed to pride themselves on their surly deportment.

Yet, this is the flavor of life as a women's rugger. Even though there are about 150 women's clubs teams across the country, the sport is still struggling for recognition, basically without sponsors, and the women who play (especially those who play for the national team) train on their own time, pay their own way, put up with the bad food and bad hotels.

So, with all the hassles, why do they play rugby? I asked a few of them how they got into the game, and why they stick with it.

Barb Bond, Number Eight: "I started playing as a sophomore at Reed College, sort of as a lark. Only one woman on the team had ever played before. Our first game, we were down something like 70-0 at the half!

(A) Before the kick-off. (B) Fierce scrum.
(C) Going high in the line out.
(D) Jen Crawford slashes through.
(E) "Number Eight" Barb Bond. (F) Tough gal, tough shirt. (G) Mary Sullivan, Kerri Heffernan collect congratulations.

12

*The third U.S./Canada International was played in Edmonton, Canada, September 3, 1989. The U.S. beat Canada 28-3.*

CAN-AM RUGBY

WOMEN'S 3RD ANNUAL
INTERNATIONAL TEST MATCH
BETWEEN

CANADA AND U.S.A.

SUNDAY, SEPTEMBER 3, 1989
ELLERSLIE RUGBY PARK

**U.S.A.**        **1989**

| | |
|---|---|
| • Annie Flavin | 1 |
| • Mary Money | 2 |
| • Karen Ryan | 3 |
| Kath Edsall | 4 |
| • Tam Breckinridge | 5 |
| Cynthia Bystrak | 6 |
| Clare Sup | 7 |
| • Barb Bond(capt.) | 8 |
| • Margie McClure | 9 |
| Pat Standley | 10 |
| Krista McFarren | 11 |
| • Jen Crawford | 12 |
| • Candi Orsini | 13 |
| Patty Jervey | 14 |
| Nancy Breen | 15 |
| Vicki Middaugh | 16 |
| Laurie Lockwood | 17 |
| JoElyn Boone | 18 |
| Morgan Whitehead | 19 |
| • Kathy Flores | 20 |
| | 21 |

The U.S.A. National Squad (still with no name) made it **THREE IN A ROW** with yet another successful outing against the Canadians in the 3rd Annual Test Match (see page 4).

In fact, on September 3, the Women's National Squad retained recognition as the North American power, defeating Canada 28-3. The third consecutive win in as many meetings, this annual event was held in Edmonton, Alberta,Canada at Ellerslie Rugby Park. The largely Canadian crowd of 250 was small compared to last year's Saranac event - perhaps among other reasons, distance makes the fans grow thinner,(although the hearts are still there). However, there were those who did travel to help cheer on the Americans to victory,

Led by returning head coach Kevin O'Brien (Beantown) & recently elected assistant coach Chris Leach (U of Minnesota), the U.S. included eleven new internationals. The Canadians were faced with a slightly different situation. Dave Brown, (B.C.) formerly chair of selectors, had recently taken on the role of head coach with veteran Steve Burgess (Ontario),remaining as assistant. Pre-game comparison showed a number of new Canadian faces being added to its three-quarter line, mainly from St. Anne's. Proof would also soon be available supporting the fact age & treachery overcomes youth & skill - the Canadians averaged 25.5 years of age, 146 lbs. & 5.8 years of individual playing experience vs. the Americans at 29.7 age, 138 lbs. & 8.6 experience.

PACIFIC COAST GRIZZLIES - (front row,l-r)J.Crawford,T.Mauldin, E.Huffer, B.Hill,D.Dennis,J.Marr,C.Harju,A.Misko (back row,l-r)A.Latham,L.Lockwood, K.Keith,J.Chue,C.Strege,C.Law,B.Bond,T.Breckinridge,B.Fugate,S.Brooks, L.Fearing. Not pictured - Sheri Hunt & Franck Boivert.

The 1989 Grizzly Tour to New Zealand marked a milestone in US women's rugby: the Grizzlies are the first territorial select side to make a sanctioned international tour. Although many women's club sides have toured New Zealand, the Grizzlies were the first true select side to make the trip. Ten of the 20 women on the tour had been listed on the 1989 US National "Depth Chart" for the national side.

WEIGHTLIFTING
America Cup II
Friendship Cup
Middle Atlantics
New Zealand Games

Grove City College

Strength
Coaches
Seminar

Dick Baldwin & Laura Combes

## 1989: THERE ARE 311 WOMEN'S TEAMS IN THE U.S.

**ONE OF THE MOST FASCINATING PIONEERS** of the 1980s was Laura Combes. A fierce competitor on and off the pitch, Laura played scrumhalf for the University of South Florida and occasionally picked up with Florida State for tournaments, including the 1979 National Championships. But it was beyond rugby where she truly broke barriers.

Laura was among the very first women to enter the world of competitive bodybuilding—and she refused to conform to its narrow expectations of femininity. Known for her extraordinary muscularity, she was considered "too masculine" for women's bodybuilding at the time. She challenged the sport's norms, refusing to wear high heels on stage and becoming the first woman to pose with a closed fist—a bold act that was actually forbidden in women's competitions.

Her impact was undeniable. Laura won the inaugural NPC Nationals in 1980 and captured the AAU Ms. America title in 1981. She competed in three professional bodybuilding shows before retiring after placing sixth at the 1982 Ms. Olympia. In 1983, she authored *Winning Women's Bodybuilding*, further cementing her role as a trailblazer.

Laura Combes passed away in 1989, but her legacy endures. In 2002, she was inducted into the International Federation of Body Builders Hall of Fame—a testament to her strength, defiance, and pioneering spirit.

Just like the women who built the foundation of U.S. rugby, Laura refused to shrink herself to fit someone else's idea of what a woman should be. Her power, grit, and unapologetic presence reflected the very spirit of the game—bold, defiant, and unstoppable.

The Grizzlies were a part of history in New Zealand as well. In order to match a US territorial select side, the NZRFU selected their first "New Zealand XV", a combined representative side from both the North and South islands. It was the first time women had ever represented New Zealand in rugby, and it brought New Zealand into the expanding circle of countries with national women's teams. The positive media attention created by this match brought New Zealand women's rugby the public support it has sought for years...and it gave the Grizzlies some moments to remember!

The Grizzlies finished the tour with 6 wins and 1 loss; they scored 188 points, with 17 scored against them. Franck Boivert provided the coaching and motivation to keep the Grizzlies playing hard through all seven matches, and his technical knowledge gave the US women a competitive edge that may have surprised their well-schooled opposition.

# Laura Combes

*The scrum half on Florida State's national championship women's rugby team was 26 year old Laura Combes of Odessa, Florida. Born in New York City, Laura moved to Florida while still in prep school so she could concentrate on her water skiing. She competed at top levels in all three events (slalom, tricks and jumping), received an exceptional performance rating and placed third in the Southern Regionals in 1975. Laura was introduced to the sport of rugby five years ago at the University of South Florida (B.A. in English Literature, 1975) and competes for USF today in as many as 40 games per year. Besides being a top level rugby player and water skier, this 5 ft. 2 in., 130 lb. athlete is also a pioneer in the sport of women's body building.*

*Laura entered her first contest about a year ago and after an encouraging fourth place finish, decided to pursue the sport of body building full-time. Unencumbered by a job, she has embarked on a training regimen which, among other things, includes a minimum of 18 hours per week in the gym.*

**RUGBY: How did you first become interested in rugby?**

COMBES: There's a sport cartel at the University of South Florida which funds money to various campus sports clubs and while putting in my requisition for water skiing I met one of the fellas, Jeep Barret, who played rugby for South Florida. He mentioned that his girlfriend was starting a rugby club and invited me out to practice. We were the first women's rugby club in Florida and probably in the Southeast.

**RUGBY: Did you give up water skiing when you started playing rugby?**

COMBES: Well, I sort of did both. During December, January and February there are very few water ski tournaments and in order to stay fit, I decided to play rugby.

**RUGBY: What is it about rugby that interests you the most?**

COMBES: I think rugby is such a pretty game: very fluid. It's un-American; a total team sport.

**RUGBY: What is the general reaction of males to your playing rugby?**

COMBES: They like it. Some of the fellas have even asked me to play scrum half for their teams. When we first began, five years ago, some of the hardest of our players, like Eric Stamets, said that women shouldn't play rugby because it's too rough, but two years later he was our coach.

**RUGBY: Do you encounter any hostility?**

COMBES: No one has encountered any kind of hostility that I'm aware of. Everybody's been pretty supportive.

**RUGBY: How many games do you play a year?**

COMBES: About forty. Florida has such nice weather that our season starts in September and ends in June. The teams from up north want to play during the winter, so they visit us during their off season.

**RUGBY: How do you train for rugby?**

COMBES: We have practice two nights a week and I try to run anywhere from twenty to thirty miles a week. I also weight train.

**RUGBY: Do you travel much to play?**

COMBES: Yes. Unfortunately Florida rugby players must travel. Last year we went to tournaments in Virginia, Colorado and Illinois.

**RUGBY: How many teams are there in Florida?**

COMBES: Four: Florida State, Gainesville, Orlando and South Florida.

**RUGBY: Do you think women's rugby will grow?**

COMBES: Definitely. Rugby is one of the few team sports open to women and as more and more women lose their fear of contact sports, it can't help but grow.

**RUGBY: What is your rugby ambition?**

COMBES: Just to better my game personally.

**RUGBY: Have any of the women down in Florida gotten involved in refereeing?**

COMBES: I've reffed a few games and really enjoy it. From playing scrum half all these years I've gotten a bird's eye view of the game and think I might be good at it. As a matter of fact one fellow asked me to sign up with the Florida Union and I might just do that.

**RUGBY: With your new interest in body building, are you going to continue playing rugby?**

COMBES: Yes, I began weight training to help me compete in other sports and the weight training led to body building. I don't want to give up other sports now because of body building. You risk injury but that's the name of the game.

**RUGBY: When did you get interested in body building?**

COMBES: A year ago. A good friend of mine, the president of our rugby club, was killed by a drunken driver in an automobile accident. After that everyone really lost interest; the team just didn't want to play anymore. It was also off season for water skiing so when someone mentioned a body building contest to me, I just decided to enter.

**RUGBY: And how did you do?**

COMBES: I placed fourth.

**RUGBY: You placed fourth without any training?**

COMBES: Well I'd been training with weights for over seven years.

**RUGBY: How did you become involved in weight training?**

COMBES: When I was seventeen I took a bad fall off a ski ramp and had to undergo knee surgery. My rehabilitation all came through weight training. When I saw what it could do for my legs, I figured it could do the same for my upper body, so I started an over-all weight training program.

**RUGBY: What is the media's attitude toward women's body building?**

COMBES: They love it! It's a novelty. Something that's caught the public's fancy.

**RUGBY: What exposure have you gotten?**

COMBES: There were three articles in the Tampa Tribune, one in the Tampa Times and I'm included in a Sports Illustrated article which will be published sometime in March. I also appeared on NBC's Real People which aired January 30th.

**RUGBY: Did you get any response from the Real People show?**

COMBES: I got a few dozen letters. Some came from children asking about basic weight training programs; some from men who now realize the full potential of women as far as muscularity is concerned; and some from women who are not involved in the sport themselves, but happy that women have gotten involved.

**RUGBY: How many women body builders do you think there are in the United States?**

COMBES: Forty or fifty, and by that I mean specifically body builders. Many women train with weights but there are only 40 or 50 true body builders.

**RUGBY: Are women body builders, as people, similar to women rugby players?**

COMBES: No, not at all. There's much more comraderie in rugby.

Few of the women body builders have athletic backgrounds, which is unfortunate because their attitude toward the sport could stand some improvement. For many, this is their first athletic endeavor and they haven't had enough experience to be gracious winners or good losers. Most of them got into the sport because they had good figures and people encouraged them, but I believe it will attract athletes as time goes by.

**RUGBY: Is women's body building growing?**

COMBES: Oh, definitely. It's really taken the general public by surprise; it's like a final frontier for women in the athletic/phy-

**Laura Combes** [Photo Barrilleaux]

sical world. Weight training in conjunction with women's athletics has really taken off and body building will grow as a result of this. I think you'll find a lot of athletes venturing into it. Not every woman can be a body builder but I think a lot of them will begin weight training.

RUGBY: How much time do you spend training for body building?

COMBES: Three hours a day, 6 days a week; I take off Sunday.

RUGBY: What does your training regimen consist of?

COMBES: Well, Monday and Thursday I train shoulders and legs. On Tuesdays and Fridays I train chest and back and on Wednesdays and Saturdays I train arms. Every afternoon we train calves and abdominals. So it's a split routine.

As for repetitions I always do five sets of eight on each apparatus. This morning, for example, I did arms which means five sets each of close grip bench presses, overhead presses, dumbbell kickbacks, cable rows, concentrated curls, French curls, reverse curls, wrist curls and cable curls.

RUGBY: Are you using free weights or nautilus machines?

COMBES: Free weights.

RUGBY: Do you have a special diet?

COMBES: I stick to a well balanced, low-calorie, low-fat diet; staying away from starches and sugar. I eat approximately 100 grams of protein and 100 grams of carbohydrates daily; mainly fruits, vegetables and salads.

Unlike the high carbohydrate diets used by athletes in endurance events, you don't want to eat too many carbohydrates for body building; especially when you're getting ready for competition. Carbohydrates retain more body fat, something which does you no good in this sport.

RUGBY: Does the body building or weight training help your rugby?

COMBES: Oh, certainly it does. Most women have such frail upper bodies that they need some protection, especially where their deltoids, shoulders, and trapezius are concerned. If someone has even a little more muscle in their upper body, the risk of injury is greatly reduced.

RUGBY: Have any of your rugby teammates tried body building?

COMBES: Because of what I've been doing lately some have been tempted to start a normal weight training program. They've seen the benefits from it, and like the way it looks, so they're trying it out.

RUGBY: There are conflicting

opinions in women's body building over what constitutes a "good body" and, consequently what the judges must look for in a contest. What are the opposing views on this issue?

COMBES: The criteria for women's body building has not been clearly delineated yet and no one really knows what we're supposed to look like; how muscular we're supposed to be.

Personally I don't think there should be any restrictions whatsoever; I think we've got to find what our potential is. The cause of this controversy is the broad spectrum of bodies entered in these contests. On one end of the scale you have the "extremely muscular" type, who may be mesomorphic, and on the other, your basic "figure development"

type. I myself am striving for muscularity.

To me "figure development" is not body building; it's shapely, it's staying in shape, but it's not body building.

Beauty, as you know, is in the eye of the beholder. Personal tastes differ and the judges are having a hard time deciding what they like. No standards have been set down yet, so in the meantime I'm going to keep training for the

look I want.

RUGBY: And that look is one of extreme muscularity?

COMBES: Well, I wouldn't say extreme, but when people look at me, I do want them to see clearly that, yes, there's a tricep, there's a bicep, etc. etc.

Many people have misconceptions. They think of all body builders as huge people, like power lifters which in reality they aren't. Body builders come in all different sizes and all work on the shape of their physique. The thing that's difficult about body building is to achieve muscular size, and symmetry, while retaining the classic shape.

Women can't be grossly huge; they must have a small waist and be very lean.

RUGBY: Are you, therefore, aiming to be the female equivalent of an Arnold Schwarzenegger?

COMBES: Yes. A fully developed woman would look much softer than a man yet the shoulders would definitely be there.

RUGBY: Would those aiming for extreme muscularity have different training programs than the figure development devotees?

COMBES: Yes. The difference is in the intensity of the excerise. If you want to build bigger muscles, you must make the resistance stronger or, in other words, use heavier weights.

RUGBY: What is the reaction of boyfriends or male friends to your body building?

COMBES: They love it. The signals are go ... all the time. They understand what I'm doing. They find it attractive and aren't threatened by it. I think it has to do with how secure people feel about themselves.

Right now I'm training with Richard Baldwin who is a medium class Mr. U.S.A. He knows what he wants and I know what I want and even though I am trying very hard to develop muscles larger than most women's, there's so much difference between his body and mine that there's no way of mistaking one for the other.

RUGBY: What is the general reaction of male body builders to women's body building?

COMBES: I think they like it a lot because it breaks up the monotony of the men's contests; after a while the men all start to look alike. I also believe that women are much better posers and men, by seeing women pose, are getting a more aesthetic view of body building.

RUGBY: With rugby and body building, women have entered into heretofore exclusive male preserves. Is the acceptance and treatment of female body builders by male body builders similar to or different from the acceptance and treatment of female rugby players by male rugby players?

COMBES: For a year or so men rejected the idea of women playing rugby because the women weren't as skilled, or they simply didn't want women playing "their" game. As the skills increased and interest in the sport was seen as genuine, however, women's rugby gained respect. The same process is

taking place in body building.

At first they just said, "Forget it; I don't like it." Now the reaction is: "It's not so bad; I kinda like it; I'm getting used to it."

I think male body builders may be a little more reluctant to accept women because the central image of their sport is that of the all-powerful male. I also think it's easier to accept a skill (rugby) that people have in common, than the way somebody looks.

RUGBY: Do you think women's involvement in male preserves like body building and rugby will change men's perception of women?

COMBES: The male conception of the ideal woman could

change drastically. Instead of being limited exclusively to the "Miss America" type, they now have the option of going with someone who is intelligent, athletic, and who shares their own interests.

I think it will broaden perspectives and make for better relationships.

Laura Combes                    [Photo - Falcon]

## Women's Weight Training
(3 Days Per Week)

| | | |
|---|---|---|
| Legs - | 2 sets of 10: | leg extentions |
| | | leg curls |
| | | calf raises |
| | | squats |
| Arms - | 2 sets of 10: | dumbell curls |
| | | dumbell kick backs |
| | | concentration curls |
| Chest - | 3 sets of 10: | bench press |
| | | incline fly |
| | | dips |
| Back - | 3 sets of 10: | bent over rows |
| | | rows |
| | | latisimus pull downs |
| Shoulders | 2 sets of 10: | lateral raises |
| | | military press |
| | | upright rows |
| | | shrugs |

# 1990s

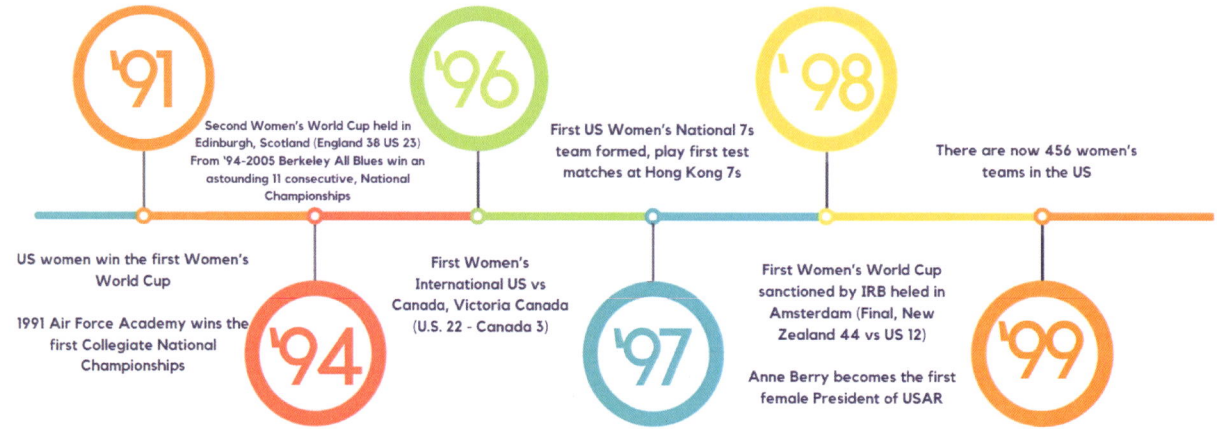

'91 — Second Women's World Cup held in Edinburgh, Scotland (England 38 US 23) From '94-2005 Berkeley All Blues win an astounding 11 consecutive, National Championships

'96 — First US Women's National 7s team formed, play first test matches at Hong Kong 7s

'98 — There are now 456 women's teams in the US

US women win the first Women's World Cup

1991 Air Force Academy wins the first Collegiate National Championships

'94

First Women's International US vs Canada, Victoria Canada (U.S. 22 - Canada 3)

'97

First Women's World Cup sanctioned by IRB heled in Amsterdam (Final, New Zealand 44 vs US 12)

Anne Berry becomes the first female President of USAR

'99

Anne Barry

**I**N 1990, ANNE BARRY BEGAN WHAT WOULD become a storied and influential administrative career in rugby. She first stepped onto the national stage as Treasurer of USA Rugby, a position she held for more than eight years. In 1992, she joined the USA Rugby Board of Directors, where her steady leadership and deep commitment to the sport helped shape the organization's direction for over a decade.

Then, in 1998, Anne broke new ground, becoming the first woman President of USA Rugby—a milestone that reflected both her personal leadership and the growing influence of women in the sport. Her tenure marked a turning point, proving that women's voices belonged not just on the field, but at the highest levels of the game's governance.

"Anne Barry was the first woman to serve as President and Treasurer of USAR. When she took over as the Treasurer, USAR had little infrastructure and was nearly $4 million in debt. Barry strengthened the organization, increased funding, and built large financial reserves that became the funding source for future international events in the US. As President of USAR she helped lead a remarkable growth in US rugby, including the acceptance of the sport by the U.S. Olympic Committee, the start of a national youth rugby development program, and the creation of the North American West Indies Rugby Association (NAWIRA). She increased funding to the USA Women's National Teams, and created the Club and Individual Participation Program (CIPP). Anne is widely regarded as the most effective leader EVER of USA rugby." (Wendy Young)

VOL. 1, NO. 1 ✳ SPECIAL EDITION ✳ 1990

# WOMEN'S NATIONAL TEAM

**1990 THE WOMEN'S COMMITTEE DETERMINES THAT THE WOMEN'S NATIONAL TEAM WILL BE CALLED THE EAGLES.**

ORDER OF BUSINESS #5: NAME FOR U.S. WOMEN'S TEAM. TWO NAMES SUBMITTED: OSPREYS, SPIRITS. THERE IS PRECEDENT AND LEGAL SUPPORT FOR USING THE TERM EAGLES. PACIFIC: GRIZZLIES, GRIFFINS NAMES USED BY MENS AND WOMENS SIDES. DISCUSSION: NATIONAL COLLEGIATE, COMBINED SERVICES, AND UNDER 25 TEAMS ALL USE DIFFERENT NAMES; USA RESOLUTIONS SHOULD BE EXAMINED TO SEE IF THERE'S A RESOLUTION BARRING THE WOMEN'S TEAM FROM ITS USE. AFTER DISCUSSION, MOVED AND UNANIMOUSLY ADOPTED:

**THE USA WOMEN'S NATIONAL SIDE SHALL USE THE TERM EAGLES FOR ITS NAME.**

**Top right:** *1991 Eagles MA Sorenson, Val Sulllivan, Annie Flavin*
**Left:** *U.S. Women's National Team—USA Presidents 15*

In 1990 the U.S. The Women's National Team, competing under the name *USA Presidents 15*, traveled to New Zealand to compete in the Women's World Rugby Festival. The *Presidents 15* posted a record of 3-1 with their only loss coming at the hands of New Zealand.

*1991 U.S. Captains, Barb Bond and Mary Sullivan hold the trophy aloft.*

## THE HISTORIC 1991
## WOMEN'S WORLD CUP

"WE RECEIVED A FORMAL INVITATION TO THE *World Cup, which had to be responded to by USARFU (now USAR). Looking back, I'm sure it was a moment for USARFU because the invitation came from the WRFU, not the RFU. Because the women were still running our own show, under the umbrella of USARFU, it would have been difficult to stop us from going. I don't recall anyone actually trying to do that. At the time, I had a rather good relationship with the staff of USARFU and with some members of the Executive Committee, and they understood our determination. We did enough to stay within the boundaries of the USARFU but still control our own game. In the end, the World Cup cost about $38,000, not including airfare for the players. Most of the trip was paid for by the players themselves."* (Jami Jordan)

The **1991 U.S. Women's National Team** was a remarkably talented and experienced squad, featuring six future Hall of Fame players: Kathy Flores, Patty Jervey, Jen Crawford, Candi Orsini, Tam Breckenridge, and MA Sorenson. (The entire 1991 team was inducted into the Hall of Fame in 2016.)

Alongside these icons were battle-tested veterans like Krista McFarren, Annie Flavin, Barb Fugate, Christine Harju, and Tara Flanigan, who, with Tam Breckenridge, formed the infamous and formidable second-row pairing known as the "Locks from Hell." The team was captained by Mary Sullivan and Barb Bond. Barb's selection as co-captain surprised many. A young No. 8 from California, she was respected as a steady, dominant player but didn't carry the same star power as some of her teammates. *"I had no idea why I was chosen to be captain,"* she later admitted. *"It was very difficult to lead a team of virtual strangers."* Yet her quiet, consistent leadership proved to be exactly what this star-studded squad needed.

February 27, 1991

I have great news!  In April, 1991, the first World Cup of
Women's Rugby will take place in Wales, and I have the honor
of representing the United States at this event.

On February 3rd in Tallahassee, FL, twenty-six US Eagles
were selected to travel to the World Cup.  All of us have
been training for years for this once-in-a-lifetime
opportunity.  Many of us have represented the US at one time
or another in previous events - at an invitational
tournament in New Zealand last August, or in test matches
against Canada.

But there has never been a World Cup.  Since rugby is not
yet an Olympic event, this World Cup is truly the pinnacle
of our sport, and the first event of its kind for women.

You may remember that my previous rugby trips were all
self-funded.  Unfortunately, nothing has changed in that
regard.  For the tour to New Zealand, each of us paid over
$1500 out-of-pocket to play for the United States.  The
World Cup tour will cost each player about $700 for air
fare, $450 for accommodations, and $200 for ground
transport; so $1350, at least, not including food or income
lost for missing two weeks of work.

Since we are representing the United States, you may wonder
why the USA Rugby Football Union is not sponsoring our tour.
The USARFU sanctions both men's and women's rugby, and
collects the same dues from all clubs.  However, the men's
Rugby World Cup is also scheduled for later this year, and
the USARFU executive board is not willing to commit any
funds to the women's event.  (That's another battle to
fight.)

So I'm writing to you for two reasons:  first, to share my
excitement and pride about making the World Cup squad; and
secondly, to ask for any help you can offer.

If you are able or interested in "passing around the hat" for me or any player on the squad, your donation will be tax deductible.  Send a check to me, but make it payable to "USARFU Women's Committee", and specify how you would like the funds to be applied:  toward the Women's World Cup tour as a whole, or to certain expenses (air fare, rooms, etc.). Each and every donation will be deeply appreciated, and 100% of the funds will be applied directly to tour expenses.

If you do not care to make a donation, I will be happy and proud to accept your best wishes as we carry the flag to Wales.  I appreciate the support you have always given me and my rugby career, and I thank you for your understanding.

Sincerely,

Women's Rugby

APRIL 8 - 14

# Female thrills
# — no frills!

Despite the problems, despite the lack of finance, the first ever Women's World Cup ran the full course. The week long event in Cardiff featured twelve teams and, as we report, the tournament at least silenced the sceptics who doubted that it would ever happen.

WOMEN'S
**RUGBY**
WORLD CUP
**91**

Getting to grips with the line-out. The USA and England forwards show that they've mastered all the subtleties of this phase of play.

The tournament itself brought together an eclectic mix of national teams, most of whom endured cold, cramped dorm rooms and harsh conditions. The weather was brutal—freezing rain, icy winds, and mud-slicked fields. In their opening match against the Netherlands, the U.S. women battled through a rain-soaked, punishing contest, barely squeaking out a win. Many players later recalled fearing hypothermia as they trudged through the freezing downpour, their resolve as tested as their skill.

But something was forged in that miserable, muddy match—a shared grit and trust that would define their campaign. These weren't just talented athletes; they were a team. And as they peeled off their soaked jerseys and huddled together against the cold, none of them could yet know that they were standing at the beginning of one of the most extraordinary chapters in U.S. rugby history.

Co-Captain, Mary Sulllivan recalls: "*After the match, we raced into the locker room to find a line of shower-heads that trickled out a small stream of lukewarm water. Each shower head had 2 or 3 players huddled under it trying to share the small dribble of water. We slowly peeled off our jerseys, jog bras, shorts and underwear with our shaking fingers. Many of us were so cold and*

*Huddle on the pitch*

The U.S. women ultimately won their pool, setting the stage for a historic final against a powerful English side playing in front of an energized home crowd. In that match, the Americans rose to the moment, delivering their most complete performance of the tournament. With precision, power, and unwavering belief, they defeated England to claim the first Women's Rugby World Cup title.

As the final whistle blew, the field erupted in celebration. Sweaty players hugged one another, laughter mingled with tears, and champagne corks popped in the cool Welsh air. Away from the noise and glory, members of the Women's Committee quietly exhaled. With no real budget, no institutional backing, and no support from USARFU, they had pulled off the impossible—bringing together players from

*cramped we could not untie our shoes, so our amazing managers crawled through the shower and untied our muddy laces and helped us take off our mud-caked cleats."*

1991 U.S. Team holds trophy

1991 U.S. Team celebrating with
First Lady Barbara Bush

four territories, getting them across the ocean, and watching them lift the World Cup.

This was more than a championship. It was a statement. It was proof that vision, grit, and sisterhood could defy indifference and overcome every barrier. On that muddy field in Wales, the U.S. women didn't just win a trophy—they changed the course of rugby history.

*"My trip to the first World Cup did not turn out at all the way I had envisioned it. It was simultaneously one of the highest points of my life, and the lowest. High, of course, because our team was so dominant, and there is nothing to compare to being a world champion. In anything, ever. The low was the profound shock and disappointment of being injured early in the first match. I was the scrumhalf and clearly remember being knocked off balance a bit by the Netherlands' flyhalf when I jumped to block her kick. I came down awkwardly on my right leg, injuring my knee. As I lay in the cold mud and freezing*

*rain, I thought, This was not supposed to happen. Substitutions in rugby were different in those years. When a player was selected to start a match, the expectation was that they would play all 80 minutes. A team could only substitute two players, and those had to be for a verified injury. It wasn't good for the team that I had to be replaced so early in the first match.*

*"Medical support was also different. We had a trainer for taping and basic injury treatment, but no team physio so there was no medical follow-up on my injury during the tour. We assumed it was my ACL, but I did not see any medical professionals for a diagnosis until we returned to the U.S. So, I worked hard to get the swelling down and return to mobility. With the help of Sharon, our trainer, I was able to participate in a full practice by the final few days of the tour. But it was still unlikely that I would be selected, as I was not 100% and would have put the team in the risky position of having to use one of*

## The Women's Rugby World Cup 1991

### WORLD CUP DINNER

CANADA
ENGLAND
FRANCE
ITALY
JAPAN
NETHERLANDS

WOMEN'S
**RUGBY**
WORLD CUP
**91**

NEW ZEALAND
SPAIN
SWEDEN
USA
USSR
WALES

*hosted by*

*at*

THE NATIONAL SPORTS CENTRE FOR WALES
SUNDAY, 14th APRIL, 1991

*Menu*

*Caribbean Cocktail*

★ ★ ★

*Chicken Chasseur*
*French Beans*
*Cauliflower au Gratin*
*Roast Potatoes*
*Potato Suzanne*

★ ★ ★

*Strawberry Gateau & Fresh Cream*

★ ★ ★

*Cheeseboard*

★ ★ ★

*Coffee with Cream*

*Wines*
*Rugby World Cup Red & White*
*by Continental Wines*

only two substitutions. And as much as I wanted to play and imagined that I could, I was still on an unstable joint.

"What I did earn, though, was a unique front row seat to history. As disappointed as I was at the time, I did not realize that I was gaining irreplaceable experience. I learned so much about the extraordinary traits of my teammates. I also got a glimpse of how coaches and players manage those high-stakes moments. And I was able to experience the ways elite competitors approached the game. While I was sad about my injury, those opportunities gave me insights I only began to understand years later. In practice and at matches, I was absorbing many coaching skills, including player selection and player management, which I would use later as a club and USA U23 coach. I don't think anyone would choose

that route to coach development, but in the long run, dealing with the injury and disappointment helped shape my coaching. And of course, I had the honor of being a part of that team of World Champions... that honor never gets old." (Scruhalf Barb Fugate)

There was no parade when the world champions returned home. No national headlines, no TV crews waiting at the airport. Few U.S. newspapers even carried the story. Most of the players were back at their jobs within a day of landing, slipping quietly from history's spotlight despite their extraordinary achievement.

But there was one moment of national recognition. In celebration of Girls and Women in Sports Day, the team received an invitation to the White House, where

## 1991 WORLD CUP U.S. ROSTER

| | | | | | | |
|---|---|---|---|---|---|---|
| Ann Barford | Center | Rutgers Renegades RFC | Patricia Jervey | Center | Florida State RFC |
| Barbara Bond (c) | #8 | Reed College | Kris Kany | Flanker | Boston RFC |
| Tam Breckenridge | Lock | Belmont Shore | Cassie Law | Flanker | Bay Area SheHawks |
| Patty Connell | Scrumhalf | Beantown RFC | Krista McFarren | Wing | New Orleans Halfmoons |
| Jen Crawford | Center | Berkeley All Blues | Joan Morrissey | Center | Beantown RFC |
| Mary Dixey | Flyhalf | Beantown RFC | Sandy Meredith | Wing | |
| Colleen Fahey | Prop | Florida State RFC | Andrea Morrell | Lock | |
| Tara Flanagan | Lock | Belmont Shore | Candice Orsini | Center | Florida State RFC |
| Annie Flavin | Prop | Beantown RFC | Jan Rutkowski | Lock | Beantown RFC |
| Kathleen Flores | #8 | Florida State RFC | Cathy Seabaugh | Flanker | |
| Barb Fugate | Scrumhalf | University of Minnesota | Maryanne Sorenson | Prop | Philadelphia RFC |
| Claire Godwin | Flanker | Florida State RFC | Mary Gail Sullivan | Fullback | Beantown RFC |
| Chris Harju | Flyhalf | San Diego Surfers | Cal Sullivan | Hooker | Florida State RFC |
| Tracy Henderson | Center | New Orleans Halfmoons | Julie Thompson | Hooker | |
| Jennifer Hertz | Prop | Chicago RFC | Morgan Whitehead | Flanker | Chicago RFC |

they were greeted by First Lady Barbara Bush. She posed for photos—rugby ball in hand, throwing it like a football—a small but symbolic gesture honoring the trailblazers who had just made history on the world stage.

At the time, few outside the women's rugby community understood the magnitude of what these players had accomplished. USA Rugby seemed almost determined to downplay the victory, fearing that the women's success might cast an unflattering shadow on the men's ongoing struggles on the world stage. While the triumph of the 1991 team was largely buried throughout the 1990s and 2000s, the growth of the women's game and the excitement surrounding subsequent World Cups brought renewed attention—and long-overdue recognition—to the American women who had won the very first title.

Another groundbreaking moment at the 1991 World Cup came when U.S. referee Laurel Lockett served as Head Referee for the England vs. Italy match. Laurel, then the highest-ranked female referee in the United States, became the first American woman to officiate an international match. She continued to break barriers, returning as a Head Referee during the 1993 Canada Cup, further cementing her legacy as a pioneer in the sport.

# 1990 TRADING CARDS

*Candi Orsini*

*Patty Jervey*

*Autumn Arvidson*

*Barb Fugate*

*Jennifer Hertz*

*Gwen Gunter*

*Mary Sullivan*

## THE DREAM OF A GLOBAL WOMEN'S COMMITTEE

**WHILE THE PLAYERS AND COACHES WERE** basking in their success, the Women's Committee was back at work fighting for resources. The success of the women's national team pressed the question of why USARFU refused to support the women's national team.

Leading this discreet inquiry was Jami Jordan, the Chair of the Women's Committee (1989-1993). *"We were running women's rugby on a volunteer basis. We didn't tend to have strong relationships with one another outside of the Committee and only met to do business. Most of our challenges were dealing with the men and the 'lowly position' of women's rugby in the USARFU pecking order. But we were a defiant group, committed to growing the women's game.*

*"Given all that we accomplished between 1979 and 1994 as a young, volunteer organization, it's pretty amazing that the women running things didn't blow up. But we weren't perfect. We fell victim to regional politics, particularly around the hiring and firing of USWNT coaches. By and large, the Women's Committee operated on a consensus basis, but we did vote on things. My memory is that we agreed on many things and that we were usually in alignment or at least mostly in alignment. But the selection of national team coaches was the most contentious. Much of that can be attributed to intense regional loyalties to certain coaches that were off putting to other regions."*

In 1994, the first International Conference on Women's Rugby was held in London. The women in attendance harbored a vision of creating the first Women's International Rugby Board (WIRB). Which they proposed would:

**Jami Jordan**

- Promote, develop and extend the women's game

- Settle all matters or disputes relating to or arising from the playing of an international match

- Control all matters relating to tours of national representative teams including the World Cup in which any union is concerned

- Control any other matters of an international character affecting the game of women's rugby

- Abide by IRFB regulations and develop a formal, integrated relationship with the IRFB. (Paper submitted by Rosie Golby, Secretary, WRFU)

Unfortunately, the dream of a women's international governing body was not to be. The IRB sent a representative to the meeting. While he was impressed with the organization and planning of the women, he recognized that a separate women's organization was a threat to the IRB's ongoing discussion with the Olympic Committee. Soon after, the IRB asked all its member nations to rein in separate women's organizations and to fold them into existing national governing bodies. But to what extent women were to be 'folded into' existing governing bodies was up to the individual member nations. The decision to disband women's leadership and curtail their autonomy was devastating to women's rugby.

In the U.S., the Women's Committee continued to operate as usual through 1994. In late 1994, USARFU folded the Women's Committee into its existing list of committees and allocated a $1250 annual operating budget.

Almost in defiance of the IRB ruling, a women's international conference was held again in 1998 in the Netherlands where women from different rugby nations met to contest the idea of 'full integration' into existing governing boards. The consensus was that there were gross disparities across countries for how national governing boards treated women's rugby. But, as if to make it painfully clear that there would be no routes for women to bring their grievances to the IRB, the IRB incongruously appointed a man to be the chair of the women's liaison committee, dismissing the experience, expertise and ability of women who had been moving mountains.

Some of the Women's Committee members stayed active and worked on USARFU committees on behalf of women's rugby, but decision-making about women's rugby fell to committees populated mostly by men. Some men were longtime allies of women's rugby and did much to support women's rugby, others were ambivalent or obstructionist. The loss of women's autonomy, leadership and ingenuity not just in the U.S. but across the globe was heartbreaking.

If you could take one lesson from their stories, it was they had confidence in themselves. They knew no system or organization was going to move women's rugby forward. The task of growing the game was on their shoulders, with few resources they successfully created the Women's National Team, the World Cup, Interterritorial Championships, Select Sides, Club Nationals, and Collegiate Nationals.

## THE 1994 U.S. WOMEN'S WORLD CUP TEAM
THE FORGOTTEN SILVER MEDAL PERFORMANCE

**THE U.S. WOMEN SHOWED UP TO THE FINALS** of the 1994 Women's World Cup having shattered the international scoring record. Over four preliminary matches they had outscored their opponent by a combined score of 364-15. The local press described their play as 'pyrotechnics' for their explosive ability to score. It was an extraordinarily talented U.S. team. The backline had four future Hall of Fame players including fullback Jen Crawford, who at the time was celebrated as the greatest back in the women's game. Jen was joined by future Hall of Fame players Candi Orsini, Krista McFarren, and Patty Jervey (who was the most capped player on the U.S. team). The forwards were also a celebrated and experienced bunch. The most decorated U.S. prop at the time and 1991 World Cup alumna Annie Flavin, was at loosehead and MA Sorensen was the steady, powerful anchor at tighthead. 1991 World Cup alumnae Tara Flanagan, Tam Breckenridge, Jan Rutkowski, Kathy Flores, Mary Dixey, Patty Connell, Cassie Law and Captain, Barb Bond provided international experience and power. It was a large and impressive roster, and the players did not disappoint over the first four games. But in the finals, they met their match on a rainy field, as the England forwards stole the day and won the match 38-23.

By the fall of 1993, the 1994 Women's World Cup was hanging by a thread. That it did finally come together was a miracle cooked up by a tenacious group of Scottish women.

The Netherlands was slated to host the '94 Cup but months prior to the tournament they ran into trouble. While women's rugby in the Netherlands

*Members of the 1994 team in Scotland, Kathy Flores in middle, Alex Williams behind and left*

was integrated into the larger Dutch Rugby Union, the organizers decided to form a separate foundation for hosting the World Cup, the Foundation for the Women's Rugby World Cup 1994. While in communication with their male counterparts, The Foundation did not create formal ties with the Dutch Rugby Union or the International Rugby Board (iRB) now, World Rugby. In October of 1993 several iRB member countries announced they would not allow their women's teams to participate in the World Cup as the event did not have formal ties with the iRB. The Dutch Rugby Union and the Foundation was forced to announce that they were postponing the tournament until 1996. This was a cancellation, not a postponement. The Dutch women's team really had no say in the matter, the iRB was miffed and made it clear that if the Dutch went ahead with the tournament, the iRB would suspend the Dutch membership. The Dutch Rugby Union threatened the tournament organizers that if the Foundation went ahead with the tournament, they would cancel the entire women's national program. The Dutch Union notified the US Women's Committee December 29, 1993, of their decision to cancel the 1994 Women's World Cup. That's when Scotland women—fully supported by the Scottish Rugby Union and the Women's Rugby Football Union stepped into the breach.

The tournament was scheduled for April 10-24, giving Scotland three months and ten days to organize the entire tournament. The lack of iRB approval meant that several women's teams would be unable to participate including New Zealand, Germany, and Italy. As iRB continued to withhold approval the organizing committee began hedging their bets calling the tournament the 'World Championship 'and the 'World Cup.' Given that some top teams were not going to be playing, some unions, including the U.S. raised concerns about calling it a World Cup. The distinction between a World Championship or a World Cup was significant as it affected the legitimacy of the

# 'We had 90 days to save Rugby World Cup. It was amazing to actually do it'

## Women's team tournament triumph set to become a play

By Laura Smith
lasmith@sundaypost.com

**Like many brilliant yet ambitious ideas, the plan to save the 1994 Women's Rugby World Cup started in a pub.**

Sandra Colamartino remembers listening in stunned silence as her teammate Sue Brodie explained her ambitious plan to stage an international rugby tournament in Edinburgh. Without any funding, experience or logistical support – and in just 90 days.

"We'd all been working towards the World Cup so when we found out by fax that it had been cancelled we were devastated," recalled the former scrum-half from Edinburgh.

"Sue called us all to a meeting at a pub in Leith and said we should host it. We all sat there thinking it was ridiculous but then she started listing all the reasons it would work. It was only an hour's flight from Holland to Edinburgh so we thought it wouldn't be too hard for the international teams to come here instead. We started to think we could actually do it."

The tournament had been scheduled to take place in The Netherlands but was cancelled just months before. Scotland

**Sandra Colamartino, top, the Scotland team that came fourth in the World Cup and a ticket for the game with Canada.**

Main picture **Lesley Martin**

had only just formed a women's side and played their first game 18 months earlier. Sandra was the captain and scored their opening try as they defeated Ireland at Raeburn Place.

Desperate for the chance to represent Scotland at the highest level, the players put in £400 each and called in favours from the tightknit rugby community, and beyond, to revive the tournament.

Sandra, who was 26 and a graphic designer at Heriot-Watt University at the time, created posters, logos and a programme.

She said: "We had to work quickly as we had just 90 days to pull it together. We phoned all the local rugby clubs and the whole community came together to offer their grounds for nothing, referees gave up their time to do it for free and people volunteered to help

transport and feed the players. We weren't sure until the last minute how many countries would come so that was a challenge. We had to form an extra team from players at Scottish universities to make up even numbers."

The organising committee had to rely on landline calls and faxes and hope the international teams would make the event.

"When I look back now, I can't quite believe how we did it. We had no mobiles, email or social media so it was all done via phone calls. We met in the pub once a week for updates and asked for help via the radio and papers," said Sandra, 54.

They hit a few snags along the way. She said: "We were shocked to hear the Russian team had arrived in Manchester with no money, accommodation or transport to Edinburgh, just Russian dolls and bottles of vodka brought as

gifts. We put an appeal out on the radio and a bus company gave them a lift, a university put them up in empty halls, and Pizza Hut delivered pizza."

Against all odds, the fledgling Scottish women's side became the unlikely saviours of the 1994 Rugby World Cup. Twelve teams competed in the capital, cheered on by record crowds. Around 6,000 people watched England beat the USA in the final at Raeburn Place, which was filmed by the BBC.

"We were so stressed out that it was a relief when we could actually just play rugby, although we were exhausted, Sue most of all as she was central to pulling it all together," said Sandra.

"In the end we came fourth with a win over Canada, which was a real bonus. Watching the packed-out final was just incredible. It felt amazing and emotional to watch that game and realise we'd actually done it. We had to hire extra stands to accommodate extra crowds at the final."

It also remains the most profitable Women's World Cup. "To date, it's the only Women's World Cup that made a profit – we charged £5 a ticket for the final," Sandra said.

As 2024 marks the 30th anniversary of the World Cup, Sandra and Sue have written a play about the extraordinary tournament called 90 Days.

They are now crowdfunding to raise the £10,000 required to stage it professionally, including a premiere at Murrayfield next April.

"It's an opportunity for us to give back to the sport we love and show how far it's come in three decades. The hope is to take the show to the Edinburgh Festival and maybe rugby clubs around Scotland," she added.

Sandra, who now runs her own chocolate company, Quirky Chocolate, remains a passionate Scottish rugby supporter. She regularly attends Scotland Women matches in Edinburgh and believes the current squad, ranked ninth in the world, is due an exciting run of form to match Scotland men's side.

Scotland Women will face Spain in Edinburgh for a warm-up match ahead of World Rugby's new global competition, WXV, in Cape Town in October.

"In Scotland, women's rugby is becoming its own entity now, which is wonderful," Sandra said. "They come close to selling out the Hive stadium near Murrayfield and there's always a good atmosphere.

"There's something very exciting happening in the team right now. They are really starting to peak and build momentum so I can't wait to see what they do next season."

*Support 90 Days at crowdfunder.co.uk/p/ crowdfunding-for-1994-womens-rugby-world-cup-show-1*

tournament. Ultimately the organizing committee took a leap, dropping 'World Championship' from their materials and moved ahead with the title, 'World Cup.' The organizers held their breath, but the iRB did not push back.

Given the 'lean, mean' nature of putting on a World Cup in under three months, the tournament organizers informed all participating teams that they were solely responsible for their organizing costs including organizing their travel, accommodations, and practice logistics. In addition, teams were required to bring their own physicians and trainers as no medical support could be provided by the tournament organizers.

Final selections for the U.S. squad were announced February 7. U.S. players were told that in addition to funding their expenses to the World Cup, they would have to pay to attend four camps. Three of those camps were scheduled to be held at Stanford (one camp had already been held at Stanford immediately after ITT's), while one was to be held in Philadelphia (the Philadelphia camp would later be cancelled). The coaches and selection committee deemed the training camps mandatory and warned players that their selection would be jeopardized if they did not attend all the camps. Never slackers, the Women's Committee got to work organizing fundraising, marketing, and kit donations. The fundraising efforts were hampered by the time frame as well as the tremendous amount of work the members of the women's committee had to take on to work out the logistics of getting a thirty-person squad as well as coaches and support staff to the World Cup. In the end, thanks to a $10,000 donation, the committee was able to raise approximately $15,000. Ruggers Inc. stepped in to provide the kit. But ultimately most of the cost of travel, lodging and food fell to individual players.

The cost for the entire World Cup experience was approximately $3,500 per player. Players from the east coast faced a larger financial burden as they had to pay for travel to the west coast for training camps. Mindful of this burden, the women's committee suggested that the players agree to a cost sharing arrangement: everyone invited to the camps would chip into a larger 'pot of money' ($5000) and those funds would be used to offset player travel costs. Moreover, west coast players agreed to house players traveling to the camps. Women's Committee member Jami Jordan recalls: *"We were concerned that players on the east coast had to assume a larger financial burden than those on the west coast, so we did the best we could at the time. We were concerned that players could become resentful of one another over costs. Whether it [the cost sharing] worked is debatable".*

Another tactic was to choose a travel squad of thirty players, thus spreading the cost sharing over a larger group. However, with only four games over a two-week period there was a recognition that many players would not get much, if any, playing time. As a result of the meager budget, accommodations in Scotland were sparse. As one player recalls, *"The hotel was spartan and often cold—and meals were not adequate for rugby players. I remember how happy I was when we had time to go to a meal with parents—we pigged out!"* Alex Williams recalls:

*"We stayed in the Braid Hills Hotel, which was the same hotel my grandmother had honeymooned in many years prior. We were always hungry and there would be a race after practice to walk (run) into town to get to the tiny "jacket potato" shop to buy a hot baked potato, heaped with toppings, before they ran out. I doubt they ever got that much business again, we literally ate them out of potatoes every day."*

Jan Rutkowski recalls:

*"My mother and aunt came over to Edinburgh for part of the tournament. Their hosts where they stayed were so excited to hear that their daughter/niece played for the US. They kept their kitchen open to have me over for*

dinner after practice one evening. My mom and aunt were on the field after the final watching me sign autographs for young girls. That's when I think my mother's opinion of me playing rugby changed."

The financial burden and loss of work time players incurred attending training camps made it difficult for the entire squad to come together for significant training time. Many believed that this lack of training time together would become the team's Achilles heel. In a postscript published by the Women's Committee, the consensus was that the U.S. squad's lack of consistent opportunities to engage in high-level training and competitions was clearly a significant impediment to their ability to win the Cup. Moreover, the players and coaches expressed frustration that their competitors, Canada and England were given the resources by their governing bodies to play a regular international schedule. The feeling was that without guaranteed funding support from USAR the U.S. Women would watch teams pass them by.

Emma Mitchell, the English scrumhalf recalls England facing similar challenges but disputes that the English women received support for a regular international schedule. "We received no support from the RFU. None. The Rugby Football Union for Women (WRFU) remained separate from the RFU until around 2006-2008. We operated under a 'pay to play' model covering all our own training and travel costs." However, the English women were able to convene more often than the U.S. "We got together as a squad as often as we could (one or two weekends a month) during the season and in the build-up to the tournament." (Emma Mitchell, correspondence 3/6/2024)

On to the games:

[Much thanks to Michael Malone, Rugby Magazine, May 23, 1994, pages 8-10 for the game reporting that informed the following]:

The scramble to put together the World Cup came together and in mid-April, twelve teams convened for the tournament. The teams were divided into four pools with the top two from each pool advancing to championship play. The U.S. found itself in pool one with Sweden and Japan. Pool two included England, Scotland, and Russia. Pool three included Ireland, France, and a combined Scottish University Side (who filled in after Spain dropped out days before the tournament). Pool four included Wales, Canada, and Kazakhstan.

Alex Williams: "The pool matches were held at clubs scattered around Scotland, so we spent a lot of time in coaches driving through the beautiful, green countryside. As it was spring, there were bouncy lambs cavorting literally everywhere. After those pool matches, our fans would tell us stories of hearing the old gents in the stands complaining about women playing the game before the match started. By the time the matches ended, they were in awe of the speedy, wide-open game we played. That USA squad definitely helped people realize maybe they weren't so dead set against women playing rugby after all."

Pool one was based out of Melrose Scotland, a charming, 'rugby mad' town about fifty miles from Edinburgh. The U.S. opened play April 11 against Sweden beating the Swedes 111-0. Fullback Krista McFarren led the US with six tries. Wing, Pam Irby scored five tries; Flyhalf Jos Bergman, four tries and four conversions, Center, Candi Orsini two tries, Center, Elise Huffer one try, and flanker, Sherri Hunt one try, Jen Crawford posted four conversion kicks. It was a scary display of U.S. firepower that immediately won over Scottish fans. Jen Crawford recalls: "As it turns out, Crawford is a very Scottish name, so they were yelling my last name REALLY loud 'Come on Craaaawwwford'!"

Four days later the U.S. kicked off against what seemed like a fit and determined Japanese side. But a few minutes into the match the U.S. was once again scoring at will. The forwards and the backs worked in synch exploding for 121 points and setting an international scoring record. The speed and the strength of the U.S. squad was frightening with the U.S. creating gaps, overloads or simply running over defenders. In the end, fullback Amy Westerman led the U.S. with five tries and three conversions. Alex Williams added three tries from the #8 spot, Brett Newton scored three tries from center, Tara Flanagan had two tries at lock, Patty Connell scored twice from the scrumhalf position and Laurie Spicer-Bordon added one try to the avalanche of points. Julie Dustrup recorded five conversions. Flanker Sheri Hunt recalls: *"One of the most inspiring moments for me was at the after-party with Japan. While we beat them 121-0, they were good sports after losing. As a team they were tactically perfect. Their players had skills and they really supported each other on the pitch."*

Over two matches in pool play the U.S. had scored 232 points. Neither Sweden nor Japan came close to the U.S. twenty-two much less the try line. The scoring tsunami had the press intrigued, it wasn't just the massive number of points, Scottish rugby fans were loving the balanced attack of the Americans and the beauty of the backline. The U.S. women were proud of their performance but concerned that they had not faced a challenge—would they be prepared for the April 17 quarterfinal match in Boroughmire against Ireland? The answer was a resounding 'hell yes.' The U.S. posted their third shutout of the tournament 76-0. As in the previous matches, the forwards fed the backline, and the hungry backs dazzled the Irish defense. The few times the Irish were able to gain possession the U.S. defense was particularly good, making several crushing tackles. Fullback Jen Crawford led the U.S. with three tries and a conversion. Wing Amy Westerman accounted for two tries, a penalty kick and three conversations, Wing Pam Irby picked up two tries, Mary Dixey, Kerry Kelly, Jan Rutkowski, Brett Newton, and Julie Dustrup each scored for the U.S. But the stakes were being raised and three days later the U.S. would face a tough Welsh side in the semifinals in Galashiels and a flaw in the U.S. system would be exposed.

## SEMIFINALS

**THE U.S. KNEW THAT WALES WOULD BE A TEST.** The Welsh had beaten Canada and Scotland to advance. While those scores had been close, the Welsh forwards had controlled a large amount of the possession. The U.S. came out early with the same game plan they had used in three previous matches—unleash a crashing fullback, force the defense to commit numbers, offload and let the magic backs do their thing. It took one minute for the U.S. to put Jen Crawford through from a penalty at the Welsh twenty-two. While the U.S. backs were once again unmatched the Welsh forwards did prove to be a match for the U.S. forwards. The U.S. was up 25-5 in the first half when Wales started a rolling maul at midfield. They successfully rolled for two and a half minutes covering approximately forty meters before forcing the U.S. into a penalty at the goal line. Wales was awarded a scrum and scored a pushover try. Captain Barb Bond recalls: *"Wales rolling mauls were crazy. We had never encountered anything like that before."*

Emma Mitchell recalls: *"...a fair bit of the game plan [for the final] came from what the coaches picked up watching the USA v Wales semi-final."* The U.S. went into the half up 25-10 and remained confident in the backline's unmatched scoring power. Five minutes into the second half Jen Crawford scored a beautiful try, taking the ball in the U.S. half and crashing through the Welsh backline, shedding tackles, and scoring to bring the U.S. to a 30-10 lead. But a few minutes later the Welsh forwards answered with another rolling maul, this one from fifteen meters out to bring the score to 30-15. The U.S. forwards were unnerved but the backs seemed unfazed and quickly answered with a scoring bonanza. While the Welsh flyhalf was content to kick for touch on most possessions, the U.S. fought to get the ball into the hands of their centers at every opportunity. The exhausted Welsh could not keep pace with the speed and handling of the U.S. backline and watched the Eagles run away with the match by a score of 56-15. Once again, fullback Jen Crawford led all scoring with five tries. Flyhalf Jos Bergmann had one try, five conversions and two penalty kicks. Patty Jervey and Candi Orsini each had a try.

## THE FINALS

**THE U.S. HAD POWERED THEIR WAY INTO THE** finals which would take place April 24, in historic Raeburn Place in Stockbridge against their 1991 finals foe, England. England had a less glamourous road to the finals, defeating Russia, 66-0, Scotland 26-0, Canada 24-10, and France, 17-6. In each match the English forwards showed their dominance, controlling the ball and feeding it to steady flyhalf Karen Almond. The English showed they were a side that could dominate possession and they trusted their backs to score points, not a lot of points, but enough points to win games. Their game plan favored efficient, technical, low- risk rugby.

An estimated five thousand spectators came to the final with an unknown number watching from the rooftops and rowhouses that surrounded the field. The match was played under grey skies that soon gave way to rain, bad news for the U.S. forwards. Karen Almond the England Flyhalf recalls: *"Our mindset going into the Final was 'confident but wary.' We knew we had the game plan and had done everything we could to prepare. Our squad was stronger, fitter and more tactically astute then the '91 team. We had also beaten them [the U.S.] in the Canada Cup. However, those USA backs were incredible and capable of tries from anywhere. We had to play at the top of our game and keep focused on our strategy; strangle them of possession."*

The match opened as usual with Jen Crawford crashing through the line on the opening kickoff and going into England territory. But at the first scrum the English pack drove the U.S. scrum back fifteen meters, the U.S. was forced into a penalty and England flyhalf Karen Almond scored a penalty kick from twenty-five meters out. In the sixth minute of the game, Jen Crawford did what Jen Crawford always did, she crashed the defensive line and dragged defenders with her over the line to put the U.S. up 5-3. But then, the rain began to fall, and the English pack began to flex. From ten meters out the English walked the ball over the line, forcing the U.S. again into a penalty, the referee awarded the English a penalty try. Jen Crawford and the U.S. backs responded, crashing into English territory and spinning the ball to wing Patty Jervey for a diving try that brought the crowd to its feet. But as the rain continued to fall the English pack continued to exert its power. Under intense pressure, the U.S.

struggled to get the ball out to the backs. The U.S. backrow and scrumhalf had little experience working under such intense pressure, while the English did a great job of continually applying that pressure. At the half the English led 24-10.

*"Our confidence was shaken in the first minute when their U.S. backs fielded the kickoff and nearly ran through our whole team! We had to refocus, remain calm and trust our game plan. I told the team they were always going to score tries; we just had to score more."* (Karen Almond)

The U.S. came out determined and were able to come away with a penalty kick in the first few minutes for a 24-13 score. But the England forwards were relentless. England #8, Gill Burns, was particularly dominant in the scrum and the lineouts, winning the ball and keeping possession away from the U.S. backline. As the clock was ticking the U.S. continued to believe in their ability to score quickly under pressure. They worked every magic trick they had to get the ball out but under pressure an errant pass went into English hands for a backbreaking score and with

# RUGBY PROFILE

# Jen Crawford

**Full Name:** Jennifer Crawford
**Height:** 5' 7"
**Weight:** 155
**Birthplace:** Fort Belvoir, VA
**Birthdate:** 7/25/64
**Present Residence:** Oakland, CA
**Occupation:** Software consultant
**College:** Stanford
**Years Playing Rugby:** 14
**Position:** Center, fullback
**Present Club:** Berkeley All Blues
**Previous Clubs:** Stanford, Beantown, Vixens, Saracens
**Number of Caps:** 11
**Eagle Matches:** Eagles versus Canada - 1988 & 1989; Soviet Union, New Zealand, England (1991 World Cup); Canada - 1992; England - 1993; Sweden, Ireland, Wales, England (1994 World Cup).
**Territorial Experience:** Pacific Coast 1983-1985, 1987-1995
**Local Union Experience:** Northern California 1983-1985, 1987-1995
**Most Valuable Teammates:** Jennifer Chue - Stanford, Annie Flavin - Beantown, Kim Mercer - Berkeley
**Most Difficult Opponents:** Patty Jervey-FSU, Krista McFarren - Maryland
**Most Respected Players** (same position): Krista McFarren, Candi Orsini (FSU)
**Favorite Players:** Sue Brooks-Old Puget Sound, K.O. Browder - Beantown, Kim Mercer - Berkeley
**Toughest Opposing Team:** England
**Best Memory in Rugby:** Winning National Club Championships with Beantown in 1986 and with Berkeley in 1994.
**Biggest Disappointment in Rugby:** Losing the 1996 National Club Championship.
**Tours:** New Zealand with the Pacific Coast in 1987
**Best Country Visited:** New Zealand
**Biggest Influence on Career:** Franck Boivert
**Area in which U.S. Rugby Needs Most Work:** We must focus on recruiting younger players, building a solid base of high school teams and retaining players after their playing careers are over to help coach, referee and administrate.
**Area in which U.S. Rugby Has Improved the Most:** Communication. The Internet has provided an easy way to keep people informed. I've received a lot more feedback from administrators than ever before.
**Other Sports:** Absolutely none
**Leisure Interests:** Letting my body heal after rugby matches, camping.
**Significant Books:** *The Bone People* - Keri Hulme
**Favorite Films:** Cinema Paradiso, Ace Ventura - Pet Detective
**Favorite TV Programs:** Wild Kingdom
**Favorite Musical Groups:** Beantown, particularly MJ.
**Favorite Character in Film or Literature:** Mrs. Madrigal from Tales of the City
**Favorite *Seinfeld* Character:** George
**Goals in Rugby:** Coaching a college women's side after retiring as a player.
**Personal Goals:** Live long and prosper.
**Best Administrator:** Krista McFarren
**Best Playing Field:** Canterbury, New Zealand
**Best Tournament:** 1987 Long Beach Tournament
**Best Coach:** John Tyler (Stanford), Franck Boivert (Eagles)
**Best Captain:** Lisa Burgess - Saracens
**Most Embarrassing Moment in Rugby:** Filling out this *Rugby* Profile and having people read it.

Jen Crawford, playing for her Berkeley All Blues club, breaks free against B. the final of the 1996 National Women's Club Championship. (Photo-Hagerty)

1996 Interview with Hall of Fame player, Jenn Crawford

time running out England had a comfortable 31-13 lead. The U.S. attempted to claw their way back into the game, but it was too little too late, and as the rain continued to fall, England celebrated a 38-23 win. England scrumhalf Emma Mitchell recalls: *"Towards the end of the game, the USA had scored another try (a second in quick succession) and I can remember feeling exhausted and thinking that, with possession, their backs were almost able to score at will and I was unsure if we would be able to hang on. We had kicked off at 2.30pm and, as I got ready to muster what energy I had to run out at Jos' conversion attempt, I heard a man from behind the posts say: 'it's alright England, it's 4pm'. As we ran out and the conversion went over, Jim Fleming blew the final whistle. Karen, Giselle, and I hugged under the posts (Jane soon joined us) and the most overwhelming initial emotion was relief followed by (as you can imagine) euphoria."*

As Jen Crawford offered about the final: *"We played on an historic field and the crowd was just fantastic. It was electric, it was energizing, it was maddening, it was painful watching England keep the ball within the pack, it was a big fat bummer, but it was fun."*

Flanker Sheri Hunt recalls: *"We really believed we were going to win right until the last moment. Emma Mitchell: I honestly think that we were the only people in Edinburgh that day who thought we had any chance of upsetting the USA side who were such huge favourites."*

*"Being a reserve and watching the final was extremely frustrating. Those were still the days where you didn't get into the game unless someone was well and truly injured and couldn't play, so there was no opportunity to try to help turn the game around. That said, it was my first World Cup, and I was so honored to have had the opportunity to play for the USA with such talented and dedicated teammates. I cherish both the memories and the World Cup silver medal."* (Alex Williams)

While the U.S. players were understandably heartbroken, the players spoke graciously about England's strategy and World Cup victory. The press continued to show the U.S. side love, complimenting them for their skill on the field as well as their gracious demeanor in a tough loss. It was notable to the players that no representatives from USA Rugby beyond members of the Women's Committee were present. The players had won silver at the World Cup and broken an international scoring record yet were met with complete silence from USAR.

While little was written about the U.S. performance after the 1994 World Cup, much of what was written focused on the loss. 1994 was a different era in coaching, many coaches at the time relied on subjective measures of players performance. It's tough to read the critique of the U.S. forwards from Head Coach Franck Boivert. In an interview with Rugby Magazine right after the U.S. loss, Boivert said, *"I'm disappointed in our tight five. I feel they quit on us. I told them before the match they had to be ruthless for 80 minutes and they didn't do it...."*

In a final match report Boivert continued to assert the loss was the result of the forwards inability to be aggressive. In a lengthy document to the Women's Committee, he called the forwards as, *"naïve, mediocre and lacking in fighting spirit. First, the absence of any fighting spirit in our forwards, who gave up very quickly. Other than the obvious problems in the scrum, it seemed that the English forwards simply wanted it much more. They were not only more aggressive in the scrum, but also in every other aspect of the game. They wanted to win. I believe too many of our players were happy just to play in the final and too few of our players played the way you need to play in a final match. It was a great disappointment because I believe the preparation was good without overdoing the motivational speeches and Joe Kelly took good care of the basics with the forwards."*

U.S. Captain Barb Bond recalls: *"The forwards did not give up nor did we lack fighting spirit. There is no doubt we were outmatched in set pieces but the reasons*

# U.S. ROSTER

| | | | | | |
|---|---|---|---|---|---|
| Jos Bergmann | Flyhalf | 5'5 | 145lb | 25 | BASH |
| Barb Bond | #8 | 5'8 | 165lb | 31 | BASH |
| Sue Brooks | Lock | 5'8 | 145lb | 28 | Berkeley |
| Patty Connell | Scrumhalf | 5'3 | 120lb | 30 | Beantown |
| Jen Crawford | Fullback | 5'7 | 150lb | 29 | Berkeley |
| Mary Dixey | Flyhalf | 5'4 | 140lb | 32 | Beantown |
| Julie Dustrup | Fullback | 5'8 | 160lb | 28 | Maryland Stingers |
| Tara Flanigan | Lock | 6'0 | 185lb | 30 | UCLA |
| Annie Flavin | Prop | 5'4 | 165lb | 32 | Beantown |
| Kathy Flores | Flanker | 5'5 | 145lb | 39 | Berkeley |
| Julie Gray | Hooker | 5'2 | 145lb | 27 | Twin City Amazons |
| Betsy Hill | Prop | 5'4 | 170lb | 38 | Peninsula Chaos |
| Elise Huffer | Center | 5'4 | 130lb | 32 | Peninsula Chaos |
| Sherianne Hunt | Flanker | 5'5 | 145lb | 32 | San Diego Surfers |
| Pam Irby | Wing | 5'5 | | 29 | Peninsula Chaos |
| Patty Jervey | Wing | 5'4 | 135lb | 30 | Florida State |
| Kris Kany | Flanker | 5'4 | 144lb | 32 | Boston |
| Kerry Kelly | Scrumhalf | 5'6 | 125lb | 34 | BASH |
| Cassie Law | Flanker | 5'8 | 145lb | 29 | BASH |
| Krista McFarren | Fullback | 5'6 | 135lb | 32 | New Orleans |
| Candy Orsini | Center | 5'6 | 135lb | 37 | Florida State |
| Brett Newton | Center | 5'4 | 144lb | 29 | Beantown |
| Beth Pepper | Hooker | 5'5 | 155lb | 34 | BASH |
| Jan Rutkowski | Lock | 5'8 | 175lb | 38 | Beantown |

| | | | | | |
|---|---|---|---|---|---|
| M.A. Sorenson | Prop | 5'6 | 172lb | 37 | Philadelphia |
| Laurie Spicer-Bordon | Flanker | 5'7 | 140lb | 29 | Beantown |
| Lisa Weix | Prop | 5'4 | 145lb | 31 | BASH |
| Amy Westerman | Fullback | 5'6 | 164lb | 27 | Beantown |
| Alex Williams | #8 | 5'10 | 185lb | 24 | Beantown |
| Christine Nixon | Lock | 5'11 | 180lb | 34 | Minnesota |
| Franck Boivert | Head Coach | | | | |
| Joe Kelly | Assistant Coach | | | | |

*for this were complex. The lack of time together as a pack was limiting, it takes time and competitions to gel into a cohesive unit. The team that played together for the final had had very few matches together. We had an amazing forwards coach in Joe Kelly but the constraints of time in preparation ahead of the tournament limited how much we could do once the tournament was in progress."*

Lock Jan Rutkowski: *"That 'we lacked fight and gave up' is absolutely untrue. I, and my fellow tight five, gave our all that day."*

Jen Crawford recalls: *"We were devastated by the loss. In the locker room after the game players looked to Joe (Assistant Coach Joe Kelly) because we were so crushed, and Franck was just not there for us. Joe's speech to the forwards after the finals was just incredibly heartfelt."*

Boivert's postmortem was long and difficult to read. More troubling, he did very little reflection on his own contributions to the outcome. At the time Boivert was juggling his role as the Head Coach of the Women's National Team with his job as the Head Coach of the Stanford men's side. He flew home to California to coach the Stanford men in the Pacific Coast Collegiate Championship between the U.S.

match against Wales and the final against England. A trip a few U.S. players felt compromised the team's preparation. He also seemed to lack an understanding of the limited power of the Women's Committee and USAR's general lack of interest in the women's game. At the time, USAR seemed determined to ignore the success of the women's program as they believed it detracted from the men's game. At that time, the U.S men's team struggled mightily in international play. Throughout the 1980's and 1990's the U.S. men made three trips to the World Cup but only managed two wins in pool play, one against Japan and one against Uruguay.

Captain Barb Bond recalls: *"I think the major 'fault' for the '94 World Cup outcome falls to USAR. Not only for the lack of support leading up to and during that tournament but for the failure to recognize that USA rugby had a unique opportunity to be competitive on the world stage for years to come following the success of the '91 team. Advice from me and, I'm sure others, that we will quickly lose our competitive advantage without investment in the women's game went unheeded."* While Rugby Magazine carried some of Boivert's critique of the team in a full-page interview, the larger

document was not seen beyond a few members of the Women's Committee and a few members of the team. Others did offer more measured observations of the U.S. performance in the final. Emil Signes, rebutted Boivert's assertion that the tight five were overmatched and under-aggressive. Emil noted that the U.S. backrow and hooker were overmatched in size by twenty pounds per person thus giving the U.S. women a decided disadvantage in set pieces. His observation was astute as the U.S. tended to favor backrow fitness and mobility over size and power. This made sense as the backrow were integral to keeping the ball alive for the explosive backline. England on the other hand understood the value of a heavy backrow. You can see the impact of the 1994 England scrum in subsequent World Cups. England continues to produce big, mobile backrow players. Gill Burns' influence can be seen in the English backrows in subsequent World Cups, such as the great, Maggie Alphonsi (2010) and 2023 player of the year, Marlie Packer. Moreover, England coaches scouted the U.S.

and noted that the U.S. flankers were instructed to drop off defensive scrums in anticipation of a backrow move. This gave England an eight-on- six advantage on their own scrums, which they took full advantage of to a crushing degree.

The U.S. forwards were the top players from some of the best club teams in the U.S. Most came from club scrums so dominant, they rarely if ever moved backwards. Moving backwards was a new experience for most of the U.S. forwards. As Krista McFarren recalls, *"I did not come from a club with a dominant pack and I gained new respect for the scrumhalfs I played with who really had to scrap, dig in, dive pass to give the backs decent ball."*

Thirty years later watching the video of the final, reading the excitement in the match reports and the notes from the Women's Committee on the 'mountains that had to be moved' to get the team to the tournament I am left believing that the 1994 team was truly one of the great U.S. teams, deserving of a celebration they never got. Their play electrified rugby and its impact can be seen today in the quality of rugby across the globe. There was no one like Jen Crawford at the time. No back line with the combination of speed, power, skill, and confidence that the U.S. displayed in every match. The forwards faced a different challenge but a 'lack of fighting spirit' was not one of those. These were elite, well tested forwards who loved and honored the game with their play. The 1994 U.S. The Women's World Cup team was a resounding success worthy of our respect. Jen Crawford: *"In the end, it's the little moments that made the hours we spent grinding it out into a special time. I don't even know how to describe it—the bond, teamwork, being a family. All of those and more—the Twin Towers from Hell donning kilts, the hotel staff quietly amused at all our antics, Betsy Hill being late for practice by saying she forgot the time, laundry day when we each took turns, pranks we played on each other. There truly is nothing like those moments. They last a lifetime."*

Keirsten Lawton prepares to clear against New Zealand during the 1996 Canada Cup in Edmonton. (Photo-Hagerty)

# New Zealand Women Win Canada C

**by James Rabbitte**

**Edmonton, Alberta**
**September 9-14, 1996**

New Zealand won the Canada Cup, a round robin among the women's national teams of the U.S., Canada, New Zealand and France. There was never any question which was the best team in the competition, as the big, fast, well-drilled and stunningly fit New Zealand side outscored its opponents 293-11 en route to the title.

**ROUND I**

U.S. 39, France 16
New Zealand 88, Canada 3
(summaries in September issue)

**ROUND II**

New Zealand 86, U.S. 8
Canada 39, France 3

The U.S. had the daunting task of facing coach Daryl Suasua's slick new New Zealand side in the second round of competition. The Eagles and the All Blacks had split their two previous matches; New Zealand scoring a 9-3 decision in 1990 and the Eagles pushing over a last minute try to win its 1991 World Cup semifinal 7-0. But women's rugby in New Zealand has taken great strides since then, evident in the All Blacks' recent 28-5 win over Australia. The New Zealanders' marked improvement was a fact that the U.S. women became painfully aware.

Swift New Zealand wing Louisa Wall, who stands 5' 10" and weighs 185 pounds, scored three tries against the U.S. Wall, a double international, was the youngest ever member of New Zealand's netball team.

(Photo-Hagerty)

## N. Zealand 86, U.S. 8

**September 11, 1996**

The All Black attack was nothing short of awesome in New Zealand's 86-8 thumping of the '94 World Cup finalists. Whether it was the rolling maul or multi-phase ball spun out to the lethal back three, virtually every New Zealand attack worked perfectly, as the All Blacks sprung for 14 tries.

"We went to school in this game," said Eagle captain Jen Crawford. "We played from the heart and we'll be back."

The match's first ten minutes were scoreless, but it didn't take long for the Kiwi try parade to begin, starting with the wings. Louisa Wall scored in the 11th minute, while other wing Vanessa Cootes scored four minutes later. The two wings – both big and amazingly athletic -- combined for eight tries on the day, Cootes leading the way with five. There were long tries and short tries; back tries and pack tries. Pretty tries and very pretty tries. Lots and lots of tries.

Also impressive was the Kiwi goal kicking. While she was off the mark in the second half, fullback Heidi Reader was dead on in the first, nailing six conversions in a row.

The U.S., its lineup altered by injuries, got a penalty from wing Amy Westerman in the 22nd minute to make it 19-3, but they would not score again until about 30 seconds from the final whistle. Flyhalf Kim Cyganik, wearing #10 for injured Jos Bergmann, scooted into the corner for a try.

Fitness was the backbone of the improved New Zealand women's game, and the national team had agreed to run a "Hennie Muller" (a brutal sprint workout) for every point allowed. So while the U.S. prepared for the conversion, New Zealand found no solace in its 86-8 lead. The New Zealand players charged the U.S. kicker as she approached the ball, and they were able to block the kick and keep the ensuing Hennie Mullers to a minimum. A fitting end to the match.

**SCORING: New Zealand:** Cootes 5T; Wall 3T; White 2T; Hirovanaa T; Richards T; Rush T; Reader T, 8C. **U.S.** Cyganik T; Westerman P.

**New Zealand**
Waters
Palmer
Thomas
Barclay
Richards
Littleworth
White
Martin
Hirovanaa
Richards
Wall
Simpson-Brown(c
Rush
Cootes
Reader

Referee: Paul Mi
* temp. replace

**Awesome**

The All Bla strengthened h rugby attitude. " is show up," sai his players. The technical adviso forced a strict fi program. The passed on train tactical moves bits to the other participants wi women's rugby bettered. The Ne Union gives th excellent suppo players of New a number of int

"We don't \ by ourselves," Simpson-Brown *(NZ)*. "It's been rugby because t are at and we w to come get us, image of the sp

"Our girls w ing at that pace," Franck Boivert multi-phase, hig tack. "We were repositioning c fense. It was a n players."

**Eagl**

Scrumhalf ? flanker Diane S first test appeara the All Black m Candi Orsini ea the most in Eagl

Promising young U.S. wing Sharon Johnson attempts unsuccessfully to round New Zeal Cootes. Besides playing tenacious defense, Cootes burned the U.S. for five tries. (Photo

1996 Canada Cup: New Zealand flexes

One of Orsini's caps had come in the U.S. win over New Zealand in the '91 Cup. "New Zealand seemed to have better mental preparation. They played 15 man running rugby. They were very well-rounded and their fitness really killed us," she commented on the current squad.

## Canada 39, France 3

**September 11, 1996**

Canada, which bowed out of the '94 World Cup quarterfinals with a 24-10 loss to eventual champion England, showed tough tackling in defeating France 39-3. Limiting France to a single penalty goal, the gritty Canadians set up a showdown with the U.S. for second place.

### ROUND III

## N. Zealand 109, France 0

**September 14, 1996**

More of the same. Lenadeen Simpson-Brown's All Black troops put forth their most impressive performance yet, somehow surpassing their two previous efforts with a 109-0 thrashing of France. A third place finisher at the 1994 World Cup, France was no slouch. But New Zealand had far too many weapons, as it upped the standard of women's rugby another notch in securing the Canada Cup.

## U.S. 22, Canada 14

**September 14, 1996**

The Eagles took second place with a 22-14 win over Canada in the Cup's final match. Fielding a host of young players that coach Franck Boivert has pegged to lead the squad into the 1998 World Cup, the U.S. tallied four tries to hammer out the hard-fought win.

"We were lucky to get out of this one," said Boivert after the match. "Due to injuries we have a new backline and were not as fit as the Canadians because we are off season. However, we are very, very happy with our young players."

In what was considered the most

exciting match of the competition, Canada took an early 3-0 lead on a penalty kick from flyhalf Annette Darby. But the Eagles responded in the 11th minute when lock Alex Williams crashed in with second phase ball and Amy Westerman converted for a 7-3 lead.

Two more Darby penalties had the hosts on top 9-7, but a try from center Westerman gave Boivert's squad a 12-9 lead at the break.

**Second Half**

Canada regained the lead early in the second half when wing Julie Foster outpaced the cover defense (14-12), and held the advantage for the better part of the half.

But U.S. captain Jen Crawford, the leading Eagle scorer at the 1994 World Cup, powered through would be Canadian tacklers for a try after taking the feed from wing Sharon Johnson. The U.S. led 17-14.

Right before the curtain fell, Crawford returned the favor for Johnson when she booted ahead for the young wing to collect the ball on the fly. Johnson found #8

Barb Bond in support for the try, 22-14.

**SCORING:** U.S. Williams T; Bond T; Crawford T; Westerman T, C. **Canada:** Foster T, Darby 3P.

| U.S. | | Canada |
|---|---|---|
| Kirk | 1 | Muller |
| Sorensen | 2 | © Kalra |
| Turton | 3 | Lacasse |
| Williams * | 4 | Fairclough |
| Fitz | 5 | Asprey |
| Kim | 6 | Denike |
| Schnapp | 7 | White |
| Bond | 8 | McMahon |
| Cyganik | 9 | Wesch |
| Lawton | 10 | Darby |
| Rowe | 11 | Hunt |
| Westerman | 12 | Walsh |
| Orsini | 13 | Pare |
| Johnson | 14 | Foster |
| Crawford © | 15 | Johnson |

\* temp. replaced by Lee
Referee: Paul Murgatroyd

**12 New Caps for the U.S.**

Twelve players made their first appearance for the U.S. They were Liz Kirk, Tricia Turton, Jen Renne, Nancy Fitz, Kalei Kim, Diane Schnapp, Kim Cyganik, Sharon Johnson, Lisa Rowe, Laura Cabrera, Therese Taylor and Kiersten Lawton.

On one of the rare times that the U.S. had possession against New Zealand, scrumhalf Therese Taylor attacks from the base of the scrum with Alex Williams in support. (Photo-Hagerty)

The U.S. Women in Edmonton: (FRONT, L-R) Amy Westerman, Barb Bond, Diane Schnapp, Cindy James, Candi Orsini, Jennifer Crawford (captain), Therese Taylor, Keirsten Lawton. (BACK) Laura Cabrera, Christie Nixon, Jennifer Renne, Jennifer Levi, Liz Kirk, M.A. Sorensen, Tricia Turton, Laurie Spicer-Bourdon, Kerry Kilander McCabe, Alexandra Williams, Krista McFarren, Kim Cyganik.

## THE 1998 WORLD CUP
### A THIRD STRAIGHT MEDAL FOR THE U.S.

**THE 1998 WORLD CUP MARKED A MAJOR MILE**-stone: it was the first women's tournament officially sanctioned by the International Rugby Board (IRB). The U.S. once again reached the finals, ultimately falling 44–12 to a dominant New Zealand side in front of 4,000 fans—but still earning their third consecutive World Cup medal.

The Americans opened the tournament with a commanding 84–0 victory over Russia, followed three days later by a 38–16 win against Spain. Four days

after that, the U.S. beat a resilient Scotland team 25–10, setting up a semi-final clash with Canada. With only three days' rest, the U.S. delivered an inspired performance, defeating Canada 46–10 and punching their ticket to the final against a powerhouse New Zealand squad coming off a staggering 134–6 win over Germany.

Heading into the final, the U.S. had outscored opponents 193–32. Veterans like Candi Orsini at center and fullback Jenn Crawford, both with 19 caps, anchored the backline, while younger stars Jos Bergman and Amy Westerman provided speed and energy. In the forwards, MA Sorensen, Barb Bond, and Nancy Fitz offered steady leadership and experience.

Despite their talent and cohesion, the U.S. faced an ascending New Zealand team that proved unstoppable. The Americans struggled to contain stars like Farah Palmer and wing Vanessa Cootes, who together scored four of New Zealand's eight tries, securing the Black Ferns' dominant victory.

The 98 World Cup saw a record sixteen teams compete and experienced heightened media attention. There was no qualification process, teams taking part were invited by the iRB.

Eagle World Cup veterans: (Kneeling, L-R) J. Bergmann, P. Irby, A. Westerman, A. Williams. (Standing M.A. Sorenson, C. Orsini, P. Jervey, Jen Crawford (captain), K. McFarren, B. Bond.

# USA Women's National Rugby Team

USA RUGBY

---

## USA Women's National Rugby Team Schedule

The Americans and their 18 - 4 win loss record commence their reacquisition of the World Cup campaign with a challenging 13 month schedule that is constructed to develop and maintain their international status as a rugby world power.

**July 4, 5 and 6 1997**
**Under 23 training and Canada test match**

A 39% increase in the number of college teams has indicated the importance of developing the student players into the player required to compete at the international level. The National Team seniors will conduct individualized training sessions with the college all stars and close the weekend with a first ever Under 23 match between the two countries plus a senior test match.

**July 17 through August 5, 1997**
**Americans tour Australia and Fiji**

The Americans will travel to Australia during the peak of the rugby season when close to a record 100,000 people, 12,200 interstate travelers will be on hand to watch the Bledisloe Cup and the Australia men's test match.

"The combination of general public, member union, corporate and hospitality tickets sold already, indicates that on July 26 we will have close to a record 100,000 people watching Australia take on New Zealand", John O'Neill said.

"Almost double the number of rugby fans will now have the opportunity to watch what is the pinnacle of Test match rugby – over 8500 New Zealanders, 12,200 interstate travelers and 50,000 Victorians [not including members]"

The women's USA versus Australia test match will be the curtain raiser to the Australia - South Africa men's test match, guaranteeing any rugby enthusiast a peek at the American trademark fast running, action packed rugby that has earned this rugby team the honor of being one of the top 3 rugby teams in the world.

**December 1 - 7, 1997**
**Inaugural Patriots Cup**

In celebration of the National Teams 10 years of existence, the first ever international rugby tournament will be conducted in Florida, with invitations to countries such as Canada, Netherlands and Scotland. The USA Rugby will not only showcase their game to a mass audience, but provide the local economy with an injection of tourist dollars.

The local economy can expect overseas and interstate visitors for the week preceding the Patriots Cup occupying the many of the flights and local hotels plus utilizing many of Florida's feature attractions.

**March - April '98**
**Two week camp with 3 games**

The American World Cup squad will be selected and provided an opportunity to gel with one another during the camp.

**May '98**
**1998 World Cup**

in Holland, Amsterdam

---

# Women's Rugby World Cup

A special 12 page supplement to Oval World June 1998

iRB
WOMEN'S RUGBY WORLD CUP 1998

written by Peter McMullan (unless otherwise credited)

photography by Wim Peperkamp (unless otherwise credited)

---

## EAGLES & ALL BLACKS ON COLLISION COURSE

The outcome of the semi-finals, on May 13, suggested nothing could prevent **New Zealand** from winning WRWC 1998. The All Black women ignored true heatwave conditions to dismiss defending 1994 champions **England** 44-11 after pounding in five second-half tries and went on to meet three-time finalists **USA**, 46-6 winners over **Canada**, for the Women's Rugby World Cup 1998 on May 16.

With the temperature topping 33C compared to 8C only a few days before, all the players and referees found the going incredibly tough with water in constant demand.

Looking ahead to their first ever final, the New Zealanders, with their line crossed only once – by England wing Jane Molyneux – had scored exactly 300 points to 26, running in 55 tries in four games.

On an individual basis, they boasted the leading points-scorer, centre Annaleah Rush (64) and one of the two joint try leaders, full-back Tammi Wilson (7), a total equalled only by England wing Nicky Brown.

Said New Zealand captain and hooker Farah Palmer: "We love and treasure the rugby in our country and that will shine through in the final. We knew we had to be patient against England and we tried to make the best use of our three-quarters in the second half."

England made a powerful and confident start to lead 6-0 with two early penalties from number eight Claire Frost, standing in for injured captain Gill Burns. But England could not hold out against relentless New Zealand pressure and by half-time the game had turned the All Blacks' way as they prepared to build on a 10-6 lead after an opening try from Rush, scorer of the winners' first 13 points to finish with 24, including a second try.

The **USA** stepped up their game at all levels, leaving **Canada** trailing in their wake with two sparkling early tries, a 31-3 half-time advantage and ultimate victory by six tries, five conversions and two penalties to two penalties. It was a result sparked by dominant individual performances from full-back Jen Crawford, who had three tries, and outside-half Jen Bergmann, who added five conversions to a great all-round effort in attack.

Canada took credit for a courageous display against their traditional North American rivals but could never match the physical strength and inscive running of the winners. Thus England and Canada had to play off for third and fourth places, England having won 72-6 when the two teams met on May 3.

In the semi-finals of the Plate competition, **Australia** needed a fourth penalty by full-back Tanya Osborne just before the finish to grab a 17-15 victory over widely admired **Spain** while **Scotland** were altogether too strong for France, winning 27-7. The Scots were only 10-7 ahead at the interval after an opening try with a classic forward catch and drive from a line-out for a try by wing forward Jayne Abeth.

On the other side of the draw **Karakhstan** qualified for the final of the Bowl with a strong finish to master **Wales** 18-13. Their opponents would be **Ireland**, 20-5 winners over **Italy** thanks to a penalty try and five penalties from outside-half Rachine Shrieves. In the second game of the tournament Ireland had lost 12-6 to Karakhstan.

In the Shield, the final was to be between **The Netherlands** and **Germany**. The Host Union came through 61-0 at the expense of **Russia** while **Germany** just squeezed past **Sweden** 20-18.

The programme for May 15 was: Bowl Final (9-10) Ireland v Karakhstan, (11-12) Italy v Wales. Shield Final (13-14) Netherlands v Germany, (15-16) Russia v Sweden.
On May 16 it was: WRWC Cup Final (1-2) NZ v USA, (3-4) Canada v England. Plate Final (5-6) Scotland v Australia, (7-8) Spain v France.

**CUP SEMI-FINALS**
USA 46: Tries Crawford (3), Kau, McPartan, Wuhrman. Cons, Bergmann (5). Pen, Bergmann (2). Wehl, Bergmann. CANADA 6: Pen, Marsh (2).
USA: J Crawford, K McPartan, P Jervey (rep M Johnston), A Weinstein, P Ida, J Bergmann, J Rowe (rep J Taylor), B Wuhrman, J Queen, D Hemgesberg, T Brodali, K Kau, J Donnelley. H Gekers, N Fax, M Harrison (rep L Kau), S Booth, M Ortega (rep T Sawicki). Canada: S Johnson (rep J Roden), C Sperling, C Walsh, L Locke, A Burly, S Wands, M Whiteclay, M MacMahon, J Plunkett (rep J Higdon), T Ramsden, J Fitzhugh, J Blackey (rep K Syrak), L Larson, M Marsh, S Hall. Referee: Gordon van't Hoofd (Holland)

**NEW ZEALAND 44:** Tries, Cotter (2), Rush (2), Kire, Richards, Rush (rep) (3) Wehl, Rush. ENGLAND 11: Try, Molyneux. Pen, Frost (2). NZ: T Wilson, V Cotter, A Rush, S Shortland (rep K Kave), L Kirk, A Richards, M Hermanns, A Vincent.

**PLATE SEMI-FINALS**
Scotland 27: Tries Abeth, Kennedy, Littlejohn, MacKenzie, Crain, Chalmers (2) Pen, Chalmers. Wehl, MacKenzie. France 7: Try, Hazzard. Cons, Lubin.

Australia 17: Try, Osborne. Pen, (4) Osborne. Spain 15: Tries, Hungria, Pen, Monribes, Gore. Ramirez, Wehl, Pena.

**SHIELD SEMI-FINALS**
Ireland 20: Pen, Shrieves (5), penalty try. Wehl, NT, Rain. Italy 5: Try, Bolini.

Karakhstan 18: Tries, Bache, Tsgarbekova, Cans, Tamasova, Pen, Tamasova (2). Wales 13: Tries, Evans, Cottles, Wehl, Evans.

**BOWL SEMI-FINALS**
Netherlands 61: Eves, Dalton (3), Van Delft, Van den Hoogen, Van Loek, Van Vest, Van Westerop, Cotter, Van den Hoogen (2), Van Westerop (3), Prins, Hoofden, Van Westerop, Wehl, Teeparn. Russia 0.

Germany 20: Sites, Albech (2), Wichheim, Cotter, Meister, Pen, Meister. Sweden 18: Tries, Nordlof, Robertsson, Cotter, Andersson, Pen, Andersson, Bergmann, Wehl, Nordlof.

 # 1998 RUGBY WORLD CUP ROSTER

| | | |
|---|---|---|
| SHALANDA BAKER | FULLBACK | AIR FORCE ACADEMY |
| JOS BERGMAN | FLYHALF | MARYLAND STINGERS RUGBY CLUB |
| BARB BOND | #8 | BAY AREA SHEHAWKS RUGBY CLUB |
| STACY BOYLE | HOOKER | PHILADELPHIA RUGBY CLUB |
| CAROL BURDICK | HOOKER | BERKELEY ALL BLUES RUGBY CLUB |
| JENNIFER CRAWFORD (C) | FULLBACK / CENTER | BERKELEY ALL BLUES RUGBY CLUB |
| TAMMY ECKERT | CENTER | BERKELEY ALL BLUES RUGBY CLUB |
| NANCY FITZ | LOCK | WASHINGTON DC FURIES RUGBY CLUB |
| SHERI HUNT | FLANKER | SAN DIEGO SURFERS RUGBY CLUB |
| PAM IRBY | WING | OREGON SPORTS UNION (ORSU) |
| PATTY JERVEY | CENTER | ATLANTA HARLEQUINS RUGBY CLUB |
| MICHELLE JOHNSON | CENTER / #8 | COLORADO OLD GIRLS RUGBY CLUB |
| KIM KALEIWAHINE | BAY AREA | BAY AREA SHEHAWKS RUGBY CLUB |
| ELIZABETH KIRK | PROP | SEATTLE RUGBY CLUB |
| KEIRSTEN LAWTON | FLYHALF | BEANTOWN RUGBY CLUB |
| KRISTA MCFARREN | FULLBACK | MARYLAND STINGERS RUGBY CLUB |
| CANDI ORSINI | CENTER | AT LARGE |
| MEREDITH OTTENS | PROP | MINNESOTA VALKYRIES RUGBY CLUB |
| ERINA QUEEN | #8 | EMERALD CITY MUDHENS, SEATTLE WA |
| JENNIFER RENNE | LOCK | WASHINGTON DC FURIES RUGBY CLUB |
| LISA ROWE | SCRUMHALF | MARYLAND STINGERS RUGBY CLUB |
| DIANNE SCHNAPP | FLANKER | BERKELEY ALL BLUES RUGBY CLUB |
| MA SORENSEN | PROP | PHILADELPHIA RUGBY CLUB |
| TERESA TAYLOR | SCRUMHALF | TWIN CITY AMAZONS RUGBY CLUB |
| TRICIA TURTON | PROP | SEATTLE RUGBY CLUB |
| AMY WESTERMAN | CENTER | BEANTOWN RUGBY CLUB |
| ALEX WILLIAMS | #8 | BEANTOWN RUGBY CLUB |

US scrumhalf Lisa Rowe has the ball out during the Eagles' victory over Scotland in the 1998 Women's World Cup. (Photo - Dixey)

**Atlantis Women in Hong Kong Women's Sevens March 1996**

Top: Emil Signes (coach), Pam Irby, Nancy Fitz, MJ Mohl, Sallie Ahlert, Amy Westerman
Bottom: Janet Marshall (manager), Tray Moens, Candi Orsini, Patty Jervey, Kim Cyganik, jos Bergmann, Suzanne Cobarruvias (manager)

## U.S. WOMEN'S NATIONAL 7S TEAM

**THE FIRST U.S. WOMEN'S NATIONAL 7S TEAM** was established in 1997. The team competed in the Hong Kong 7s tournament against 5 national sides. Played over two days, the tournament required teams to play in 2 pools of 6 matches plus a semifinal and a final. The top 2 teams would play a total of 7 games. The U.S. played well, winning all their pool play matches and beating England in a thrilling semifinal 17-5 to advance to the finals against New Zealand.

The U.S. lost 43-0 to the New Zealand Wild Ducks, one of the few teams in the tournament that was not a recognized national team.

The tournament brochures and USAR materials sent to players clearly refer to the team as the U.S.

National 7s Team. However, the pioneering 1997 was never recognized or capped.

Much of the vision and 'sheer will' to create a national women's sevens team came from player and 7s advocate Sallie Ahlert. While women across the globe were playing sevens the problem was there were no national teams. That's when the legend—the emperor—Emil Signes stepped forward. Emil was the founder and Head Coach of Atlantis Men's and Women's rugby teams. In 1996 the Atlantis women competed in the Hong Kong Women's Sevens tournament. Founded in 1976, Hong Kong 7s was one of the top 7s tournaments in the world and 1996 was the first year Hong Kong included women in the tournament.

The 1996 women's tournament was a poor affair for women's teams. The women played on a poorly

**1996 National Women 7s Camp Philly**

lined, muddy soccer field as the original stadium field was under water following torrential downpours. Initially, the organizers cancelled the tournament on the opening day. But reasonable heads prevailed and the soccer field was located nearby. The Atlantis women played three matches in one day, defeating Asia Pacific, Timaru NZ and a combined Japanese team, outscoring their opponents 181-0. The BBC's Ian Robertson watched the matches and raved about Atlantis' performance to the Hong Kong Rugby Union, with his endorsement and the lobbying of Emil Signes, the organizers agreed to include a women's division in the 1997 Hong Kong Tournament. But the tournament would be held a week prior to the mens tournament.

Sensing the moment, Emil returned home and organized the first U.S. National Women's Sevens selection camp in August of 1996. Forty-four players

**Jardine Fleming Unit Trusts**

**Hong Kong Invitation Women's Rugby Sevens**

SEVENS

Arabian Gulf • Australia • Canada • England • Fiji • Holland • Hong Kong • Japan • New Zealand • Scotland • Singapore • USA

**ABERDEEN STADIUM**
**MARCH 15-16, 1997**

Souvenir programme

## USA
### Eagles

| Players | | |
|---|---|---|
| | Jos Bergman | Krista McFarren |
| | Janine Cochran | Tracy Moens |
| | Nancy Fitz | Suzie Parker |
| | Keirsten Lawton | Anita Pease |
| | Jen Lucas | Lisa Rowe |
| **Coach** | Emile Signes | |
| **Manager** | Sherie Hunt | |
| **Playing strip** | Red, blue, white, tie-dyed | |

*The US is one of the pioneers of women's rugby. The nation's first recorded women's team was at Colorado State University in 1972. Since then the sport has surged and the national team won the first ever World Cup in 1991 and were runners-up in 1994.*

27

*Janine Cochran, UCLA; Nancy Fitz, Washington Furies; Sheri Hunt, UCLA; Kiersten Lawton, Beantown; Jennifer Lucas, Washington Furies; Krista McFarren, Maryland Stingers; Tracy Moens, New Orleans Halfmoons; Sue Parker, Maryland Stingers; Anita Pease, New Orleans Halfmoons; Lisa Rowe, Maryland Stingers*

were invited to the camp. The attendees represented twenty-nine women's clubs, seventeen LAUs and seven territories. Ten players came directly from college teams. The camp was grueling, the first two days included individual speed, strength and endurance tests and the final two days were matches. Following the August gathering a second camp of thirty players was organized from which the first, ten, national team players were selected.

In late September the first U.S. women's national team was announced. The team's average age was 30 years old with the youngest players, Keirsten Lawton and Lisa Rowe, at 25 and the oldest, Tracey Moens-Henderson at 39. Six of the ten were capped 15s players. Krista McFarren led with 11 caps, while the other 5 averaged 2 caps a piece. They were small, 5 players were 5 '5, and the team's average weight was 140lbs—the lone 'big girl' on the team was Nancy Fitz at 6'0 and 160lbs. The team was one of the most professionally accomplished including two physicians, one attorney, a chemical engineer, a chemist, an investment analyst, an exercise physiologist, and an environmental scientist.

The players paid their own way to tryouts and practices in Philadelphia, San Diego, Washington DC and Los Angeles, as well as Hong Kong. The Hong Kong tournament, a full international event, took place March 15-16, 1997.

*Left to right: Anita Pease, Sherri Hunt, Janine Cochran, Tracy Moens, Lisa Rowe, Sue Parker, Kiersten Lawson, Jen Lucas, Krista McFarren, Nancy Fitz. Front: Emil Signes and Al Caravelli*

Once in Hong Kong the team trained twice a day with additional chalk talks. They stayed in an odd, inexpensive hotel, the BP International. Where one player noted that it had to be 'the only hotel in the world where the lobby measured bigger in square meters than all the rooms combined.' The hotel staff was less than enthusiastic to be hosting rugby teams. So much so that the players were forbidden from eating in the hotel restaurant. To add insult to injury, the team arrived to find their donated jerseys were all mens large. Coach Al Caravelli had the jerseys altered before the first match. In rainy, humid Hong Kong, the team took the field in heavy cotton, tie dyed red, white and blue jerseys.

HONG KONG 7S RESULTS

**First Day (Emil Signes review)**

**US 26 Scotland 5:** The U.S. began strongly with Lisa Rowe scoring in the first. Tries were by Lisa Rowe (2), Sue Parker and Nancy Fitz, while Kiersten Lawton added three conversions.

**US 10 Hong Kong 7:** The U.S. had two tries called back. The U.S. scores were by Janine Cochran and Krista McFarren.

**US 43 Arabian Gulf 0:** Janine Cochran and Kiersten Lawton each scored two tries, with one each by Rose, McFarren and Jennifer Lucas. Lawton converted 4 of 7 tries.

**US 53 Singapore 0:** Janine Cochran and Sheri Hunt each scored a hat trick, and Anita Pease,

*1998 U23 player Hedwig Aerts*

final loss to England in 1994. The U.S. drew first blood when Lisa Rowe covered a McFarren kick inches from the back of the try zone. Lisa Rowe also scored the second try on a run following a McFarren assist, for a 10-0 lead. England scored to make it 10-5 with several minutes to play but Sue Parker followed with a 95m try converted by Lawton that made the score 17-5.

**US 0 New Zealand Wild Ducks 43 (Championship Final):** Nine minutes into the 20-minute game the U.S. were only down by one try, but New Zealand scored on the last play of the half, and then had their way in the second half to finish with a convincing win.

*"Our first game was against Scotland, we were all gathered in a huddle before the match and I remember Al Caravelli telling us all that we were pioneers in the sport, how honored he was to coach us, and how proud we should be stepping onto the pitch as the first 7s USWNT. There wasn't a dry eye in the huddle. One funny story about our final match against New Zealand—we were losing badly and in the last minutes of the second half, I recall something not feeling right. I started counting the number of US players on the field.... 1, 2, 3, 4, 5, 6...1, 2, 3, 4 5, 6!!! I yelled to Emil, "we only have 6 players on the field!!!" ..like things weren't bad enough."*

—Anita Pease

Kiersten Lawton and Sue Parker scored one each. Lawton had 4 conversions.

**Results, Second Day:**

**US 29 Fiji 0:** McFarren, Lawton, Parker, Pease and Moens scored tries and Lawton had 2 conversions.

**US 17 England 5 (Cup Semifinal):** This was a huge game for the US; two players—Hunt and McFarren—had played in the World Cup 15s

Following the successful 1997 Hong Kong debut of womens 7s, the organzers cancelled the 1998 Hong Kong women's tournament due to the 1998 women's 15s World Cup. The U.S. selected a 7s national team in 1998. The U.S. won the Magnificent Sevens Tournament in Toronto, outlasting a field of 102 teams.

By 1999 the Hong Kong organizers decided to hold the women's event on Friday of the Hong Kong

Sevens, and to hold the final in Hong Kong Stadium following the men's play Friday evening. Returning to the final, the U.S. lost again to New Zealand (0-29).

In 1997 the first U23 Women's National Team was formed. Penn State Coach Peter Steinberg was appointed Head Coach. The U23s faced Canada in the first ever, U23 international match at the 1997 Can Am series.

— — —

## COLLEGIATE RUGBY
### 1991, THE FIRST NATIONAL CHAMPIONSHIP

**THROUGHOUT THE 1970S AND 1980S, WOM**-en's rugby thrived in a unique, hybrid space—part college team, part community club. Until the early 1990s, few collegiate rosters were made up entirely of undergraduates; most included graduate students, alumni, and local residents. This mix of ages and experience created a distinctive culture: spirited, inclusive, and fiercely independent.

College towns became the natural incubators for the sport. In the 1970s, towns like Madison, WI; Tallahassee, FL; and Chapel Hill, NC, offered cheap rent, lively music scenes, and co-op living. Many also had strong feminist communities, artists, and writers, along with university fields that were easy to access. These towns became fertile ground for women to discover rugby, form teams, and push the boundaries of what women could do in sport.

As players graduated, they carried the game with them, planting seeds for new teams across the country. Many modern clubs trace their roots back to pioneering programs at schools like the University of Wisconsin, Texas A&M, Florida State University, UC San Diego, and the University of Virginia. By the mid-1980s, college teams started drawing more traditional-age students, creating a dynamic—and sometimes uneven—landscape where young novices faced off against experienced, older players from club-dominated rosters. Florida State University, with just a handful of undergraduates, dominated both collegiate and club competitions, proving that skill and strategy could outweigh age or numbers.

The Women's Committee, aware of the risks in mixing club and college teams, began working with ambitious students to create a legitimate collegiate pathway. Two of the most precocious were Roshna Wunderlich and Colleen Lanigan at the University of Virginia. Like many early women administrators, they were barely out of college themselves, yet they took on the enormous task of building a system from scratch.

Roshna and Colleen didn't just follow a roadmap—with the help of experienced women's committee members like Jami Jordan—they built new roads, shaping the structure of collegiate women's rugby and leaving a legacy that would guide generations to come. Their work captured the pioneering spirit of the era: fearless, inventive, and utterly committed to expanding the game for all women.

— — —

## 1991 NATIONAL COLLEGIATE CHAMPION
### THE U.S. AIR FORCE ACADEMY

**THE INAUGURAL NATIONAL COLLEGIATE** Championship was held in 1991 and hosted by Northern Virginia Women (NOVA). Chris Casatelli was the president of NOVA and did much to organize the tournament. But even at the first championship teams were not yet fully 'collegiate.' The guidelines for the 1991 Collegiate Championships were that 85% of the team members had to be enrolled as undergraduate

# WOMEN

**By Christine Casatelli**

## Women's U-23: A Major Success

Women's rugby in the U.S. took a giant step in the right direction this month when the women's national side for players under 23 years of age took the pitch at the National All Star Championship in Tampa, Florida.

The Under 23s lost 20-0 to the Northeast Rugby Union side in its first game but won their last match, 23-22, in a nail-biter against Southern California. Former Yale player Hedwig Aerts hit a conversion on the last play of the game for the U-23 win.

### Encouraged

Peter Steinberg, head coach of the Under-23s, said he was encouraged by the play of these up-and-comers but added that there is still much work to be done to lift everyone to the same level. "I think that the team bought into the communication concept, and it helped us," he said. "Our decision-making was not what I had hoped, and therefore, we suffered both in our ball retention and in our ability to keep the ball alive."

As for next time, Steinberg said his players will focus on taking the ball into contact. "We should have worked on this basic skill a little more."

There will be plenty of opportunity for this new crop of national team trainees to improve — if Steinberg gets his way.

A native of England, Steinberg enrolled in graduate school at Penn State in 1994 and started coaching their women's team while he recuperated from a rugby injury. After two years as an assistant under Charlie Smith, he took over the helm and has been the head coach of the Penn State women for the last two years.

Penn State has been to the Final Four for the last six years and won the National Collegiate Championship this year in front of their home crowd.

### U-23 Genesis

The idea for the women's Under-23 side was born a couple of years ago, when Air Force women's coach and USA Rugby National Collegiate Director Alan Osur talked about getting a women's All-American program going. "I think this all came from the North Adams camp in the summer of 1996," Steinberg said. "We were all together and began to talk."

### U-23s vs All American

Steinberg said that he always preferred coaching an under-23 team rather than an All-American team, because it was more inclusive and would encourage players to play after college. He was apointed as the first women's under-23 coach in June 1997.

> *The Under-23 side will help players cross the great divide from college to club by breaking down barriers.*

### U-23 Objectives

The U-23 team has two goals, Steinberg said. "The first is to develop players for the national team; therefore, we wanted high-potential players," he said. "The second is to encourage players to play after graduation."

According to Steinberg's plan, the Under-23 side will help players cross the great divide from college to club by breaking down barriers. "I have heard many times that players only want to play with their college teams," Steinberg said.

The inducement the Under-23 side has is that players who have graduated must be an active member of a club team to be eligible. This gives U-23 squad members an incentive to play for at least one more year after college. Hopefully by then, they will appreciate the challenge and camaraderie of their new club and will continue to play for many years.

### Eagles & U-23s

As with all developmental team the selection of the coach sho come from a recommendation fr the national coach — and the U is no exception. Steinberg h worked with Women Eagles He Coach Franck Boivert to coor nate coaching and share inform tion about players.

"We try to implement a simi style to the senior Eagles and many of the drills that Franck e ploys," Steinberg said. "The id is that when a player gradua from the U-23 side, she understar the style of the Eagles and that transition is as smooth and easy possible."

### New Eagles

The system seems to work. ready, the U-23 side has yiel Eagles. Jen Sikora, Justine Sleez Tess Napili and Catherine Bo got their first taste of national-ca ber play with the Eagles in Cana Two other members of that gro — Penn State's Stacy Boyle a and Air Force Academy's Shalar Baker — went on to Australia w the National team, eventually ea ing caps in test matches.

### Selection Criteria

Right now, there are roughly players from all over the U.S. on U-23 roster, with a bias toward pl ers from the East Coast.

Steinberg said he and his ass tant coaches are solely responsi for selecting players for the tea One criterion for selection was t the players had to attend an U-camp, but Steinberg said he was able to keep to that for the Natio

**The US Women, winners of the 1998 Magnificent 7s: (FRONT, L-R) Eckert, Parker, Madden, Fitz, Wilson, Rodriguez, Jones. (BACK) White, Spirk, Caravelli, McCoy, Pease, Lucas, Signes, Tyler.**

March 26, 1999: Eagle Women following the final in Hong Kong Stadium

Standing: Al Caravelli (coach), Ines Rodriguez, Jane Mitchell, Erina Queen,
Nancy Fitz, Diane Schnapp, Anita Pease, Emil Signes (coach)
Kneeling: Kim Cyganik, Michele Mullen, Laura Cabrera, Lisa Rowe
Front: Kristina Caravelli (mascot)

students. The Air Force Academy, a roster of 100% undergraduate students, defeated Boston College for the first National Collegiate Championship.

"The 1992 National Collegiate Championship required that 100% of the rostered players be enrolled under-graduate students. This 1992 National Championship was hosted by the Air Force Academy and came on the heels of a long debate about who should govern women's collegiate rugby (as well as the format of the national championships). It was an interesting debate because, in the long term, it seemed clear that men's and women's collegiate teams should be governed together but there was a real disparity in access to resources and overall interest in the women's game from collegiate men or USA Rugby. The people who really cared about wom-en's collegiate rugby were the women's clubs because they knew their vitality and future depended on the women's collegiate game. The women who had just won the World Cup were also heroes to many collegiate players—they represented a possibility that never had existed for women. Nevertheless, it was clear that the issues facing collegiate women were more aligned with the issues facing collegiate men and so it was decided to identify with college rugby as opposed to women's rugby." (Roshna Wunderlich)

"In the 1980s UVA hosted the Virginia Women's Invitational Tournament. As we fostered the growth of collegiate programs across the Virginia Rugby Union (VRU), which was also happen-ing in neighboring states, we faced the dilemma every year of creating fair brackets of play with strong club teams and fledgling inexperienced

*First U23 Roster*
*U.S. v Canada*

the ball,

**U-23 Eagles**

| | |
|---|---|
| Wolanin | 1 |
| Ellefson | 2 |
| Dubovick-a | 3 |
| Lunkenheimer | 4 |
| Sanner-b | 5 |
| Kesselman | 6 |
| Steele | 7 |
| Stewart | 8 |
| Kio | 9 |
| Aerts | 10 |
| Copenhaver | 11 |
| Schooler | 12 |
| Borek - c | 13 |
| Gibson - d | 14 |
| Hawkins - e | 15 |

Referee: Terry Day
Replacements: a-
Ward, c-Brown, d-Sl
e-Foster, y-Thomps
Under-23s: Aerts
Schooler (T); Baker(
Southern Cal: Bi
Raskin (T); Kuerster

collegiate teams. We were the first tournament to create a separate division for true collegiate teams, and also premiere several budding high school programs from the Northern Virginia area in exhibition matches. It was exciting to see so many women of all ages and skill sets coming together in one venue. There was a feeling and vibrant energy that our sport was about to have a growth spurt, with older and younger players working together to create a unified future. We were ready to create the collegiate championships." (Colleen Lanigan)

"One of the biggest challenges we faced was timely communication. No one had computers—email didn't exist so we communicated by LETTERS. I am amazed that we organized national championships by mail and through landline telephone conversations. The

communication challenges really showed and at the first collegiate championship some things went disastrously wrong. Overall miscommunications often led to unnecessary conflicts." (Roshna Wunderlich)

"Since the Women's Committee was still essentially running women's events under the auspices of USAR, we felt we could not hold a separate collegiate event. Human resources were just too scarce. We decided to hold the event alongside the Women's Club Nationals in Washington D.C. over Memorial Day weekend. From a collegiate schedule standpoint, this made no sense. College students were out of school and had been for weeks at that point. But teams came anyway. Several men on the Collegiate Committee were in an uproar that we were going ahead with the event. They publicly

**Roshna - top row, far left. Colleen - top row, second from right.
Current UVA coach, Nancy Kechner - front row, middle behind the ball.
Roshna and Colleen were the only two undergraduates on the team.
The others are graduate students or community members.**

**1991 National Collegiate Champions, The U.S. Air Force Academy**

called the women organizers 'irresponsible'. Did I mention that the women's college teams came anyway? We only allowed 25 minute halves during the first collegiate championships. The feedback from the teams afterwards was that they didn't want 25 minute halves, they wanted regulation time. Roshna is also correct in her recount of the struggle between the Women's Committee and the Collegiate Committee. At some point though, both committees recommended that the administration of women's collegiate rugby come under the Women's Committee. However, the USA Rugby Board did not agree and moved it to the Collegiate Committee anyway."
(Jami Jordan)

## COLLEGIATE CHAMPIONS

1991 Air Force Academy v Boston College
1992 Boston College v UCONN
1993 UCONN v Air Force Academy

1994 Air Force Academy v Boston College
1995 Princeton University v Penn State
1996 Princeton University v Penn State
1997 Penn State v Radcliffe College
1998 Radcliffe College v Penn State
1999 Stanford University v Princeton University

Radcliffe (left) and Penn State prepare to scrummage during the 1998 Women's National Collegiate final.
(Photo - Giagrande)

# Rugby

### "All The News That's Fit"

## #1 Penn State University

(FRONT, L-R) Cronin, Long, MacDonald, Brown, Thorn, Knudsen, Freyvogel, Dedoes, Hollenbeck, Kio, Kuchine, Tagliaferri, Dickey, Infantino. (BACK) Helsey, Hollendower, Steinberg, Boyle, Sikora, Meisenhelder, Gaulrapp, Sellers, Planinsek, Metzger, Shank, Ellefson, Mas, Schloss, McKenna, LeBlanc, Kuntz.

## #2 Radcliffe

(FRONT, L-R) Halligan, Lantz, Yee, McGuire, Zielinski, Lundquist, Rifkin, Steele, Wallison, Magill, Cable, Payne, Hatcher, Remeika, Ward, Esty, Lee. (BACK) Connors, Gartner, Nemethy, Austin, McMahan, Ivey, Gearty, Antar, Phillips, Pindyok, Gaines, Haugland, Case, Schwertfeger, Gilbride, Adair, Brooks, Dixey.

## #3 Air Force

(FRONT, L-R) Newcomb, Phelps, Smith, Harris, Zrebiec, Milliani, Waldrep, McBrayer, Berkhahn, Lee. (BACK) Petrina, Kelly, Demma, Peterson, Baker, Lynch, Scott, Zicarelli, Victoreen, Carter, Storm, Brings, Jordan, Osur

---

PROFILE:

# Shalanda Baker

Shalanda Baker,
1997 MVP Back

**Name:** Shalanda Baker
**Height:** 5' 6"
**Weight:** 145 pounds
**Birthplace:** Austin, TX
**Birthdate:** December 24, 1976 (20)
**Residence:** Colorado Springs, CO
**Occupation:** Student/Cadet
**College:** US Air Force Academy
**Marital Status:** Single
**Years Playing Rugby:** 3
**Position:** Wing, fullback
**Present Club:** Air Force
**Eagle Matches:** US "Red" vs. US "White" intrasquad, March 1997
**Territorial Experience:** Western RFU 1995 & 1996, Collegiate All-American 1995, 1996, 1997
**Local Union Experience:** Eastern Rockies 1995 & 1996
**Most Valuable Teammates:** Julie McCoy (West)
**Most Difficult Opponent:** Justine Sleezer (Red & White match)
**Most Respected Player** (same position): Krista McFarren
**Favorite Player:** Mona Rayside, New Orleans Halfmoons
**Toughest Opposing Team:** US "White" team, Pacific Coast RFU
**Best Memory in Rugby:** Getting the phone call from the US selectors to play in the Eagle intrasquad game.
**Biggest Disappointment in Rugby:** Losing our National Collegiate semifinal match three years in a row.
**Tours:** New England, spring 1996, England, spring 1997
**Best Country Visited:** England
**Biggest Influence on Career:** Air Force coach Alan Osur
**Area in which US Rugby Needs Most Work:** We must focus on developing the game at the grass roots level.
**Area in which US Rugby Has Improved the Most:** Most people in the rugby community have developed a much more professional approach to the game.
**Other Sports:** Volleyball, basketball, track
**Leisure Interests:** Hiking, camping, mountain biking
**Significant Books:** Catcher in the Rye, To Kill a Mockingbird
**Favorite Films:** The Color Purple, Boys on the Side
**Favorite Recording Artist:** Natalie Merchant
**Favorite Character in Film or Literature:** Oliver Twist
**Favorite Seinfeld Character:** George
**Goals in Rugby:** To play for the US in an international match.
**Personal Goals:** To graduate from the Academy.
**Best Playing Field:** Penn State, Air Force Academy
**Best Tournament:** 1997 Champagne Classic
**Best Coach:** Alan Osur
**Best Captain:** Julie McCoy
**Best Manager:** Suzanne Cobarruvias
**Most Embarrassing Moment in Rugby:** Spraining my ankle while celebrating after scoring a try in the US intrasquad game.

Air Force fullback Shalanda Baker, a three-time All-American. (Photo-Sean Hagerty)

# Rugby

### "All The News That's Fit"

August 12, 1996
Vol. 22, No. 7
$3.00

# Collegiate Women:
## The new force in U.S. rugby

Two-time All American Tracy Dubovick, a prop on the Princeton teams which won Women's National Collegiate Championships in both 1995 and 1996. (Photo-Hagerty)

Jamie Burke, UVA

A young Pete Steinberg with the 1997 Penn State Team

The Penn State women's team won the 1997 National Collegiate Championship.
(Photo - Hagerty

*Gina Raimondo, governor of Rhode Islans and Secretary of Commerce under President Obama was the scrumhalf for Radcliffe Rugby 1990-1993.*

**Gina Raimondo**

## HIGH SCHOOL

**HIGH SCHOOL AND YOUTH TEAMS CONTINUED** to be rare in the 1990s. However, Karl Barth was building the Summit High School program which would become a dominant program for decades. Karl began coaching the Summit team in 1997, which is remarkable given how few girls high school teams there were in the country at that time.

In his time at Summit, the team has won fifteen state championships and numerous tournaments outside of Colorado. Eighty-four Summit players have received scholarships to play at NIRA, D1 Elite, D1 and D2 programs. Karl was on the forefront of a burgeoning youth movement in rugby and was selected to be the first Head Coach of the U.S. U19 program and Defensive Coach for the U20 women. His 30-year commitment to youth rugby changed the face of women's rugby in the U.S. As Wendy Young

noted, *"Today, women's rugby in the United States stands stronger than ever, a testament to the collective efforts of individuals like Karl Barth and the Summit High School girls rugby program."*

### CLUB RUGBY

1990 Belmont Shore
1990 **Belmont Shore** v Bay Area SheHawks (Bash)
1991 **Beantown** v Florida State University
1992 **BASH** v Berkeley All Blues
1993 **BASH** v Beantown
1994 **Berkeley All Blues** v BASH
1995 **BASH** v Berkeley All Blues
1996 Beantown v Berkeley All Blues
1997 Berkeley All Blues v Maryland Stingers
1998 Berkeley All Blues v Maryland Stingers
1999 Berkeley All Blues v Beantown

**1998: U19 Summit Colorado U19 Women**

# High School Ruggers Give Glimpse of Future

**by Christine Casatelli**

Meet Julie Houts, probably among the world's smallest loosehead props at 5-foot-4 and roughly 100 pounds. But don't give her a hard time, or she'll knock you right on your keister. Just 18 years old, Julie has been playing rugby for four years at Lake Braddock High School in Burke, Virginia.

"I started playing rugby so I could tackle my sister," said Julie, who sometimes plays scrumhalf. Her sister Leslie also played at Lake Braddock and is now a loosehead prop at Mary Washington College in Virginia. The two sisters will be reunited on the pitch this fall when Julie arrives as a freshman.

Making the transition from high school to college rugby was a little scary because the level of play was higher, Leslie said. "I'm 5-foot-4 and 110 pounds, so I'm not very big, but I have good technique." That's technique she learned as a high school player.

### Lake Braddock High

Founded in 1988, Lake Braddock is one of the oldest girls' high school rugby teams in the country. The CIPP-registered team usually plays college squads and an occasional club B side to get its rugby fix.

"We lose, but the kids don't mind," said head coach Jamie Jisa, a NOVA Women's RFC player who has been coaching the team since 1991. "They just want to play," she said. "And when we score, it's big time."

Win or not, Lake Braddock has the reputation of turning out talented players ready for college competition. Tony Brown, the coach at Vassar College, has been heavily recruiting the Lake Braddock players, Jisa said.

There are roughly 162 high school rugby teams in the U.S. Only a handful of them are girls' teams, or boys teams that allow girls to play. Although Canada is working hard to boost its number of girls high school teams, the U.S. is lagging way behind. The result of Canada's early effort may be felt by the Americans in a big way by the time the 2004 Canada Cup rolls around...or sooner.

Fortunately, there are pockets of activity around the country for girls' high school rugby. Teams are springing up when schools — often worried about parents and insurance — permit them to take shape.

### Parkhill High

USA Rugby President Gene Roberts coached a girls' team last Spring at Parkhill High in Kansas City, Missouri. The girls at Parkhill were the driving force behind the creation of their team, he said, but it will take a long time before others around the country get motivated enough to start their own teams.

"In reality, it'll be 20 years before we see the real affect of high school players on the Women Eagles," Roberts said. With limited funds, it's a question of priorities at the National Office. "We will get the fastest fix from the college program," he said. "But if we're looking at 20 years down the road, we've got to go to the high schools and convince administrators and parents that rugby is a viable sport."

### Ali Black

But once the girls play, it's hard for them to walk away. At least that's what Ali Black said. She played hooker for four years at Lake Braddock and is hoping to play as a walk-on for Georgetown or American University in Washington, D.C. when she starts school at Northern Virginia Community College in September.

"I went to my first practice and that's all it took," Black said. Although she played on other athletic teams in high school, she said, "rugby is my sport now."

After she gets her degree at NOVA C.C., Black wants to transfer to Penn State and play for the nationally ranked Nittany Lion women ruggers.

### Marshfield High

Sometimes, though, the girls have to play with the boys. Erin Ward, a junior at Marshfield High in eastern Massachusetts, is one of two girls on the boys' team. "Girls' sports are too boring, like in softball, you just stand there," said Ward, a flanker. "I like contact in field hockey, so rugby was perfect."

Ward's teammate, wing Jolienne Antonino, has been playing rugby for two years. At 5-foot-7 and 125 pounds, winger Antonino said there are still aspects of her game that she is working to improve. "I'm not good at running into big people," she said. Despite a black eye, sprained ankle and cleat marks on her legs, Antonino said she loves the sport. Her parents, however, do not. "They tried to talk me out of it," said the sophomore. "My father is the worst. I'm supposed to be daddy's little girl."

Jim Jordon, co-captain of the Marshfield squad, said having girls play rugby is not a big issue on his team. "I kind of forget they're there."

### Oak Ridge High

At Oak Ridge High in El Dorado Hills, California, a group of girls watched the boys play rugby and decided to start a team of their own last spring. "At first they thought it was funny," said Erinn MacBride, a hooker whose brother played stand-off. "Then we showed them that we could really play and that we weren't wusses."

Making history as California's first high school girls' rugby rivalry last spring, the Oak Ridge girls played the neighboring Del Campo Cougars three times, losing the first match (5-0), tying the second (0-0) and winning the third (5-0). "We improved 100 percent in just one season," she said.

MacBride, who has never even seen women play, already has high hopes. "I want to play for the National team."

### Kentwood High

Jane Becker will be a senior next month at Kentwood High in Kent, Washington, a suburb of Seattle, and she already has two years of experience under her belt. "Rugby is a real team sport where everyone works together — I like that."

About half the players on the Kentwood girls' team are serious about the sport, and the other half play because it's cool, said the 5-foot-8, 140-pound flyhalf. One of the very serious ones, Becker is so determined to improve her skills that she hangs out at the boys games with her jersey, hoping that the coach will put her in. "The boys from other teams hit me a lot harder because they don't want to look stupid," Becker said she doesn't mind the extra abuse. "Playing with the boys helps me to take my game to a higher level."

What Becker does mind, however, is the lack of coaching. "The coaches spend all their time with the guys. There are so many girls who want to play," Becker said, describing efforts of other high schools around the area. "There was an awesome turnout," she said, but the coaching fell through so the teams disbanded. "I guess we'll have to wait until the women players retire so they can come back and coach."

Becker is looking at Princeton for college because it's a good school and, well, because the Tigers have been National Collegiate champs for two years. "I want to see how far I can go in rugby," said Becker, who already plays on the Pacific Northwest select side with club players. "I would love to be an Eagle someday!"

# SUMMIT DAILY NEWS

Volume IX, Number 287    **WEDNESDAY**    June 3, 1998

## Crunch!

Summit County's Lisa Gravina, with the ball, is surrounded by opponents and teammates as she controls the ball in a recent match at Rainbow Park. The game was between the Summit Youth Rugby under-19 team and Denver's Black Ice team.

**The Berkeley All Blues went on a tear throughout the 1990s winning eleven National Championships between 1994 and 2007**

1990 Belmont Shore

# Beantown Over Berkeley For Women's Club F

by Jim Hoehn

**Chicago, IL**
**May 25-27, 1996**

Number 8 Alex Williams punctuated Beantown's forward dominance with a pair of second-half tries, as Beantown rallied for a 28-10 victory over the Berkeley All-Blues in the final of USA Rugby's 1996 Women's National Club Championship.

With its forwards controlling possession against the wind, Beantown (Boston, MA) overcame a 10-8 halftime deficit to win its first national title since 1991 and sixth since the inception of the Women's Club Championship in 1979.

"I think their forwards wore us down a little bit," said Berkeley No. 8 Kathy Flores, wearer of nine Eagle caps. "They controlled the scrum. We were a little smaller up front. Give credit to Beantown. They were able to play to their strength and keep us away from ours."

In the second half, Beantown used its rolling maul to control the ball and the clock, allowing Berkeley's explosive backline few opportunities on the muddy pitch.

"We've been working on that maul," said Williams, a member of the 1994 Eagles World Cup squad. "I think our forwards put great pressure on them in the second half. It feels pretty darn good."

## First Half

Beantown, with six capped Eagles in its lineup, took advantage of the wind in the first quarter, driving inside the Berkeley 10 in the 14th minute. From a quick tap at the Berkeley 5, veteran flyhalf Mary Dixey scored in the right corner to put Beantown in front 5-0.

Berkeley answered on its ensuing possession, spinning right on third phase to wing Alison Stoddard, who covered the final 10 meters to tie it, 5-5.

Berkeley, which finished second last year after winning the national title in 1994, got its backline untracked in the 35th minute with a 70 meter scoring movement. Center

Beantown and Eagle flanker Laurie Spicer-Bourdon is surrounded by Berkeley defenders in the final of the 1996 Women Championship. Beantown topped Berkeley 28-10 to claim their sixth national title. (Photo-Hagerty)

Jane Mitchell broke through and carried inside the Beantown 30, dishing to outside center Jen Crawford. Mitchell remained in support, taking the return feed from Crawford to put Berkeley on top 10-5.

Keirston Lawton's 20 meter penalty goal from the left post pulled Beantown to 10-8 at the half.

## Second Half

Beantown capitalized on a Berkeley infraction to establish field position and then turned the pressure into go-ahead points. Berkeley was penalized for hands in the ruck at the Berkeley 42 and Beantown kicked to touch at the Berkeley 10. Berkeley was penalized again after the lineout, with Beantown carrying to the goal. Beantown then stole the ball against the head on a scrum at the Berkeley two, with Williams picking up and burrowing over to put Beantown in front 13-10 at the nine minute mark.

Beantown's forwards then began to assert themselves, both in

the scrum and through an almost unstoppable rolling maul. Beantown's backline helped maintain possession, bringing the ball back to the forwards in the second half.

"We had a lot of faith in our forwards," said Dixey, possessor of five Eagle caps. "We wanted to keep the ball in tight."

Berkeley was penalized trying to stop Beantown's maul in the 20th minute, and Lawton converted from 20 meters to increase the lead to 16-10.

Beantown maintained field position on the restart. From a scrum at the Berkeley 10, Beantown's forwards pushed to the 5. Scrumhalf Kerry Kilander picked up in the loose, handing off to an alertly supporting Williams for the diving try. Lawton's conversion pushed the lead to 23-10 with 10 minutes left.

From a scrum in the final minute at the Berkeley 15, Beantown spun weakside right to wing Mary Sullivan. Kilander trailed and took the feed for the final score in the right corner.

"Their control was awesome,"

Stoddard said. "They also won our ball on a few key scrums and lineouts. There were only two or three of each, but they were enough to change the momentum."

| Beantown | | Berkeley |
|---|---|---|
| Graichen | 1 | Stoner |
| Palmacci | 2 | Burdick |
| Kimball | 3 | Wadford |
| *Rutkowski | 4 | Bukowski |
| Connolly | 5 | Burrows |
| *Spicer-Bourdon | 6 | Micheli |
| Derzon | 7 | Schnapp |
| *Williams | 8 | Flores* |
| Kilander | 9 | Fong |
| *Dixey | 10 | Darrow |
| Friel | 11 | Stoddard |
| Carrier | 12 | Mitchell |
| *Newton | 13 | Crawford* |
| *Sullivan | 14 | Kane |
| Lawton | 15 | Jackson |

**Referee:** Jerry McLemore (USARFU)

* capped Eagle

## Quarterfinals

Eight teams gathered in Chicago for the 1996 Women's National Club Championship, and Saturday's quarterfinals produced the following results:

Beantown 64, Ozark Ladies 5

Bay Area SheHa Twin Cities Ama

Berkeley All Blu Minnesota Valky

Maryland Stinger New Orleans 5

Five time ch ('82, '83, '86, '87 face defending ch time title holder Ba (BASH) in one s day, while 1994 cl All Blues would the Maryland Stir

**Semi**
**BEANT**
**BAS**
May 25, 1996

Utilizing bot forwards and th backs, Beantow defending nati BASH in Sunday scoring four tries a 17-0 lead into th overmatched ag side, threatening only once or twice each half.

Beantown dominated from the kickoff, opening their account in the sixth minute with a try by wing Michele Friel, which fullback Keirsten Lawton converted, 7-0.

Eagle Alex Williams, a 5' 10", 190 pound #8, scored Beantown's second try on a multi-phase play which originated from a short lineout near BASH's line. Lawton converted, and then, after missing penalties in the 30th and 33rd minutes, nailed one in the 38th to send Beantown into the half with a 17-0 lead.

### Second Half

Any hopes of a BASH comeback were dashed two minutes after the restart, when a kick ahead into their end zone was mishandled and Beantown center Nicole Carrier was there for the touchdown, 22-0.

Beantown's Lawton missed on a penalty in the 21st minute but her ricochet off the posts eight minutes later resulted in a try. Beantown recovered the rebound, formed a maul and scrumhalf Kerry Kilander crossed for the try, 27-0

Kim Henderson, a 1995 All American from Princeton, sparks the Maryland Stingers' backline into action during their 18-12 semifinal loss to Berkeley. (Photo-Hagerty)

| Beantown | | BASH |
|---|---|---|
| Graichen | 1 | Weix* |
| Palmacci | 2 | Teague |
| Kimball | 3 | Kuiken |
| *Rutkowski | 4 | Martin |
| Connolly | 5 | Carn |
| *Spicer | 6 | Feigenbutz |
| Derzon | 7 | Meredith* |
| *Williams | 8 | Bond* |
| Kilander | 9 | Kelly |
| *Dixey | 10 | Leal |
| Friel | 11 | Cote |
| Carrier | 12 | Bowler |
| *Newton | 13 | Moose |
| *Sullivan | 14 | Csapo |
| Lawton | 15 | Zdarko |

Referee: Fred Thomas
* capped Eagle

### BERKELEY ALL BLUES 18, MARYLAND STINGERS 12

Berkeley's 18-12 win over Maryland in Saturday's second semifinal was both closely contested and highly entertaining, featuring five tries from two talented backlines.

Berkeley had a slight wind advantage in the first half, but they never really made good use of it, with Eagle fullback Jen Crawford missing makeable penalty attempts in the 2nd and 12th minutes. And although the Blues dominated territorially, they weren't able to cash in until the half was nearly over.

A try by Berkeley flyhalf Cat Darrow finally broke the ice in the 37th minute, and then wing Allison Stoddard scored two minutes later

Beantown and Eagle center Brett Newton advances the ball during her team's 27-0 semifinal victory over BASH. (Photo-Hagerty)

at the end of a 70 meter, multi-phase movement. Crawford missed both conversions and Berkeley went into the intermission with a 10-0 lead.

### Second Half

Just as Berkeley controlled the first half, Maryland called the tune in the third quarter. Like Berkeley, the Stingers also had difficulty translating their territorial advantage into points, as center Toni Rawlings missed a penalty attempt 13 minutes in and then Eagle flyhalf Jos Bergmann misfired on a drop goal a minute later.

The faith of Maryland's supporters was rewarded in the 17th minute, however, as wing Sue Parker got possession with room to maneuver. Parker scored between the posts and Rawlings converted to reduce Berkeley's lead to three points, 10-7.

Maryland's try seemed to energize Berkeley, and their excellent backline, particularly Kim Green, Rachel Jackson and Jen Crawford, made some impressive attacks. One long Berkeley movement was driven out of bounds at Maryland's two, and scrumhalf Mary Daisy Fong touched down following the ensuing lineout. Crawford missed the conversion (15-7), but in the 22nd minute Berkeley had some breathing room.

The Stingers, which featured both youth (Princeton's 1995 All American scrumhalf, Kim Henderson) and experience (veteran Eagle wing Krista McFarren) refused to fold. They were rewarded in the 30th minute when wing Sue Parker outsprinted the Berkeley cover to score her second try and reduce the deficit to 15-12.

Maryland committed an infraction on the ensuing kickoff reception, however, and Jen Crawford's penalty in the 32nd minute would end the scoring at Berkeley 18, Maryland 12.

| Berkeley | | Maryland |
|---|---|---|
| Woolford | 1 | Signes |
| Burdick | 2 | Lanier |
| Craig | 3 | Carrera |
| Bukowski | 4 | Heimann* |
| Burrows | 5 | St. Clair |
| Micheli | 6 | Martin |
| Schnapp | 7 | Ogg |
| *Flores | 8 | Mohl |
| Fong | 9 | Henderson |
| Darrow | 10 | Bergmann* |
| Stoddard | 11 | Pease |
| Mitchell | 12 | Drustrup* |
| Green | 13 | Rawlings |
| Jackson | 14 | Parker |
| *Crawford | 15 | McFarren* |

Referee: Jeremy Turner
* capped Eagle

## How They Got There

**East:**

*Beantown*
*Maryland*

Beantown and Maryland emerged from Atlanta's East Club Championship the weekend of April 27-28th and represented the East in the National Club Championship. Beantown defeated Southeast 35-5 and Boston 49-0, while Maryland handled Boston 43-10 and Southeast 27-0. Beantown then topped Maryland 19-5 in the final to take the top seed.

**Midwest:**

*Twin Cities Amazons*
*Minnesota Valkyries*

At the Midwest Club Championship in Minneapolis, the Twin Cities Amazons and the Minnesota Valkyries earned the two Midwest seeds in the National Club Championship. Twin Cities defeated Madison 25-0 in one semifinal, while the Valkyries beat Chicago 27-12 in the other. Twin Cities went on to defeat the Valkyries 28-8 in the final.

**West:**

*New Orleans*
*Ozark Ladies*

New Orleans and the Ozark Ladies finished atop the Western Club Championship in St. Louis on April 27-28th. New Orleans defeated the Oklahoma University Roses, while Ozark topped the Colorado Old Girls.

**Pacific Coast:**

*Berkeley*
*BASH*

Perennial U.S. powers Berkeley and BASH emerged as the two national representatives from the Pacific Coast.

| Player | Position | Height | Weight | Age |
|---|---|---|---|---|
| Martha Bosworth | Lock | 5-9 | 165 | 35 |
| Nicole Carrier | Center | 5-1 | 135 | 23 |
| Sonya Church | Wing | 5-8 | 165 | 31 |
| *Patty Connell | Scrumhalf | 5-3 | 120 | 33 |
| Mary Connolly | Lock | 5-9 | 145 | 24 |
| Anne Derzon | Flanker | 5-3 | 120 | 32 |
| *Mary Dixey | Flyhalf/FB | 5-5 | 140 | 35 |
| Heidi Erlacher | Lock | 5-8 | 170 | 28 |
| Michele Friel | Center | 5-4 | 136 | 26 |
| Dee Graichen | Prop | 5-5 | 160 | 31 |
| Amy Heroux | Hooker | 5-1 | 130 | 23 |
| Susan Keliher | Lock | 5-9 | 165 | 29 |
| Kerry Kilander | Flanker | 5-8 | 150 | 28 |
| Betsy Kimball | Prop | 5-5 | 155 | 44 |
| Keirsten Lawton | Flyhalf/FB | 5-5 | 145 | 24 |
| Annette Lee | Scrumhalf | 5-1 | 120 | 26 |
| Karen Micciche | Center | 5-5 | 138 | 28 |
| *Brett Newton | Center | 5-4 | 146 | 31 |
| Gina Palmacci | Hooker | 5-1 | 155 | 32 |
| Kelli Pearson | Flanker | 5-8 | 140 | 26 |
| Kathleen Pignone | Hooker/Prop | 5-3 | 140 | 26 |
| *Jan Rutkowski | Lock | 5-8 | 180 | 40 |
| Liz Satterfield | Prop | 5-6 | 165 | 23 |
| *Laurie Spicer-Bourdon | Flanker | 5-7 | 135 | 31 |
| *Mary Sullivan | Wing | 5-8 | 148 | 34 |
| Sharon Wall | Prop | 5-6 | 176 | 25 |
| *Alex Williams | #8 | 5-10 | 190 | 26 |
| Hillary Woodruff | Flyhalf | 5-6 | 145 | 28 |

* capped Eagle

## Beantown RFC -- 1996 National Champion

(FRONT, L-R): Dowd, Kimball, Kilander, Connolly, Derzon, Spicer-Bourdon, Carrier, Palmacci, Rutkowski, Newton, Friel, Graichen, Lawton, Sullivan, Dixey, Church, Pearson. (BACK) Lyons, Kimmel, Holzhauer, Morrissey, Wall, Bosworth, Lee, Erlacher, Heroux, Gandy, Clark, Satterfield, Williams, Connell, Keliher, Woodruff, Micciche, Pignone, DeSmet, Armstrong.

# Berkeley All Blues Claim Women's National

story and photos
by Michael Malone

**Bloomington, MN**
**May 24-26, 1997**

Featuring a flashy backline and superb defense, the All Blues of Berkeley won the 1997 Women's National Club Championship, withstanding a comeback from the resourceful Maryland Stingers in the final to prevail 25-14. The final served as the farewell match for veteran Berkeley player and coach Kathy Flores, and the end result could not have been sweeter for the inspirational #8 or her teammates. Commented Berkeley fullback/US captain Jen Crawford, "Kathy's retiring made the win extra special."

The Washington Furies won the second tier Plate competition. Led by internationals Nancy Fitz and Jen Renne, Washington topped Colorado 49-20 in the Plate final.

## Cup

**Final:**

### BERKELEY 25, MARYLAND 14

A stiff wind blew from north to south in the Cup final, and it was the Berkeley All Blues that enjoyed its benefit in the first half. Very wary of Maryland's backline speed, Berkeley aimed to keep the ball out of the hands of Krista McFarren, Lisa Rowe, Jos Bergmann and the rest of the lethal Stinger backs. Berkeley repeatedly used its loose forwards to crash on inside passes from the backs, and then spun to the outside backs on 3rd and 4th phase, which almost always led to tries. Berkeley scored twice in the first 15 minutes to claim a 10-0 lead, and extended its advantage to 20-0 before the half.

"We've been playing kind of up and down all season," stated Flores, "and I was hoping we'd peak at the nationals. We came on hard in the first 10 minutes, and I could really feel the power of the whole fifteen. Our team came together, and what a game to come together for."

Led by hard hitting flanker

The Berkeley All Blues kick ahead during their 25-14 victory over the Maryland Stingers in the final of the 1997 Women's National Championship.

Diane Schnapp and playmaker/flyhalf Jane Mitchell, Berkeley got the first score when a kick was mishandled by Maryland fullback McFarren, giving Berkeley a lineout deep in the Maryland end. The ball was spun down the line to wing Rachel Jackson, who scored in the corner, 5-0.

The All Blues' efforts were again rewarded five minutes later when Maryland committed an infraction at their own 15. Jane Mitchell fed to crashing fullback Jen Crawford for the score, 10-0.

Maryland nearly got on the board when wing Kim Cyganik initiated a 2 on 1 counterattack with

McFarren, but Crawford, playing safety, was there to break up the final pass.

Berkeley continued to employ the inside passing game to hold onto the ball and stay in the Maryland end, while loose forwards Flores, Schnapp and Jill Vialet quelled any hint of Stinger firepower.

Led by flyhalf Jos Bergmann, Maryland finally mounted a rally in the 25th minute. Superb recycling saw the Stingers string together 10+ phases and travel from their own 30 to the Berkeley 5, but the effort died when Bergmann missed a penalty kick after a high tackle.

Berkeley center Kim Cobb landed a 22 meter penalty shot at the half hour mark (13-0), and two successive penalties against the

Stingers marched Maryland back into its own red zone. The quick tap was spun to center Kim Green for the try. Cobb stroked the conversion and Berkeley went into the half up 20-0.

### Second Half

Gaining the substantial wind at the turnaround, Maryland sought to break McFarren free from Berkeley's shackles. But save for a 15 minute stint, Berkeley owned nearly all second half ball; the efforts of locks Bukowski and Burrows in the lineouts were on par with their literary namesakes' skills with the written word. With flankers Schnapp and Vialet tireless in support, Berkeley recycled possession flawlessly; Maryland #10 Bergmann was forced to put in the most tackles of any Stinger de-

fender.

The Stingers finally ca break in the 49th minute. Berg was off on a tough-angled p shot from 35, but hustling Sarah Schooler, a 1996 All-A can at Radcliffe, grabbed the fired shot on the bounce touched down. Bergmann's version made it 20-7.

Maryland pressured agai in the 60th minute was awa: scrum when Berkeley full Crawford knocked on a mete the All Blues' line. Berkele some breathing room after st the put-in and booting to touc the ensuing lineout was wo Maryland and spun from Berg to an inserting McFarren fo score. Bergmann converted ar score stood at 20-14.

Wing Rachel Jackson turns the corner on her way to Berkeley's first try in the National final agains Maryland Stingers.

But the Stingers would get no closer. With flanker Schnapp patrolling the loose like a linebacker, any ensuing Maryland attack was stuffed before it had a chance to flourish. Speedy flyhalf Mitchell, who helped England to the 1994 World Cup title, kept the Maryland cover off balance with her crafty dummies and incisions through the defense, and the All Blues forwards continued to hammer away at Maryland. A final try went to Blues wing Katie Wharton, and the whistle sounded with Berkeley on top 25-14.

"That was the best we played all year," said a joyous Crawford. "It was that special feeling when you've got it together as a team. We were able to shut down Krista, Jos and the rest of their backline. We kept hammering away in the 3rd, 4th and 5th phase, and they eventually wore down."

"They're a very solid team," commented Maryland's Bergmann. "We tried to play a complete game and came up short. Our team fitness was a huge factor in our win over Beantown, but we were a little tired from that game. We were hoping to improve upon last year's 4th place standing and we did, so we're happy with that."

| Berkeley | | MD Stingers |
|---|---|---|
| Benning | 1 | Signes |
| Burdick | 2 | Lanier |
| Wadford | 3 | Neuburger |
| Burrows | 4 | Heiman |
| Bukowski | 5 | Mohl |
| Vialet | 6 | Rawlings |
| Schnapp | 7 | Crandell |
| Flores | 8 | Klaren |
| Dennis | 9 | Varella |
| Mitchell | 10 | Bergmann |
| Wharton | 11 | Rowe |
| Cobb | 12 | Schooler |
| Green | 13 | Kane |
| Jackson | 14 | Cyganik |
| Crawford | 15 | McFarren |

Referee: Kevin Hanley

### And the MVP is...
### Diane Schnapp

With a tip of the cap to sparkplug Jane Mitchell and the ever-dangerous Jen Crawford, Berkeley won its championship in the forwards, and none was finer than flanker Diane Schnapp, earning her *Rugby Magazine's* MVP vote.

Berkeley scrumhalf Deb Dennis attacks during the Blues' 17-12 overtime victory over BASH in semifinal.

Schnapp's crushing tackles repeatedly left dispirited Maryland ballcarriers on their backs, and she consistently provided the link work in the loose that was so vital to the Berkeley gameplan.

### Flores Steps Down

The final was the sweetest of swan songs for Berkeley veteran Flores, who earned nine caps on the international level to go with her two national championships. She now seeks to develop women's collegiate rugby in Northern California, and vows to continue helping out with the Berkeley All Blues. "If they still want me around, I'll be happy to lend a hand," a tearful Flores stated following the final.

### Semifinals

En route to the semifinals, Berkeley defeated Boston 32-8, and Maryland withstood a tough challenge from the local Twin Cities Amazons, 21-17. The stage was set for the semifinals, with all of the 1996 final four teams again in the running. Both semifinal matches were a treat for spectators; one a tense, dramatic nail biter, the other

a wide open gunfight.

### BERKELEY 17,
### BASH 12

The Bay Area battle between BASH and Berkeley was every bit the tight affair that most expected, the match going into sudden death overtime before a result was finalized.

The first score went to four-time national champ BASH. Center Brett Newton, the hardest hitter in the tournament, showed her skill with ball in hand by grabbing a loose ball and traveling half the pitch to touch down, giving BASH a 5-0 lead.

Berkeley answered almost immediately. A multi-phase ball was spun down to wing Katie Wharton for a try, converted by center Kim Cobb for a 7-5 Berkeley lead that held up until the half.

### Second Half

BASH, shut out by Beant[...] in last year's semi, took the lea[...] a late try by wing Debbie Cote[...] 7), and appeared to be headed[...] the final. Rookie flanker Kalei [...] capped for the US in the '96 Ca[...] Cup, kept the dangerous Berk[...] attack at bay with numerous [...] hits. But Berkeley's wealth of [...] session eventually wore down [...] BASH defense. With six min[...] remaining, Berkeley controlle[...] lineout at the BASH one and [...] tempted to push it over, but [...] denied. Scrumhalf Deb Dennis t[...] tried to burrow in herself, but [...] too was denied. Off a 5 meter scr[...] Berkeley opted for the weak s[...] but flanker Kim broke off [...] bundled wing Rachel Jackson [...] touch just as Jackson prepare[...] dive in.

# WORLD CUP SEVENS SP[...]
Commemorative Official merchandise from the World Cup Se[...]

HONG K[...]
9[...]

Berkeley (left) and BASH awaiting a lineout during the semifinal.

**1998 Eastern Rockies Territorial Side**

## TERRITORIAL CHAMPIONSHIPS

**FROM THE EARLY 1980S UNTIL THE MID-1990S** the route to the Women's National Team was through the Territorial Championships. Club players competed to represent local 'territorial teams' (New England, Eastern Pennsylvania, SoCal, South, etc); from those teams players would be chosen for one of four, larger territorial teams (East, West, Pacific and Midwest). The annual playoffs of the four territories was an opportunity to see the best players in the country going head-to-head. The advantage of territorial play at the time was it allowed players and coaches to develop against good competition and be seen by national selectors.

## NOTABLES
### THE WOMEN'S COMITTEE

**THE MEMBERS OF THE WOMEN'S COMMITTEE** were rarely recognized or thanked for the work they did for over twenty-five years but their contributions to women's rugby are undeniable. On the slimmest of margins and with constant opposition, they laid the foundation and built women's rugby at every level. The rugby we enjoy today is a direct result of their work.

*"We were running women's rugby on a volunteer basis. We didn't tend to have strong relationships with one another outside of the Committee and only met to do business. Most of our challenges were dealing with the men and the 'lowly position' of women's rugby in the USARFU pecking order. But we were a defiant group, committed to growing the women's game.*

*"Given all that we accomplished between 1979 and 1994 as a young, volunteer organization, it's pretty amazing that the women running things didn't blow up. But we weren't perfect. We fell victim to regional politics, particularly around the hiring and firing of USWNT coaches. By and large, the Women's Committee operated on a consensus basis, but we did vote on things. My memory is that we agreed on many things and that we were usually in alignment or at least mostly in alignment. But the selection of national team coaches was the most contentious. Much of that can be attributed to intense regional loyalties to certain coaches that were off putting to other regions."* (Jami Jordan)

**1991 Eastern Rugby Union Team**

USARFU WOMEN'S COMMITTEE

# 1974 - 1994

**Alissa Augello** - Midwest, Founder of the Women's Committee, First Chair
**Marsha Birkby** - Midwest, WRFU Women's Rep
**Marcia Borge** - Midwest, Women's Committee Chair
**Leslie Brant** - West
**Tam Breckenridge** - Pacific
**Paula Cabot** - Pacific, Women's Committee Chair
**Chris Casatelli** - East
**Lee Chichester** - East Secretary
**Suzanne Cobarruvias** - West
**Darlene Connors** - East
**Ellen Cunningham** - Pacific
**Janeen Dell'Aqua** - Pacific
**Lisa Gardner** - Midwest
**Pat Glenn** - Liaison to USARFU and National 7's coordinator
**Trudy Grout** - Midwest
**Leslie Jamison** - So Cal
**Jami Jordan** - Mid-Atlantic, Women's Committee Chair
**Betsy Kimball** - East, Women's Committee Recording Secretary
**Colleen Lanigan** - East, Women's Committee Chair
**Mary Larkin** - Midwest, National Events Coordinator
**Krista McFarren** - East, Convenor of Selectors
**Vicki Middaugh** - Midwest
**Tracey Moens** - West
**Kathy Morrison** - Pacific, Coaching Committee Liaison
**Elaine Recchiuti** - West, Convenor of Selectors
**Jennie Redner** - Midwest, Women's Committee Chair
**Lisa Riehl** - Midwest
**Kim Sheridan** - Midwest
**Julie Silverstein** - Midwest
**Diane Terwilliger** - Women's Committee Chair
**Judy Tixler** - East
**M.L. Wernecke** - East, Treasurer
**Janine Wright** - Fundraising
**Roshna Wunderlich** - East

## IN SUPPORT OF WOMEN'S RUGBY

## Back in 1992...

| | |
|---|---|
| *Yearly tuition at private university (fees, room and board)* | **$16,950** |
| *Yearly tuition at public university (fees, room and board)* | **$7330** |
| *Monthly rent* | **$447** |
| *Per capita income* | **$20,504** |
| *Adults with a bachelor's degree* | **21.4%** |

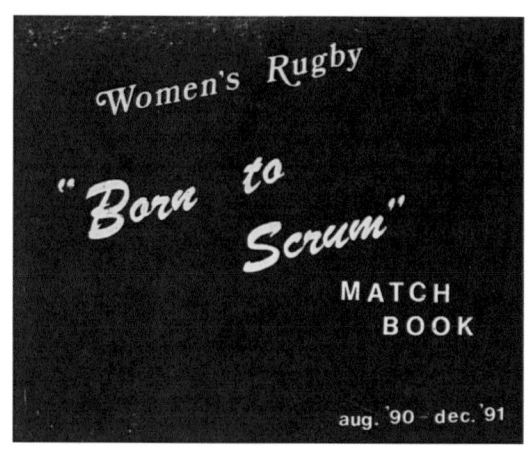

Women's Rugby
"Born to Scrum"
MATCH BOOK
aug. '90 – dec. '91

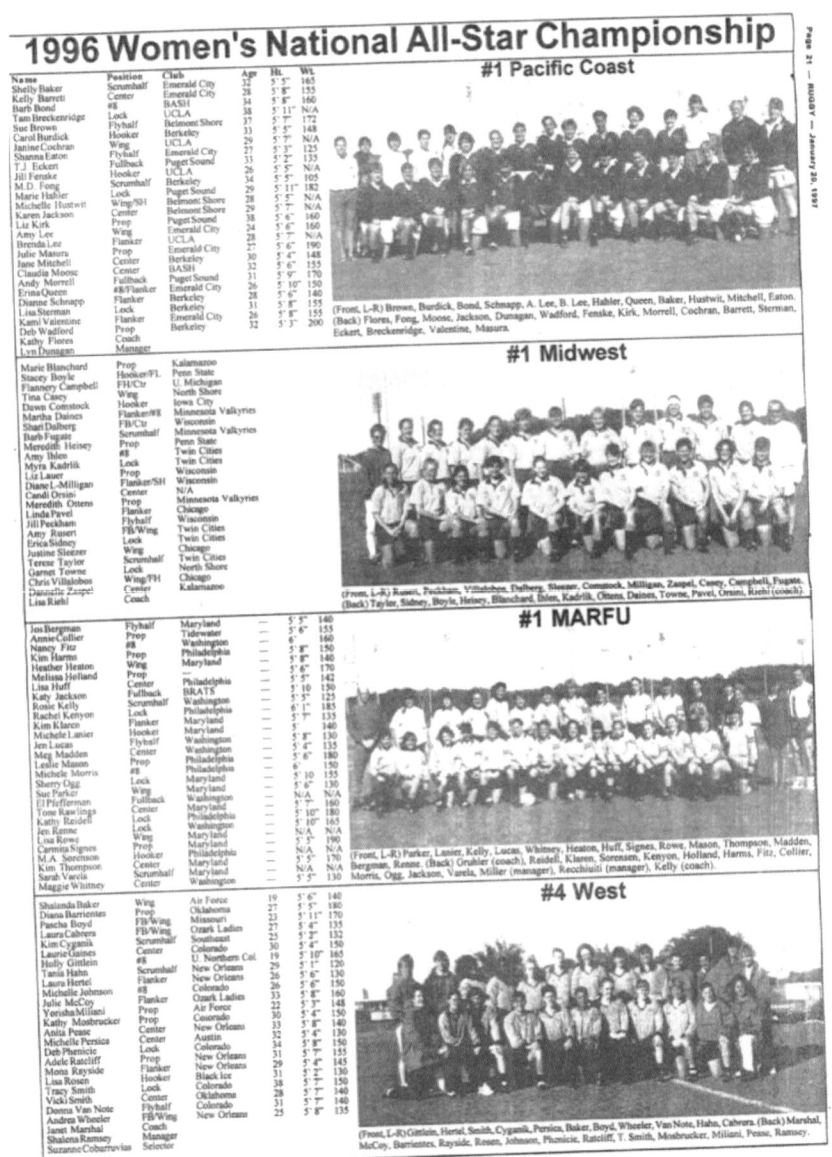

1996 Women's National All-Star Championship

# 2000s

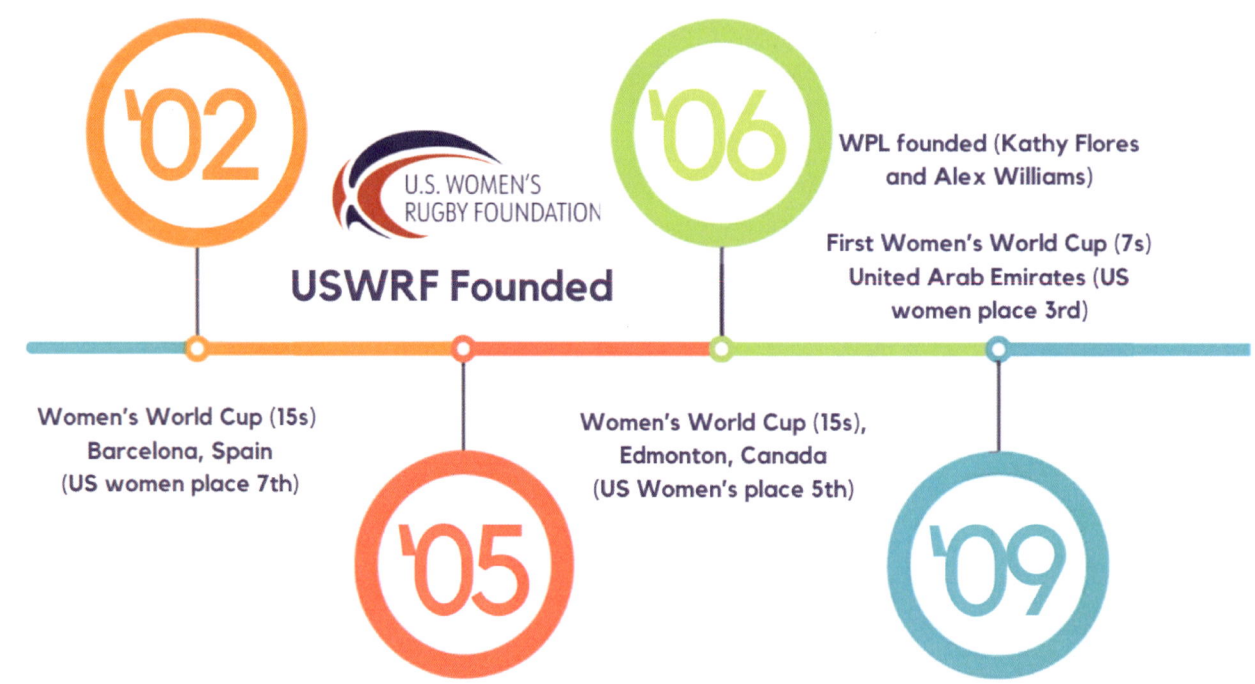

'02

U.S. WOMEN'S RUGBY FOUNDATION

**USWRF Founded**

'06

**WPL founded (Kathy Flores and Alex Williams)**

**First Women's World Cup (7s) United Arab Emirates (US women place 3rd)**

**Women's World Cup (15s) Barcelona, Spain (US women place 7th)**

'05

**Women's World Cup (15s), Edmonton, Canada (US Women's place 5th)**

'09

**2**000-2009 WAS A BUSY DECADE FOR WOM-en's rugby. Kathy Flores became the first woman to serve as the Head Coach of a National Team; Anne Barry was two years into her reign as the first female President of USAR; the U.S. 7s Team came into being with Julie McCoy the first woman to serve as the Head Coach of a National 7s team; the dream of varsity collegiate rugby was realized and the Women's Premier League was organized.

In 2006 Wendy Young started *Your Scrumhalf Connection* as a blog. In the ensuing 20 years YSC has grown into one of the most respected news sources for women's rugby. Wendy has branched out in broadcasting. *Wendy Young began her rugby writing career in 2006 when she was playing with the University of Oklahoma rugby team. At first her writing was on a blog called WRFU—Women's Rugby, in 2008 she rebranded to a new website that was focused on covering international women's rugby titled Your Scrumhalf Connection. In 2021 the site again transformed and now curates women's rugby stories from across the globe with a focus on large rugby events.*

**Kathy Flores**

YSC RUGBY

## THE COLLEGE GAME

**THE EARLY 2000S BELONGED TO WOMEN'S collegiate rugby**. After decades of struggle and grass-roots organizing, collegiate women's rugby finally came into its own as a recognized sport—a place where high school and youth players could aspire to compete at the college level.

In 2002, women's rugby was added to the NCAA Emerging Sports list. The decision to single out women's rugby, rather than men's, sparked difficult conversations within the rugby community. Yet the choice made practical sense: collegiate men's rugby programs, often with rosters exceeding 100 players, faced an almost insurmountable challenge in gaining NCAA recognition. Athletic directors saw an opportunity in women's rugby—it could contribute to Title IX compliance while also offering one of the first full-contact sports for female athletes on campus.

This milestone marked a turning point, signaling that women's rugby was a legitimate collegiate

*2002 USMA*

athletic pursuit, opening doors for the next generation of players.

In 2002 Eastern Illinois University elevated the club women's rugby program to varsity status under the direction of Frank Graziano. The first collegiate varsity program in the U.S., Eastern Illinois would dominate collegiate rugby for a number of years before falling victim to a lack of administrative support from EIU. The program produced a number of great players including 2016 and 2024 Olympic Captain Lauren Doyle, Becky Carlson the founder of NIRA and Head Coach of Quinnipiac and Michelle Reed, Head Coach of Sacred Heart.

2002 PANTHERS not only finished with an undefeated 11-0 mark, but also became the nation's first official NCAA Division I women's rugby squad

**2002 Panthers not only finished with an undefeated 11-0 mark, but also became the nation's first official NCAA Division I women's rugby squad**

**2003 Bowdoin Polar Bears**

In 2003 Bowdoin College in Maine, elevated their women's program to varsity. Under the leadership of long-time Head Coach MaryBeth Mathews, Bowdoin became the most successful D3 program in the country. Bowdoin won a number of D3 NIRA 15s Championships. In 2012 MaryBeth opened the Polar Bear Rugby Camp, the first rugby camp for girls. After 29 years of coaching at Bowdoin, MaryBeth stepped down in 2023.

In 2004 Southern Vermont University became just the third varsity program in the country. Unfortunately SVU dropped rugby in 2006.

In 2004 Norwich University elevated their successful club program to NCAA varsity status. Norwich, under the leadership of Austin Hall, became a powerhouse, winning six D3 National Championships. Most notably was the 2013-14 team, with a record of 40-0, including the USA Rugby College 7s National Championship, the ACRA Division I National Tournament

**2013-2014 Norwich University**

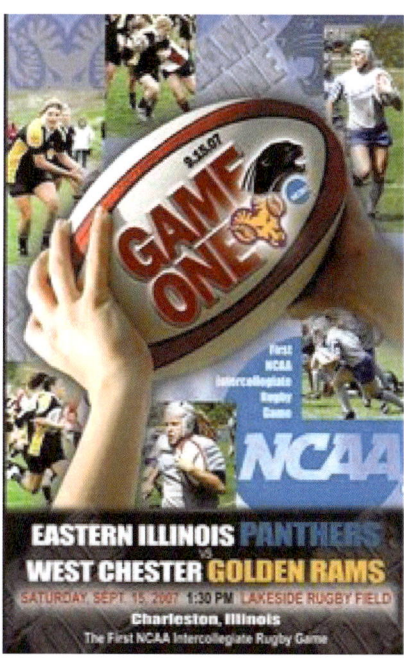

*2007 Eastern Illinois v West Chester University*

15s Championship, and the ACRA 7s National Championships. In 2024 Norwich repositioned themselves as a NCR D1 program.

West Chester University became the first NCAA Division II women's rugby program in the country in 2004. West Chester, has been under the guidance of Head Coach Tony DeRemer for over 20 years. Like Bowdoin, that coaching stability allowed the program to become a model for collegiate programs.

Sept 15, 2007, Eastern Illinois v West Chester was the first, women's intercollegiate varsity game.

In 2010 Quinnipiac University in Connecticut added women's rugby as a D1 varsity program. It was the first program to begin a program 'from scratch' as Quinnipiac had no club program to elevate.

In 2013, Harvard University elevated their successful club program to varsity status.

In 2014 the U.S. Military Academy and Brown University elevated their women's programs to D1 varsity and American International College elevated their program to D2.

**2014 Brown University,
Head Coach (Kathy Flores on the far right in red shirt)**

2015 USMA

2013 Harvard University
(photo Rose Lincoln)

**2015 Quinnipiac University, National Champions
(Ilona Maher back row, middle)**

2017 Mount St. Mary's Program

**2015 Sacred Heart University Team**

In 2015 National Collegiate Women's Varsity Rugby Association (NCWVRA) hosted the first championship. Quinnipiac University defeated Army 25-22 to win the championship.

In 2015, Dartmouth College and Sacred Heart University elevated their teams to D1.

The University of New England became a D3 varsity program and Central Washington University, D2. Eastern Illinois University dropped their women's program.

2015: NCWVRA changed its name to NIRA

2016: Notre Dame College and Molloy College elevated their programs to D2, and Castleton College elevated their club program to D3.

2017: Mount St. Mary's College became a D1 program, Long Island University, Post College and Queens University became D2 programs.

2018: Central Washington State University dropped out of NIRA and returns to club status

2019: NIRA moves from a Tier system to NCAA Divisions Competition (D1, D2, D3)

The National Small College Rugby Organization (NSCRO) was founded in 2007. NSCRO would become National Collegiate Rugby Association (NCR) the world's largest collegiate rugby organization, serving programs across all divisions. The evolution and success of NCR has led to a long standing feud with USA Rugby culminating in a 2025 lawsuit filed by NCR.

The 2002 D1 Collegiate Championships may go down as the most competitive championship of all time. Played in cold, windy conditions in Blaine, Minnesota, four teams: Navy, Air Force, Penn State and the University of Illinois squared off with no team willing to break.

Laura Murphy captured the match for Rugby Magazine, June 2002. *"In the first semi-final, Penn State defeated Navy 17-14, stealing the win in the final*

*seconds of the match when PSU wing Leah Ackerman streaked her way down the sideline to score with no time remaining. Her score broke Navy's heart and sent Penn State into the finals against Air Force.*

*"Air Force made it into the final by defeating a tough Illinois team 7-5 in overtime. The match was a low scoring defensive struggle. It's difficult to imagine, but the match ended 0-0 in regulation time. The first score of the game came in the final minutes of the first overtime when Illinois's outside center scored to give the Illini the lead. But with less than two minutes left in overtime, the Air Force scrumhalf powered over the line to tie the match. The Zoomies were able to convert and take the win over an exhausted and heartbroken Illinois team.*

*"The final was yet another close match as Air Force came back in the second half to defeat Penn State 12-7. In all three matches, the wind was a significant factor, as teams playing against the wind tended to find themselves bottled up in their own end for much the half. PSU scored in the first half off a driving lineout and was able to convert the try to lead 7-0. In the second half, Penn State was forced to deal with the wind and played much of the match in their own half. Air Force was able to score twice to take a 12-7 lead and hang on to win their second national championship."*

*"The game was a defensive battle, and a tactical battle. Every play, every set piece, was crucial. Penn State, playing with the wind and up a player due to a yellow card, put lock Stacy Jones over for a try, converted by Meghan O'Melia, and led 7-0 at halftime.*

*"With the wind in the second half, Air Force was able to put lock Tiffany Williams over to make it 7-5. Still Penn State held onto the lead. But No. 8 Erin Harms took a quick tap on a penalty and scored with 12 minutes left. Adrianna Vonderbruggen converted, and Air Force led 12-7. There followed a torrid final period in which McDonald helped earn her MVP award with her defense and leadership."*

# Air Force Over Penn State In Women's DI Final

### By Laura Murphy

**Blaine, MN**
**May 4-5, 2002**

The Air Force Academy rallied to overcome Penn State 12-7 and win the 2002 Women's Division I Collegiate Championship. The tournament was marked by three come-from-behind wins in heart-stopping matches between closely matched teams. Air Force, which had appeared in the first eight Final Fours from 1991-98, returned there after three years of Elite Eight elimination to capture its third Women's DI title. They had defeated Illinois 7-5 in overtime to reach the final.

Penn State, itself a two time DI champion in its ninth Final Four appearance and third consecutive final, fell short for the second straight year after taking the title in 2000.

Navy has the ball out during its loss to Penn State in the semifinal. (Photo-Jen Doan)

The Air Force defense converges on a Penn State ballcarrier during the Zoomies' victory in the final. (Photo- Jen Doan)

They had beaten Navy 17-14 in the closing moments of the other semifinal to advance to the championship match.

Illinois fended off a valiant Navy rally to earn third place 19-17.

### Semifinals:
### PENN STATE 17, NAVY 14

Navy got an early lead on a try from center Lindsay Bellomy that Bridget Seymour converted for a 7-0 lead. Navy had to make it stand up for most of the game as defenses dominated play and Penn State could not get on the board in the first half.

### Second Half

Penn State scored an unconverted try early in the second half by tighthead Carrie White, then took a narrow lead 31 minutes into the second half on another unconverted try by #8 Kathryn Gloyer, 10-7.

When Navy was awarded a penalty try, converted by Seymour, on a Penn State high tackle in the closing minutes of the game to go up 14-10, it appeared that a determined Navy side was about to advance to their first final. But Penn State refused to relent, and wing Leah Ackerman evaded several tackles just before the final whistle to touch down. Meghan O'Melia converted to give Penn State a dramatic 17-14 victory and a date in its third straight DI final.

# Women's DI National Champion - Air Force

**Air Force:** (KNEELING, L-R) Williams, James, Hartert, McNair, Harms, McDonald, Ferrara, Whittaker, Winters, Labowitch, Hamilton-Brown, Vorderbruggen. (STANDING) Shackelford (coach), Mittelstadt (coach), Daluz, Delgiorno, Smith, LeCompte, Kastrop, White, Hartzell (coach), Williams, Bailey, Rotering, Politte, Dietz, Smith, Belanger, Osur (coach). (Photo-Jen Doan)

Stanford vs California

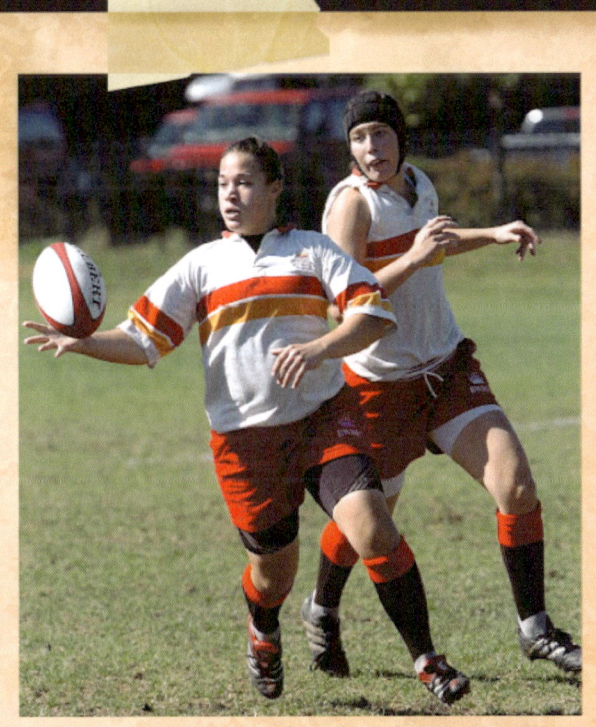

**Frankie Male of Brown University with 2009 College player of the Year Emilie Bydwell in support**

*Almost Gameday*

**Top right:** *Chico State 2001 National Champions*
**Bottom right:** *University of Illinois*

## COLLEGIATE CHAMPIONS 2000-2009:

## Collegiate Champions: USAR D1

### USAR D1

2000: Penn State v Princeton University
2001: Chico State (Cal) v Penn State
2002: Air Force Academy v Penn State
2003: Air Force Academy v University of Illinois
2004: Penn State v Princeton

2005: Stanford University v Penn State
2006: Stanford University v Penn State
2007: Penn State v Stanford University
2008: Stanford University v Penn State
2009: Penn State v Stanford University

## Collegiate Champions: USAR D2

### USAR D2

2000: Plymouth State University v East Stroudsburg University
2001: Northern Iowa University v University of Nevada
2002: Northern Iowa University v University of Minnesota
2003: University of Dayton v Northern Iowa University
2004: Temple University v Providence College

2005: Providence College v Temple University
2006: UC Santa Cruz v Plymouth State University
2007: Iowa State University v UC Santa Cruz
2008: Shippensburg State University v University of Minnesota Duluth
2009: Shippensburg State University v Stonehill College

**2009 Massachusetts Institute of Technology (MIT) NSCRO National Champions**

*NSCRO Small College*

2007:  Stonehill College V Marist College

2008:  Bryant University v Gettysburg College

2009:  MIT v East Stroudsburg University

## Collegiate Champions: NSCRO Small College

| 2007 | 2008 | 2009 |
|---|---|---|
| Stonehill College | Marist College | MIT |
| Marist College | Gettysburg College | East Stroudsburg Univ. |

## U.S. WOMEN'S NATIONAL TEAM

**THE 2002 WOMEN'S RUGBY WORLD CUP WAS** the second World Cup sanctioned by the iRB. The tournament was held in Barcelona, Spain. Sixteen nations competed. Fourteen of the sixteen teams taking part were the same as in 1998 but two lowest ranked European teams (Sweden and Russia) were replaced by teams from Asia (Japan) and Oceania (Samoa).

The competition took place May 13-24. New Zealand defeated England 19-9 to claim a second consecutive title. The U.S struggled, losing to France and Australia early on but rallied to beat Spain for a seventh place finish. 2002 was the fourth World Cup for Hall of Fame player, Patty Jervey and the first World Cup for future Hall of Fame player, Phaidra Knight. The U.S. was represented at the Tournament by USAR

*2000 U.S. v Canada (Canada 17 –U.S. 10)*

President Anne Barry, the first woman to lead USAR and the first woman to lead a national governing body.

In 2002 the first U.S. U19 girls team was chosen. February 2003 the U.S. played Canada and Wales U19 teams

# NEWSBRIEFS

## Women Eagles Named For 2000
### USNT

The 2000 women's Eagle side has been named for the August clash against Canada at Saranac Lake and for September's Canada Cup.

The squad mixes new and old, with nearly half its members uncapped. Captain of the side is lock Nancy Fitz and six members are former U-23 players graduating to the senior ranks for the first time. Others secured their place on the Eagle roster with strong showings in the women's development match last month.

"The match against Quebec gave people an opportunity to play for their spots," program director Peter Steinberg said, noting that athletes such as Justine Sleezer and Cynthia Gehrke staked their claim with big games against the Canadian province. "One advantage is that we got a look at people in positions they don't normally play at the club level. The development team will continue to be a valuable stepping stone."

### Jen Crawford

The Eagles chances for success have been boosted by the fact that former Eagle fullback and captain, Jen Crawford, is staging a comeback.

"Her experience is going to be key, as well as her rugby ability," said Steinberg. "We are still in a rebuilding process from the last World Cup, and we'll have young players around her who will learn an enormous amount."

The Eagles assemble on July 29 for the one-off match against Canada. Last year, the USA posted a 16-11 win over their North American rivals at Saranac Lake, but then lost their first-ever match to the Canadians, 18-15, later in the year.

The Canada Cup, meanwhile, sees the world's best women's teams head to Winnipeg, Manitoba in late September. The Eagles are scheduled to play England (9/23), New Zealand (9/27) and Canada (9/30).

A new head coach for the women's national squad should be appointed prior to the Can-Am camp. USA Rugby's three month search is nearing a conclusion and an announcment is expected shortly.

### Forwards

Jen Crouse (lock), Nancy Fitz (lock) (captain), Cynthia Gehrke (prop), Marie Hahler (lock), Amy Heroux (hooker), Megan Himan (hooker), Liz Kirk** (prop), Phaidra Knight (prop), Sue Landsittel* (prop), Kerry McCabe (flanker), Becky Metzger* (flanker), Amanda Micheli (flanker), Jessica Olive** (flanker), Meredith Ottens (prop), Erina Queen (No. 8), Lisa Rowe (scrumhalf), Diane Schnapp (flanker), Alex Williams (lock).

### Backs

Hedwig Aerts (center), Shalanda Baker (fullback), Laura Cabrera (fullback), Jennifer Crawford (center), Kim Cyganic (wing), Shari Dahlberg (flyhalf), Catherine Darrow (flyhalf), Stacey Davis (wing), Lindsay Davison (wing), Yancy Graf (center), Heather Hale (center), Patti Jervey (center), Justine Sleezer (scrumhalf).

\* = CanAm only
** = Canada Cup only

## Under-19s In Australia

The US Boys Under-19 team is currently in Australia on an 18-day tour that kicks off the program's bid to return to the U-19 World Championship. Thirty-six players have been chosen to represent the US in a demanding five-match itinerary.

# 2002 RUGBY WORLD CUP ROSTER

| | | |
|---|---|---|
| HEDWIG AERTS | FLYHALF | NEW YORK RUGBY CLUB |
| KRISTIN BAJA | CENTER | WASHINGTON FURIES RUGBY CLUB |
| LIBERTY CAPLAN | FLANKER | UNIVERSITY OF NORTHERN IOWA |
| JENNIFER CROUSE | SECOND ROW | BEANTOWN RUGBY CLUB |
| KIMBERLY CYGANIK | SCRUMHALF | MARYLAND STINGERS RUGBY CLUB |
| SHARI DAHLBERG | SCRUMHALF | WISCONSIN WOMEN'S RUGBY CLUB |
| STACEY DAVIS | WING | EAST BAY BULLDOGS RUGBY CLUB |
| JILL FENSKE | HOOKER | UNIVERSITY OF CALIFORNIA, LOS ANGELES |
| NANCY FITZ (C) | SECOND ROW | WASHINGTON FURIES RUGBY CLUB |
| STACY FOLEY | FLANKER | KEYSTONE RUGBY CLUB |
| CYNTHIA GERHKE | HOOKER | WISCONSIN WOMEN'S RUGBY CLUB |
| HEATHER HALE (VC) | CENTER | WASHINGTON FURIES RUGBY CLUB |
| PATRICIA JERVEY | WING | ATLANTA HARLEQUINS |
| ELEANOR KARVOSKI | WING | NEW YORK RUGBY CLUB |
| ELIZABETH KIRK | PROP | SEATTLE RUGBY CLUB |
| PHAIDRA KNIGHT | PROP | WISCONSIN WOMEN'S RUGBY CLUB |
| ELIZABETH LAKE | PROP | MINNESOTA VALKYRIES |
| KERRY MCCABE | BACK | BEANTOWN RUGBY CLUB |
| REBECCA METZGER | FLANKER | MARYLAND STINGERS RUGBY CLUB |
| MEREDITH OTTENS | PROP | MINNESOTA VALKYRIES |
| INES RODRIGUEZ | FLYHALF | KEYSTONE RUGBY CLUB |
| MYRA SANDQUIST-REUTER | SECOND ROW | TWIN CITIES AMAZONS |
| JENNIFER SIKORA | FLANKER | KEYSTONE RUGBY CLUB |
| KATHRYN STEWART | FULLBACK | NEW YORK RUGBY CLUB |
| REBECCA WALLISON | CENTER | NEW YORK RUGBY CLUB |
| ALEXANDRA WILLIAMS | NUMBER 8 | BERKELEY ALL BLUES RUGBY CLUB |
| | | |
| MARTIN GALLAGHER | HEAD COACH | |
| TAM BRECKENRIDGE | FORWARDS COACH | |
| GEORGE METUARAU | BACKS COACH | |

# 2002 U19 ROSTER

| | |
|---|---|
| AMBER BENLIAN | PENN STATE |
| SOPHIA CHYTRY | UC BERKELEY |
| SARA EDWARDS | LITTLETON HARLEQUINS |
| COLLEEN EYNON | UNIV OF DAYTON |
| HALEY FRENCH (C) | LOBO WOMEN |
| BREANNA GULLECKSON | MIAMI UNIVERSITY (OHIO) |
| BLYTHE HAGAN (C) | HAVERFORD HS |
| MARINA HAMMON | ANTIOCH |
| JOJO HOFFMANN | DIVINE SAVIOR HOLY ANGELS HS |
| KIM HOLMES | KENT CRUSADERS HS |
| LISA KAUFMAN | LOBO WOMEN |
| ALEX MASSIE | AT LARGE |
| KARLEY MCVERRY | DOWNINGTON |
| WENDY DA COSTA MIRANDA | SUMMIT TIGERS HS |
| SANDY NELSON | KANSAS CITY DRAGONS HS |
| JACKIE POTERAJ | LITTLETON HARLEQUINS |
| NIAMA REDDICK | CHICO STATE |
| CRYSTAL SERRANO | USNA |
| JEN WEBER | CORNELL UNIVERSITY |
| KHANH VU | OREGON STATE UNIVERSITY |
| SARAH WILSON | WORTHINGTON HS |
| ANDREA ZEIGLER | KENT CRUSADERS HS |
| | |
| KARL BARTH | HEAD COACH |
| LISA ROSEN | DIRECTOR |

# US Women U-23s Go 1-2 In New Zealand

**US Women U-23s:** *(FRONT, L to R) Starkey, Snodgrass, Jaspers, Butts, Boyle, Whitmore, Magrini, Gilbert,Logan. (MIDDLE) Brethel, Bruce, Kinsler,Ringgenberg, Vitale, Dombronski, Anglade, Stromme,Ogden. (BACK) Kellner, Zdanczewicz, Aerts, Pope, Stolba, Merritt, Arghazadeh, Meyers, Brown, Kress.*

### The Fight for Compensation

In 2003, Kathy Flores was named Head Coach of the U.S. Women's National Team, a position she held until 2010. She led the squad at the 2006 and 2010 Women's Rugby World Cups. Her appointment was historic: she was the first woman and the first woman of color to serve as head coach of any women's national rugby team.

At the time, compensation for coaches and players was rarely discussed, and it was assumed that those working with women's teams would do so for little or no pay. Despite her impressive résumé and experience, Kathy's salary was embarrassingly low—and what little she earned, she reinvested into the program to support staff and players. As Assistant Coach **Candi Orsini** recalls: *"For the 2006 World Cup I was not paid, though my travel was covered. For the 2010 World Cup, I had to reapply for my role and received a stipend of roughly*

*$5,000 plus travel. Kathy was paid around $20,000. We were fortunate at the time to have Anne Barry's protection—she made sure we were at least in the conversation."*

Meanwhile, male national team coaches were generously compensated. Orsini notes: *"I believe Eddie O'Sullivan, head coach of the men's national team at the time, was being paid $300,000. The men stayed in nice hotels; the women stayed in university dorms and military bases. Male players weren't paid either, but booster clubs contributed to coaches' salaries and provided stipends and gifts to both players and staff."*

The situation was even bleaker at other levels. Barb Fugate, U23 coach from 2000–2008, recalls: *"Players weren't paid, and managers like Jane Tierney, who managed two World Cups, weren't compensated either. At best, travel expenses were covered, and USA Rugby provided kit. I was only ever paid a stipend for one year—maybe $2,500—at the very end of my term. The first seven years were unpaid."*

**2006 Women's World Cup Team**

The lack of resources and recognition prompted action. Danita Knox, Chair of the U.S. Women's Rugby Foundation (USWRF), recalls a turning point in 2005: *"A group of 'old girls' attended the Churchill Cup in Canada to support the Women's National Team. The U.S. women lost early and were told they couldn't stay for the rest of the tournament because there wasn't enough money to cover food and housing. It was embarrassing for the team, and we were furious. Six of us decided to take matters into our own hands and address the limited funding and lack of investment from USA Rugby. From winning the first Women's Rugby World Cup in 1991 to consistent high-level performance, the Women Eagles were the most valuable asset USA Rugby had."*

The USWRF was formed with the initial goal of supporting the Women's National Team. But after engaging with women across the country, it became clear that their mission needed to be broader, encompassing youth, collegiate, and club rugby. For the past twenty years, the organization has worked tirelessly behind the scenes—fundraising, advocating, and supporting initiatives to grow and sustain women's rugby nationwide.

The 2006 Women's Rugby World Cup took place in Edmonton, Alberta, Canada from August 31 to September 17, 2006. New Zealand won, defeating England 25-17 in the final, for their third consecutive title. The U.S. played well with some terrific wins over Scotland, Australia, and Ireland. But an early round loss to England put the U.S. in a position to place no better than 5th.

*"In 2006 there was zero compensation for players. But all our flights and stays (including a warm-up camp in Minnesota) were paid for as well as our gear. And we got to take four non-rostered reserves. I do remember it was a beautiful summer when we arrived and a freezing fall by the time we played our final game against Scotland. I had played in the 2002 World Cup in Barcelona, but because Kathy and Candi were coaching in 2006, and Patty Jervey was still playing, the presence of the old guard was palpable—they had been such epic role models—there was a lot of pride in who our coaches were, but it also cast somewhat of an inescapable shadow, like it was hard for the 2006 team to find its own identity. We felt we did ourselves and our predecessors proud in so many ways (4-1 record at the tournament), but the fifth place finish felt anti-climactic for sure." (Hedwig Aerts)*

# 2006 RUGBY WORLD CUP ROSTER

| | | |
|---|---|---|
| HEDWIG AERTS | FLYHALF | NEW YORK RUGBY CLUB |
| KRISTIN BAJA | CENTER | NEW YORK RUGBY CLUB |
| CLAUDIA BRAYMER | SCRUMHALF | ALBANY SIRENS RUGBY CLUB |
| JAMIE BURKE | PROP | BERKELEY ALL BLUES RUGBY CLUB |
| LAURA CABRERA | WING | BERKELEY ALL BLUES RUGBY CLUB |
| ERIN CARTER | LOCK | BERKELEY ALL BLUES RUGBY CLUB |
| ANNIE COLLIER | PROP | NEW YORK RUGBY CLUB |
| KATIE COX | NUMBER 8 | ATLANTA HARLEQUINS RUGBY CLUB |
| JENNIFER CROUSE | LOCK | BERKELEY ALL BLUES RUGBY CLUB |
| CARRIE DUBRAY | PROP | NEW YORK RUGBY CLUB |
| ASHLEY ENGLISH | FULLBACK | BERKELEY ALL BLUES RUGBY CLUB |
| HEATHER HALE | FLYHALF / FULLBACK | WASHINGTON FURIES RUGBY CLUB |
| PATRICIA JERVEY | CENTER | ATLANTA HARLEQUINS RUGBY CLUB |
| ELLIE KARVOSKI | WING | NEW YORK RUGBY CLUB |
| LEE KNIGHT | SCRUMHALF | NEW YORK RUGBY CLUB |
| PHAIDRA KNIGHT | FLANKER | NEW YORK RUGBY CLUB |
| PAM KOSANKE | CENTER | CHICAGO NORTH SHORE RUGBY CLUB |
| KELLY MCMAHON | FLANKER | NEW YORK RUGBY CLUB |
| DANIELLE MILLER | HOOKER | SEATTLE WOMEN'S RUGBY CLUB |
| PAT NEDER | WING | ATLANTA HARLEQUINS RUGBY CLUB |
| TINA NESBERG | NUMBER 8 | BERKELEY ALL BLUES RUGBY CLUB |
| MEREDITH OTTENS | PROP | MINNESOTA VALKYRIES RUGBY CLUB |
| KATE POPE | LOCK / NUMBER 8 | PHILADELPHIA WOMEN'S RUGBY CLUB |
| MARIE WALLACE | HOOKER | BERKELEY ALL BLUES RUGBY CLUB |
| KEENYA WARNER | CENTER | NEW YORK RUGBY CLUB |
| KRISTIN ZDANCZEWICZ | FLANKER | MINNESOTA VALKYRIES RUGBY CLUB |
| | | |
| KATHY FLORES | HEAD COACH | |
| CANDI ORSINI | ASSISTANT COACH | |
| KRISTA MCFARREN | ASSISTANT BACKS | |

**U.S. and All World player Phaidra Knight scores over Ireland**

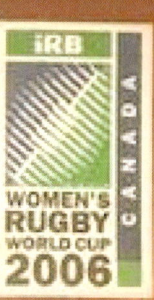

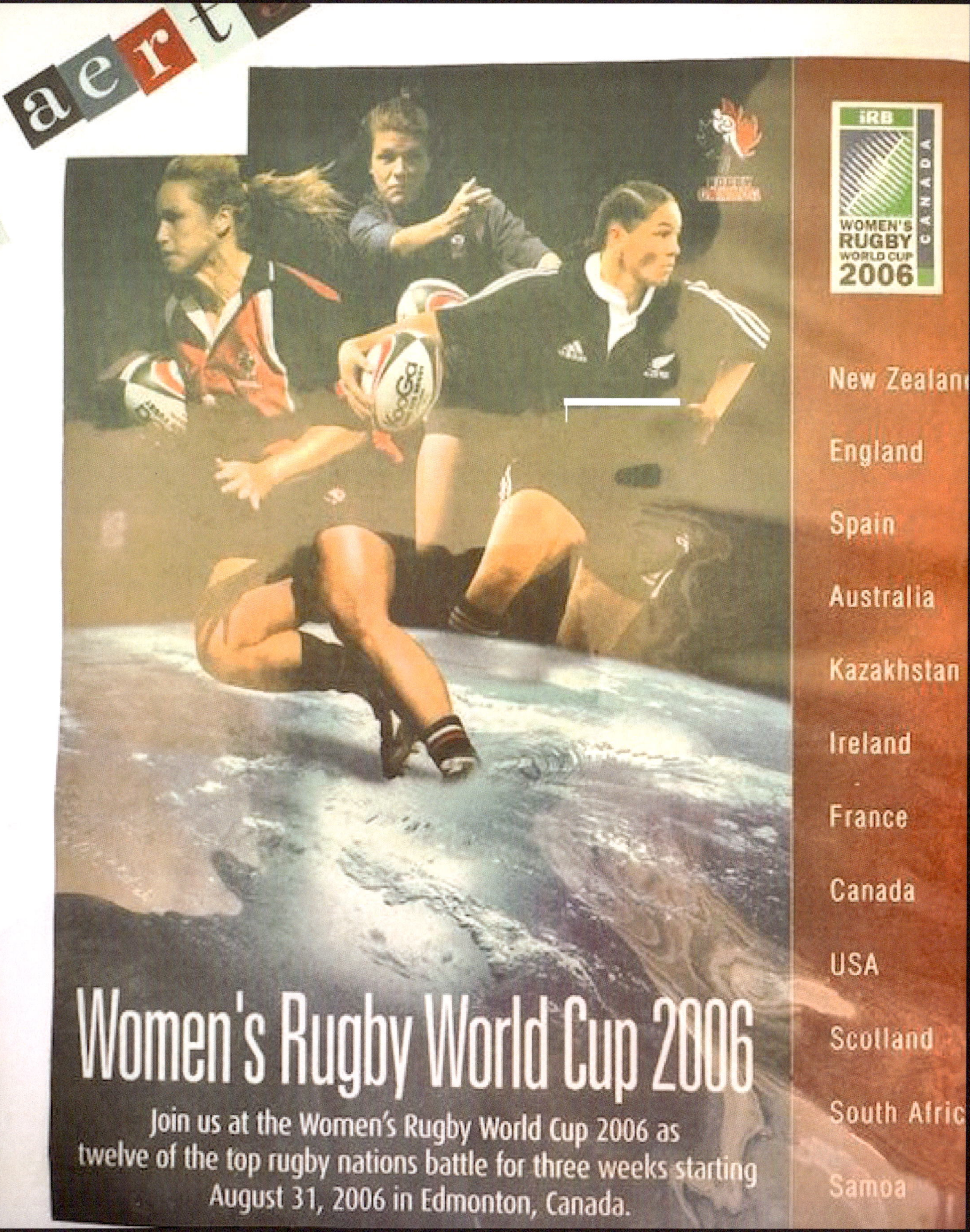
aert
iRB
WOMEN'S RUGBY WORLD CUP 2006
CANADA
New Zealan
England
Spain
Australia
Kazakhstan
Ireland
France
Canada
USA
Scotland
South Afric
Samoa
Women's Rugby World Cup 2006
Join us at the Women's Rugby World Cup 2006 as twelve of the top rugby nations battle for three weeks starting August 31, 2006 in Edmonton, Canada.

2006 World Cup U.S. beat Ireland 24-11

Tina Nesberg scores for the U.S. (10) v Australia (6)

# 2006 World Cup Trading Cards

## 2009 Nations Cup

Churchill Cup

The 2009 Nations Cup was played in Oakville Canada and featured five teams: England, U.S, Canada, South Africa and France. The U.S. placed second overall, losing one match to England.

The U.S. U20 side played a U20 Nations Cup at the same time in London, also claiming second place to the England side.

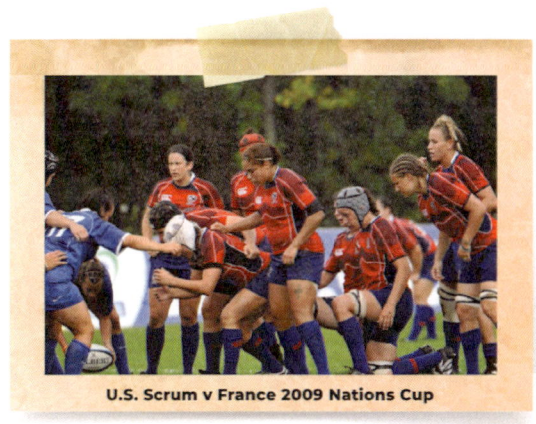

U.S. Scrum v France 2009 Nations Cup

Action photos by Bill English

**Eagle Women in Hong Kong - March 2000**

**Top, L to R: Emil Signes (coach), Greg Schor (coach), Kerry McCabe, Yancy Graf, Anita Pease, Erina Queen, Ines Rodriguez, Al Caravelli (coach)**
**Bottom: Tracy Moens (manager), Lisa Rowe, Sue Parker, Kyle Caravelli, Kristina Caravelli, Jane Mitchell, Diane Schnapp, Laura Cabrera**

**Eagles at Hong Kong Women's Sevens 2002**

**Top, L to R: Chris Ryan (manager), Al Caravelli (coach), Ellie Karvoski, Pam Irby, Melody Peterson, Kerry McCabe, Tyshawn Henry, Emil Signes (coach), Beet McKinnon (trainer)**
**Bottom, L to R: Daniela Mogro, Jen Sinkler, Lindsay Davison, Kristin Baja, Meredith Whalen, Pam Kosanke**

## THE STORY OF U.S. 7s

IN 2002 THE U.S. AGAIN FIELDED A TEAM IN the Hong Kong 7s. Coached by Emil Signes, the U.S. women lost a close semi final match to New Zealand and missed the finals. In many ways the 2002 tournament was a turning point as Hong Kong, the largest 7s showcase in the world, was pressed to fully integrate the women into the tournament. The inclusion of elite national women's teams provided a preview of what Olympic 7s could be.

From 2001 to 2006, Emil Signes coached the USA U23 Women's 7s Team, a squad that competed against senior All-Star 7s teams, helping to develop the next generation of elite players.

In 2006, Julie McCoy was named Head Coach of the U.S. Women's National 7s Team, a position she held from 2006–2009 and again in 2015–2016. A physician and neurologist by training, Julie brought a unique combination of leadership, strategy, and analytical skills to the role. She had extensive experience with the national program, serving as Assistant Coach for the Women's National 15s Team from 2002–2004 and the Women's 7s Team in 2005. Julie also coached the West 15s and 7s teams from 1999–2001, played for the U.S. Women's National 7s Team in 1998, and captained the Atlantis 7s in 1999.

Under her guidance, the U.S. Women's 7s team achieved a historic milestone in 2008 by winning the Hong Kong Sevens tournament—a feat unmatched by any U.S. team, men's or women's. The victory elevated the profile of women's 7s in the U.S. and prompted athlete board member Jenn Joyce to advocate for increased funding for the 2009 World Cup team.

The first Women's Rugby World Cup 7s was held on March 6–7, 2009, in Dubai, integrated into the Men's World Cup 7s tournament. Sixteen teams competed at the inaugural event, with Australia narrowly defeating New Zealand 15–10 to claim the title. The U.S. team finished in third place, going 2–1 in pool play and narrowly losing a hard-fought semi-final to New Zealand, 12–14, demonstrating the growing strength and competitiveness of American women's 7s rugby.

**Eagles at 2009 Rugby World Cup**

# 2009 RUGBY WORLD CUP ROSTER

AMY DANIELS

CHRISTINA MASTRANGELO

ELLIE KARVOSKI

INES RODRIGUEZ

CHRISTY RINGGENBERG

JENN STARKEY

JESSICA WATKINS

PAM KOSANKE

JEN SINKLER

KELLY WHITE

ALISON PRICE

LAUREN HOECK

JULIE MCCOY (HEAD COACH)

Training Squad

Phaidra Knight

Teena Mastrangelo

Pam Kosanke

Christy Ringgenberg

Jessica Watkins

Ines Rodriguez

Alison Price

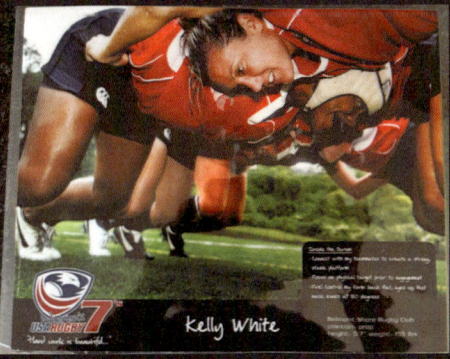

Kelly White

Jen Sinkler

## COMPENSATION FOR 2009 COACHES AND PLAYERS

**HEAD COACH JULIE MCCOY BROUGHT SOME** master level fundraising skills to the 2009 U.S. program. As such the 2009 Women's National 7s team was the first team to fund assistant coaches and players.

"I paid myself a daily stipend of $300 a day for days worked out of our budget. I paid my assistant coaches $150 per day (the first time ever assistants were paid for their work).

"I hosted the first ever month-long residency program in Little Rock, Arkansas, before the World Cup. The players were paid $100 a day for days they worked. Further, the players expenses were covered by our program for previous tours, as well. The model of 'pay to play' was eliminated in 2006. There was however, a 'pay to tryout' fee which was a cost sharing arrangement (prospects paid $100 per camp).

"The funds came from both USAR and private investors arranged by myself. We left $30k in the 7s budget, money that was later used to fund the 2010 15s World Cup team. In addition to raising funds for the World Cup 15s team, I raised funds for Kathy when she was the 15s coach to send the pool of players to Bermuda to play England as a warmup—I did that [fundraising] for about three years.

"I fought with USAR constantly for program funding. I remember the entire women's 7s budget in 2006 was $30,000. I was able to get it up to $300,000 by 2009. In 2009, my private contributor put in writing that his funds wouldn't be triggered until USAR had contributed the full amount they had promised. In 2012, we were asked to submit a budget for Women's 7s development and a plan. I was on the USAR board at the time. We flew to Denver to present a plan for $350, 000 per year for five years. USAR responded that we would get $7,000 per year. In essence it was up to me to raise the other $343,000. That's when I said 'screw it'; if I have to cover those expenses I want to run a program independent of USAR so ARPTC was born in 2014. I became tired of being told what I could do with the money I was raising. When I left, Nigel (CEO of USAR) contacted Serevi (later rebranded as Atavus) to develop a 7s program. Few folks know that I was offered the Head Coaches position in 2015 and again in 2016 for Tokyo. I was also asked to take over the High Performance Managers role. I was clear I was not interested in that path but as it was offered, when I said 'no', USAR had grounds to fire me with cause'. It was ugly, the way coaches were played in those years. The irony was it was all done to save money but by 2016 USAR went bankrupt. I was in such a tough spot. I loved the program and the players, so I decided not to sue or go to the press." (Julie McCoy)

## WOMEN'S PREMIER LEAGUE

**THE WOMEN'S PREMIER** League (WPL) was founded in 2009 with the goal of developing a larger, deeper pool of players for the U.S. Women's National Team. The league launched with eight pioneering clubs: **Beantown, Berkeley All Blues, New York Rugby Club, Washington DC Furies, Twin City Amazons, Keystone Rugby Club, Minnesota Valkyries, and Oregon Sports Union (ORSU).**

Though the concept of a premier women's league had been discussed for years, bringing it to life required extraordinary vision, dedication, and coordination. The heavy lifting—planning, organizing, advocating, and stewarding the league—was undertaken by Alex Williams, then USA Rugby High Performance Director, Women's National Team coach, and longtime WNT player. Alex was uniquely positioned for the task, earning the respect and trust of the rugby community while leveraging the connections necessary to unite teams and resources.

The creation of the WPL was a transformative moment for U.S. women's rugby, establishing a high-level domestic competition that strengthened the national team pipeline, provided a platform for elite athletes, and raised the profile of the sport nationwide. Yet, the league also exposed significant challenges. The financial burden of competing in the WPL placed stress on participating teams, affecting recruitment, team cohesion, and coaching. While the WPL was undeniably a shining moment for women's rugby, it also highlighted the limitations of USA Rugby's pay-to-play model and the need for sustainable support to ensure the long-term growth of the game.

Alex Williams (right) with Kathy Flores at 2004 National Championships

In 2008, I became the Women's High-Performance Director of USAR. My remit was developing and running all the women's national team programs. I was not charged with any domestic competition structure. That said, I intended to do what I could to create a high-level, competitive domestic league for women—an idea that many of us had been discussing for years. After I started the job, I researched the various men's elite domestic leagues that had failed over the years (Anne Barry was a great help; she held so much institutional knowledge!). I started drafting a document that captured the elements I felt would be required for a successful elite women's league.

Some of those key elements:

- *The highest quality competition possible. The top teams in the country, regardless of geographic location*

- *An even competitive schedule (ideally, all teams play all other teams during the league season, although we ended up with a seed-based divisional structure)*

- *An even financial burden for all teams (account for vastly differing travel expenses)*

- The league had to be a cooperative venture, meaning all participating teams had to have equal voices and had to come to agreement on all the major league rules & requirements (this is where a lot of the men's leagues failed, they could never all get on the same page, and were unwilling to compromise).

- We had to have a mechanism for promotion and relegation, to ensure the level of competition remained as high as possible and that teams not originally in the league could 'ascend up' based on performance

I met with Kathy Flores, a close friend and, at the time, Head Coach of the Women's National Team. Kath was completely on board and gave suggestions about the things she felt were most important from the perspective of the national team. We worked it out that she would take on the important role of conveying to prospective teams how vital a competitive domestic league would be in the development of elite caliber players—potential WNT players— while also ensuring other divisions, her scouting for WNT players would include them. She also sat on the first Governing Council. Her presence helped get people on board who were not initially supportive of the league. Kath was a vital piece of getting the WPL off the ground.

I met with Dan Payne, who was at that time USAR's Director of Competition, and told him I was working on putting together a new, elite level women's domestic league that would sit above the current D1 structure and while using some USAR resources would be a self-governed league, **not** a USA Rugby governed league. Dan was fully supportive.

I met with Richard Every, who ran USA Rugby's elite referee development and assignment program. I explained what the league would look like and that we would require National Panel/A-Panel referees for the matches, with the league paying their travel. I felt it important that WPL athletes be refereed in the style and to the level of the international game. He was fully supportive and was a terrific partner to the league. I told him that all matches had to be videotaped (to specific quality requirements) and the video uploaded within a specified short time frame after the match, so that all teams would have equal access to all match video for self- and opponent assessment purposes. He was thrilled with that, as it allowed him to review the performances of the referees he assigned to the matches and again, he was terrific—every week he watched all four matches and not only used them as assessment and training opportunities for his referees but also sent out his assessment of each match and referee performance to the head coaches and invited dialogue with the coaches about how the referees were performing and the things Richard was seeing from the teams that coaches might think about adjusting to better align with the way the referees were managing the games, with an aspiration to be at an International standard.

Once I had those background pieces in place, Kath and I called a meeting at the next USAR Club Nationals. We presented it as a request for all teams to attend a meeting with the USAR Women's High-Performance Director and the WNT Head Coach to discuss a proposal for a new, high-performance domestic league, the WPL. We had a good response, and most of the teams across the divisions at Nationals sent someone to the meeting. We knew there would be opposition, so we were as careful as possible to present it as an opportunity to support the WNT by raising the overall level of domestic play, to emphasize the cooperative nature of the league, and to be clear that there would be a promotion/relegation mechanism. The overall response was positive, though there were people/teams worried that the WPL would destroy women's club rugby. We continued to battle that concern through the league's first years, though the opportunity for top D1 teams to challenge for promotion to the WPL was a critical positive step.

I then drafted an initial League Agreement which covered the league structure, governance, requirements for inclusion, etc., and worked out a mathematical means of determining the inaugural top eight teams from the results of Nationals over the past several years. I sent a formal invitation to eight teams to join the new WPL. One of the teams declined to participate and we moved up the number nine team from the mathematical standings determination.

Then we did a lot of work to get all eight teams on board with the League Agreement. This was one of the key requirements that I insisted on—every year, every team had to have the opportunity to discuss and debate everything in the very detailed League Agreement until agreement was reached. We achieved this by holding a mandatory full-day League Meeting the day after the WPL Championships each year. This was an effective way of hashing out details and getting every team on the same page every year.

The League Agreement covered every detail I could think of that would help to ensure we achieved our goals:

- Governance structure: a Governing Council with 3 reps elected from among the 8 teams and a USAR representative (initially me, as Chair)

  ▷ The GC had regular calls to ensure the league was progressing as planned

  ▷ For the first 2 years, Dre Khoury (of the DC Furies) and I did the bulk of the week-to-week work of running the league, it was hours of work every week, sorting out all the issues that arose and putting out fires. Dre was phenomenal and she took over that role when I stepped away.

- Highest possible level of competition

- International caliber referees

- Trained Assistant Referees and a dedicated (and trained) #4 per match (supplied by the home team)

- Requirements for size and quality of match pitches

- Requirements for detailed, standardized match report submissions, including rosters and disciplinary actions

- Requirements for athlete eligibility

- Requirements for videotaping matches to specific quality parameters and uploading to a specified platform by a specified deadline

- Implementation of a promotion/relegation mechanism starting in Year 2

- Every team to have equal decision-making power regarding league requirements

- Mandatory attendance at the annual league meeting

- Teams were required to annually sign a League Agreement by specified deadline and pay an annual league fee

- The tracking of travel expenses for a designated number of rostered athletes and coaches, with the intent to implement cost sharing to offset the different travel schedules

- Teams were required to host each other to keep costs down (if hosting was requested), so we included hosting guidelines to try to ensure provision of reasonable sleeping and eating experiences

Financial Commitment:

- Required League Fee announced months in advance and to be paid when the League Agreement was signed

- Covered all travel expenses for referees (since they were National Panel, they flew from all over)

- Covered all WPL Championship expenses, including the Annual Meeting

- We always intended to find league sponsors, but struggled with that goal in the first few years

*The teams made some changes in the first few years, underscoring the goal that all participating teams have equal say in determining how the league would operate each year. Managing the many WPL requirements was a beast for each participating team. The teams did a great job sorting out how to manage everything that had to be done to participate in the league, much of which they likely had not had to manage before, or at least not to the WPL's level of specificity and excellence. For many teams, this included a significant increase in fundraising, to help cover the increased cost to participate in the WPL. It took the combined efforts and work of all those people on every team to complete that first year, and then to keep it going year after year. I'm in awe of the many people who kept the WPL going for so long. I'm also proud of the part I played in getting it off the ground.*

## HIGH SCHOOL DOMINANCE

**IN 2000 JOHN KLEIN BECAME HEAD COACH OF** the Divine Savior High School rugby team. Under his leadership the DSHA rugby team won 15 consecutive Midwest championships, 14 Wisconsin state championships, and 7 national high school championships. Divine Savior won the national title 2004 through 2009 and was runner up 2000-2001.

In 2008 Sebastian River High School in Florida established the first girls varsity program.

**Divine Savior Holy Angels High School Team**

## Girl's National Invitational HS All-Tournament Team

**Prop**
Kentwood, Jill Dempsey
DSHA, Mandy Moore
Ft. Collins, Emily Stednick
**Hooker**
Kentwood, Jessica Ainley
Summit, Casey Mclain
**Lock**
Wayzata, Jenny Peck
DSHA, Renee Bordeaux
**# Eight**
Summit, Allegra Hoopingarner
Ft Collins, Mehgan Obermann
**Flankers**
Ft Collins, Sarah Hunt
DSHA, Allison Urbanski
Kentwood, Emily Graham
Summit, Katie Beardsley
**Scrumhalf**
Downington, Amy Manidis
Wayzata, Gina Schoeneberger
**Flyhalf**
Ft Collins, Ashley Lock
Kentwood, Sunny Shervey
**Center**
Wayzata, Kendra Stritch
Summit, Charlotte Allan
Ft Collins, Chesly Ward
**Fullback**
DSHA, Colleen Brennan
Summit, Anita Molina
**Wing**
Kentwood, Carina McBroom
Wayzata, Perssis Meshkat
DSHA, Katie Collins
**MVP**
Mehgan Obermann, #8, Ft Collins

## COACHES, REFEREES, ADMINS

**BECKY CARLSON MADE HISTORY IN 2010 WHEN** she became the first female NCAA Division I women's rugby head coach, taking the helm at Quinnipiac University. Quinnipiac was the first NCAA D1 program to be built entirely from the ground up—not elevated from a club—making Becky's role both groundbreaking and foundational for the sport.

A co-founder of NIRA and a key architect of the NCAA women's rugby initiative, Becky went on to lead Quinnipiac to three consecutive NIRA/NCAA D1 National Championships in 2015, 2016, and 2017. She also served as NIRA Coaches Chair from 2016–2020, helping shape the direction of varsity women's rugby nationwide.

Becky's roots in the game run deep. From 2000 to 2003, she played flanker and center at Eastern Illinois University, the first NCAA women's rugby program in the country. She then served as an assistant coach there from 2004 to 2006 before moving into national leadership as manager of the USAR Emerging Sports Initiative.

Beyond the pitch, Becky has become a prominent advocate for women in coaching. She is the founder of the influential Fearless Coach blog, a powerful platform supporting and amplifying the voices of women coaches. In 2024, she graduated from Tulane University School of Law, continuing to expand her influence as a builder, advocate, and changemaker in women's sports.

**Patty Jervey** is one of the most iconic figures in U.S. and world rugby history. In 2006, she became the first player—male or female—to compete in five Rugby World Cups (1991, 1994, 1998, 2002, and 2006). At her final World Cup appearance, she was 42 years old, a testament to her extraordinary longevity and elite performance.

From 1989 to 2006, Patty earned 40 caps with the U.S. Women's National Team as a wing and center and

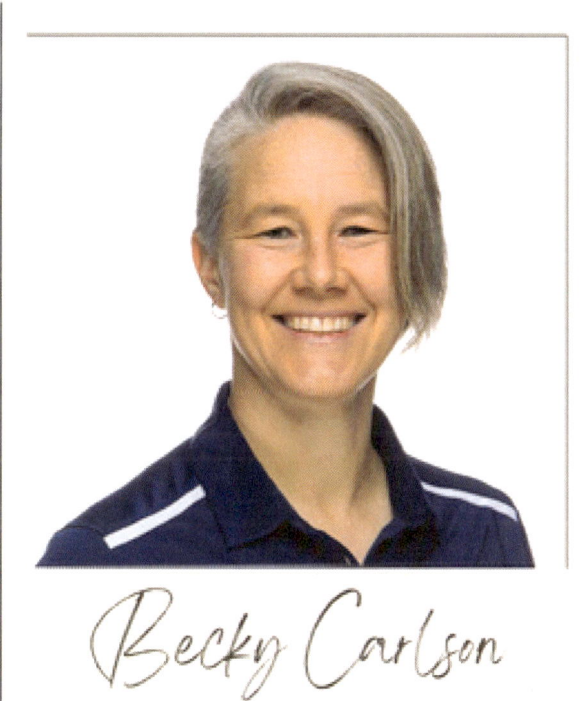

*Becky Carlson*

*Patty Jervey*

became the all-time leading scorer for the Eagles. Her brilliance on the field helped define a generation of women's rugby and set the standard for future players.

Patty's achievements have been widely recognized. She received the Distinguished Service Award from The American Sports and Arts Museum and Archives in 2008, became the first woman inducted into the World Rugby Hall of Fame in 2014, and was inducted into the U.S. Rugby Hall of Fame in 2015.

After her international career, Patty returned to her club roots with the Atlanta Harlequins, where she led the team to a national championship in 2012 at age 48 and a fourth-place finish the following year. Her legacy as a teammate, record-breaker, and inspiration to generations of rugby players is unmatched.

**MaryBeth Mathews:** Marybeths' rugby career spans nearly five decades—from 1976 to the present—marking her as one of the most enduring and influential figures in the sport. A versatile and dynamic player who excelled at fullback, flyhalf, wing, and No. 8, Marybeth was a member of Beantown's inaugural team in 1976. Just a year later, she co-founded the Portland, Maine women's club, leading the team to victory at the first National Club Championship in 1977. She returned to Beantown in 1988, capturing two more National Club Championships. From 1988 to 1992, she represented the USA Rugby East ITTs, cementing her reputation as a fierce competitor.

But Marybeth is best known for her extraordinary coaching legacy. In 1994, she became Head Coach at Bowdoin College, where she built one of the most respected women's rugby programs in the country. Over nearly three decades (nine years as a club program and twenty as a varsity team), she mentored generations of players and helped shape the growth of women's collegiate rugby.

Her leadership extended well beyond Bowdoin. She served as U23 Coach for Maine (2003–2012), NERFU

MaryBeth Mathews

U23 Head Coach (2007–2012), and NRU U23 Assistant Coach (2010–2013). In 2012, she became president of ACRA (American Collegiate Rugby Association), playing a key role in the formation of NIRA. That same year, she founded the Polar Bear Rugby Camp, the first and only camp in the country exclusively for girls.

For her lifelong contributions to the sport, Marybeth received the USWRF Lifetime Achievement Award in 2023. She continues to serve the rugby community as a board member of USWRF and the Portland Rugby Football Club. Her impact on the game—as a player, coach, and leader—has been profound, shaping the trajectory of women's rugby for generations to come.

**Anne McClain, Lieutenant Colonel USMC** was a member of the U.S. Women's National Team from 2004–2006 and again from 2010–2012. A tenacious hooker, Anne's rugby career spanned collegiate, club, and elite levels. She began playing at the U.S. Military Academy (1998–2002), later joining Clifton Rugby Club in England (2002–2004), followed by stints with the Atlanta Harlequins and the Seattle Rugby Club.

*Anne McClain*

She captained the USA Rugby South Women's XV All-Stars from 2009 to 2011, then went on to coach the program in 2012 and serve as an assistant coach for USA Rugby's Women's All-Star Team.

Her commitment to the U.S. Army prevented her from competing in the 2006 Women's Rugby World Cup, but Anne's story would soon transcend the rugby pitch. In 2013, she was selected by NASA as part of Astronaut Group 21, becoming the youngest astronaut on NASA's roster at age 34. Five years later, in 2018, she launched to the International Space Station as an Astronaut and Flight Engineer, completing two spacewalks totaling 13 hours and 8 minutes.

A decorated combat veteran, Anne's military honors include the Bronze Star Medal, Air Medal with Valor, two Air Medals, two Army Commendation Medals, two Army Achievement Medals, the Iraqi Campaign Medal with two Service Stars, the Global War on Terrorism Service Medal, and three Overseas Service Ribbons. She also wears the Combat Action Badge, Senior Aviator Badge, and Air Assault Badge.

Most recently, on March 14, 2025, Anne launched as commander of NASA's SpaceX Crew-10 mission, leading research, technology demonstrations, and maintenance aboard the microgravity laboratory. From the rugby field to outer space, Anne McClain has exemplified leadership, courage, and excellence at the highest levels.

**Julie McCoy:** In 2006, Julie McCoy was named Head Coach of the U.S. Women's National 7s Team, a position she held from 2006–2009 and again in 2015–2016. A physician and neurologist by training, Julie brought an extraordinary breadth of skills and leadership experience to the program. Before taking the helm, she served as Assistant Coach with the Women's National 15s Team (2002–2004) and with the Women's National 7s Team in 2005. She also led the West 15s and 7s All-Star teams from 1999–2001, captained Atlantis 7s in 1999, and represented the U.S. as a 7s National Team player in 1998.

In 2008, Julie made history by coaching the U.S.

*Julie McCoy*

Women's 7s Team to victory at the Hong Kong 7s tournament—a feat unmatched by any U.S. men's or women's team since. This landmark win helped spark momentum for the women's game, prompting athlete board member Jenn Joyce to push USA Rugby to increase funding for the 2009 World Cup campaign. The victory also proved to be a crucial stepping stone toward rugby's eventual elevation to the 2016 Olympic Games.

As a player, Julie was a dynamic center and flanker, competing with the New Orleans Half Moons, Little Rock Women's Rugby, West Territory 15s and 7s All-Stars, Atlantis, and the U.S. Women's National 7s Team.

In 2014, Julie and Tania Hahn co-founded the American Rugby Pro Training Center (ARPTC), one of the most ambitious development initiatives in U.S. women's rugby. Staffed largely by female coaches, ARPTC created critical pathways for girls and women, helping shape the next generation of elite athletes.

Few truly understand the depth of Julie's personal and financial investment in the women's game. Her unwavering commitment and unapologetic approach helped transform the U.S. women's 7s program from a pay-to-play model into a high-performance, world-class pathway—leaving a legacy that continues to influence the sport today.

**Emil Signes:** While a successful 15s coach for over thirty years, Emil is synonymous with U.S. 7s. In 1986 he founded Atlantis Rugby and began laying the foundation for international women's 7s. The extent of his 7s coaching is mind boggling. *"Between 1986 and mid-2014 Atlantis—men, women, boys, girls—fielded 206 squads at 145 tournaments in 31 different countries. Between 7s and 15s, men and women, club and All-Star, his teams have won 14 national championships. (Wendy Young, 2014, Scrumhalf Connection. As Alex Goff noted, Rugby would not be an Olympic sport were it not for one man—Emil Signes."* (Alex Goff, Rugby Magazine, 2009).

Emil Signes

*"Emil essentially grew the women's 7s game worldwide. It started by taking a U.S. Women's 7s team across the globe—first becoming Champions internationally in Benidorm Spain (1992). Pretty much after that Emil would ring me and say, " Hey, do you think we could get the women together to go to Hong Kong, Brazil, Ireland, Thailand, Borneo, Cuba, Spain, Trinidad and Tobago--just to name a few. He would cajole tournament organizers, inspire players, organize tours, and coach (both the U.S. Women's 7s AND 15s team. While he was always giving us a lesson—thus nicknames like 'the Professor' and 'the Emperor', he was also listening. Every player that interacted with Emil felt truly valued and will forever remember their experience. The role call of players that he has impacted in the U.S. women's rugby community at every level is unparalleled."* (Krista McFarren)

**Dana Teagarden:** In 2009, Dana Teagarden made history when she became the first woman to referee at an IRB Sevens World Series Tournament, earning selection to the 7s Women's World Cup panel in

Dubai. The following year, she was chosen for the 2010 Women's Rugby World Cup Referee Panel and broke new ground again by officiating the international test match between the Netherlands and Hong Kong—becoming the first woman to referee a senior men's 15s international match.

Between 2006 and 2014, Dana refereed three Rugby World Cups (2006, 2009, 2010), the Women's Six Nations, and a total of 23 international test matches, establishing herself as one of the most accomplished referees in the history of U.S. rugby.

Before her groundbreaking refereeing career, Dana was an accomplished flyhalf and center, playing for the U.S. Air Force Academy, Florida State University, Las Vegas, and the U.S. Women's National Team. In 1991, as a member of the Air Force Academy team, she won the first Women's Collegiate National Championship and was named Co-MVP of the tournament.

Today, Dana continues to serve the global game as a member of World Rugby's panel of referees, inspiring

Jessica Watkins

Dana Teagarden

and often personally sponsoring future generations of female officials worldwide.

**Jessica "Jess" Watkins** was a member of the 2009 Women's Rugby World Cup Sevens team. At only 21 years old, she was the leading scorer for the U.S. squad and was voted the "fastest woman in rugby." A standout at Stanford University, Jess won the 2008 D1 National Championship, made her first U.S. National Sevens team that same year, and earned First Team Collegiate Rugby All-American honors from 2008 to 2010.

After her rugby career, Jess went on to an extraordinary path in science and space exploration. She earned a Ph.D. in Geology from UCLA and became a postdoctoral fellow at the California Institute of Technology, where she also served as an assistant coach for the women's basketball team.

In 2017, Watkins was selected as a member of NASA Astronaut Group 22. She continued breaking barriers as an Aquanaut in 2019 during the NASA Extreme Environment Mission Operations (NEEMO) and in

2021, she became the first Black woman assigned to a mission on the International Space Station.

In April 2022, she launched aboard SpaceX Crew-4 for a six-month mission to the ISS, returning in October 2022. Jess Watkins stands as a powerful example of athletic excellence, academic achievement, and trailblazing space exploration—the kind of women rugby can produce.

**Alex Williams** was inducted into the U.S. Rugby Hall of Fame in 2018, becoming only the fourth woman to receive this honor. Her impact on American rugby has been both historic and wide-reaching. Alex was a member of five Rugby World Cups—three as a player (1994, 1998, 2002) and two as an assistant coach (2006, 2010). Over her storied career, she was part of nine National Championships, winning five as a player and four as a coach, and was named MVP of the D1 National Club Championships in 1996 and 2002. At the time of her retirement in 2004, Alex was the second most capped U.S. woman in history.

Alex began her rugby career at Radcliffe/Harvard in 1988, later playing for Beantown (1991–2000) and the Berkeley All Blues (2001–2004). She earned selection to the New England, East Coast, Northeast, and Pacific Coast All-Star teams. Her coaching career was equally distinguished: she served as assistant coach for the Northeast Select Side, Berkeley All Blues, and San Diego Surfers, head coach of Berkeley and the Pacific Coast Grizzlies, and was the U.S. Women's National Team Forwards Coach.

Off the field, Alex was a trailblazer in rugby governance and development. She served as the U.S. Rugby Women's High Performance Manager (2008–2012), co-founded the Women's Premier League (WPL) and sat on its Governing Council (2009–2012). She was also a USAR Director (2004–2006), member of the USAR Congress (2006–2008), and contributed to the

*Alex Williams*

USAR Women's Competition Committee and Collegiate Management Council. From 2013 to 2018, she served as Executive Director of Southern California Youth Rugby, furthering opportunities for the next generation of players.

Alex Williams' legacy is defined by excellence as a player, visionary leadership as a coach, and transformative impact as an administrator—cementing her place as one of the most influential figures in U.S. women's rugby history.

### Back in 2002...

| | |
|---|---|
| *Yearly tuition at private university (fees, room and board)* | **$26,854** |
| *Yearly tuition at public university (fees, room and board)* | **$11,966** |
| *Monthly rent* | **$681** |
| *Per capita income* | **$30,795** |
| *Adults with a bachelor's degree* | **26.7%** |

# 2010s

'10 — Women's World Cup (7's) Moscow, Russia. (US women place 3rd)

2010 World Cup (15's), London England (US women place 5th).

Dana Teargarden becomes first woman to officiate a senior men's international match

'13

'14 — National Intercollegiate Rugby Association (NIRA) founded

Quinnipiac defeats Army 24-19 to win the first NIRA Championship

World Cup (15's), Paris, France (US women place 4th)

Patty Jervey becomes first woman inducted into the World Rugby Hall of Fame

'15

'16 — Phaidra Knight inducted into the World Rugby Hall of Fame (the first African American woman), 35 US caps, 3 World Cup teams, Named to the IRB 'All World Team'.

2017 World Cup, (15's) Belfast, Ireland (US Women place 4th)

First Olympic 7's team, Rio de Janeiro (US women place 6th)

'17

'18 — 2020 Olympic 7's, Beijing, China (US Women place 6th)

Women's World Cup (7's), San Francisco. (US women place 4th)

Girls Rugby Inc founded

'20

**T**HE SIXTH WOMEN'S RUGBY WORLD CUP was held in England from August 20 to September 5, 2010. Kathy Flores made history as the first woman, and the first woman of color, to serve as head coach of any national rugby team, with Hall of Fame player Candi Orsini serving as her assistant coach. The tournament concluded with New Zealand narrowly defeating England 13–10 to claim the title.

The U.S. opened with a dominant 51–0 victory over Kazakhstan, followed four days later by a hard-fought 22–12 win over Ireland, setting up a highly anticipated pool match against England. Despite a strong performance, the U.S. fell 37–10, eliminating them from the semi-finals. The team rebounded in the placement rounds, defeating Ireland 40–3 in the fifth-place semi-final and narrowly edging Canada 23–20 to secure fifth place.

The tournament drew unprecedented attention. All 2,500 seats for the opening two days of pool play sold out, and even after capacity was increased to 3,200, the third day was completely full. The semi-finals attracted over 6,000 spectators, while the final drew 13,253 fans, setting a world record at the time for a women's rugby international. The event reached a global audience as well, with an estimated half a million viewers worldwide, according to IRB figures, underscoring the growing visibility and popularity of women's rugby on the world stage.

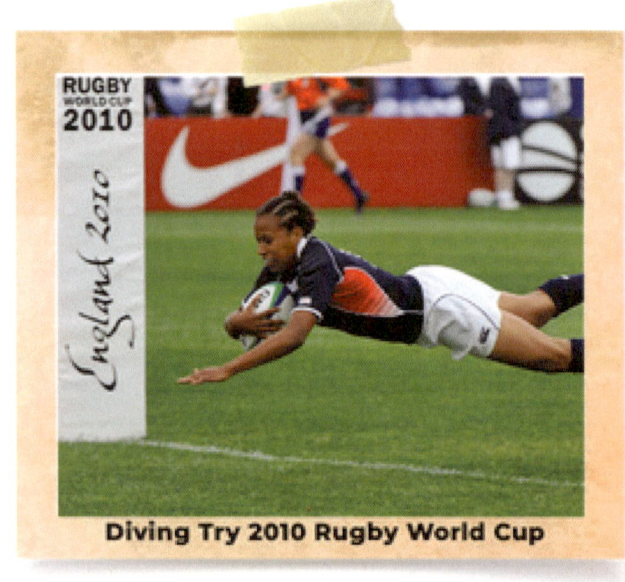

**Diving Try 2010 Rugby World Cup**

**2010 Women's Rugby World Cup**

# 2010 RUGBY WORLD CUP ROSTER

| | | |
|---|---|---|
| JAMIE BURKE | PROP | BEANTOWN |
| FARRAH DOUGLAS | PROP | KEYSTONE |
| LARA VIVOLO | PROP | NEW YORK |
| LISA BUTTS | HOOKER | BERKELEY ALL BLUES |
| KITTERY WAGNER | HOOKER | BEANTOWN |
| MAURIN WALLACE | HOOKER | BEANTOWN |
| SHARON BLANEY | LOCK | BEANTOWN |
| STACEY BRIDGES | LOCK | TEXAS A&M UNIVERSITY |
| JILLION POTTER | LOCK | MINNESOTA VALKYRIES |
| MELANIE DENHAM | FLANKER | BEANTOWN |
| PHAIDRA KNIGHT | FLANKER | NEW YORK |
| BECKETT ROYCE | FLANKER | OREGON SPORTS UNION |
| KRISTIN ZDANCZEWICZ | FLANKER | MINNESOTA VALKYRIES |
| BLAIR GROEFSEMA | NUMBER 8 | BERKELEY ALL BLUES |
| CLAUDIA BRAYMER | SCRUMHALF | SIRENS |
| KIM MAGRINI | SCRUMHALF | KEYSTONE |
| EMILIE BYDWELL | CENTER | BEANTOWN |
| AMY DANIELS | CENTER | BEANTOWN |
| MELISSA KANUK | CENTER | MINNESOTA VALKYRIES |
| LYNELLE KUGLER | CENTER | TWIN CITIES AMAZONS |
| VICTORIA FOLAYAN | WING | BERKELEY ALL BLUES |
| NATHALIE MARCHINO | WING | BERKELEY ALL BLUES |
| VANESHA MCGEE | WING | NEW YORK |
| ASHLEY ENGLISH | FULLBACK | BERKELEY ALL BLUES |
| ASHLEY KMIECIK | FULLBACK | EMERALD CITY MUDHENS |
| CHRISTY RINCCENBER | FULLBACK | MINNESOTA VALKYRIES |
| | | |
| KATHY FLORES | HEAD COACH | |

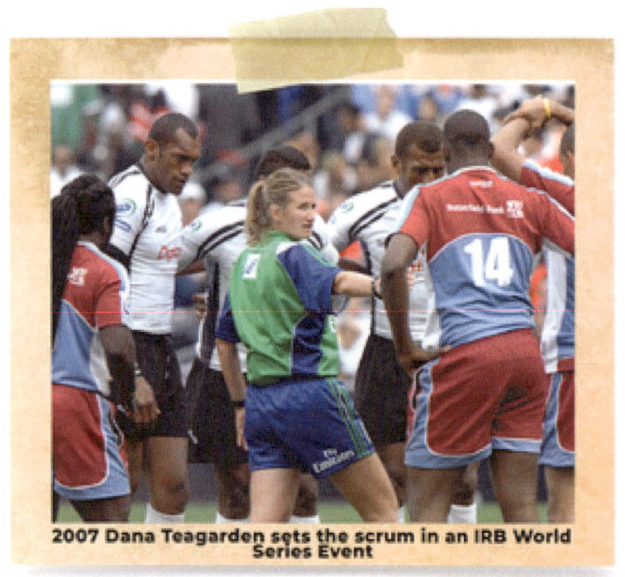

2007 Dana Teagarden sets the scrum in an IRB World Series Event

2011 England v Scotland - 6 Nations

Anne McClain - NASA

## USA WOMEN'S NATIONAL TEAM

**DANA TEAGARDEN BROKE NEW GROUND AS A** referee in international rugby. She became the first woman to officiate at an IRB Sevens World Series tournament and was selected for the Women's 7s World Cup in Dubai in 2009. In 2010, she joined the Women's Rugby World Cup Referee Panel and made history by refereeing the international test match between the Netherlands and Hong Kong, becoming the first woman to referee a senior men's 15s international match.

Over her distinguished career, Dana officiated at three Women's Rugby World Cups, the Women's Six Nations, and 23 international test matches between 2006 and 2014, paving the way for future generations of female referees in both the men's and women's game.

**2011**, England v Scotland in 6 Nations. U.S. referee Dana Teagarden (center in red) is introduced as the Head Referee. This marked the first women's test match at Twickenham officiated by an all female crew.

In 2013, Anne McClain, a hooker for the U.S. National Team was selected by NASA as part of Astronaut Group 21, becoming the youngest astronaut on the NASA roster, at age 34. In 2018 she was selected as an Astronaut and Flight Engineer on the International Space Station. She completed two spacewalks totaling 13 hours and 8 minutes. A decorated combat veteran, her U.S. Army commitments prevented her from participating in the 2006 Women's World Cup.

## 2013 Women's National Team

**HSBC 2015-16 Plate Winners**

**USA Rugby Action**

The World Rugby SVNS (HSBC SVNS), a series of international sevens tournaments for women's national teams run by World Rugby held the inaugural series in 2012–13. The series provides elite-level women's competition between rugby nations. National teams compete for the title by accumulating points based on their finishing position in each tournament. The 2012–13 season began with six core teams (Australia, Canada, England, Netherlands, New Zealand and the U.S.). The number of core teams was increased to eight in 2013-14 (all reached the quarter final from the 2013 Rugby World Cup Sevens). For the 2014–15 series, the number of core teams increased to 11. In 2018-19 the U.S. placed second in the series.

**Naya Tapper Fend**

**Ryan K Carlyle Scoring A Try**

# 2013 USA Rugby Team

# 2013 RUGBY WORLD CUP ROSTER

JILLION POTTER

KELLY GRIFFIN

VANESHA MCGEE (C)

DEVEN OWSIANY

KIMBER ROZIER

CHRISTY RINGGENBERG

VICTORIA FOLAYAN

KATHRYN JOHNSON

IRENE GARDNER

EMILIE BYDWELL

NATHALIE MARCHINO

RYAN CARLYLE


RIC SUGGITT (HEAD COACH)

# 2014 RUGBY WORLD CUP ROSTER

|  |  |  |
|---|---|---|
| KATHRYN AUGUSTYN | HOOKER | BERKELEY ALL BLUES |
| KITTERY WAGNER | HOOKER | GLENDALE RAPTORS |
| JAMIE BURKE | PROP | GLENDALE RAPTORS |
| SARAH CHOBOT | PROP | GLENDALE RAPTORS |
| NAIMA REDDICK | PROP | SAN FRANCISCO GOLDEN GATE |
| HOPE ROGERS | PROP | PENN STATE UNIVERSITY |
| SARAH WILSON | PROP | GLENDALE RAPTORS |
| LAUREN DALY | LOCK | SAN DIEGO SURFERS |
| CARMEN FARMER | LOCK | SEVERN RIVER |
| SARAH WALSH | LOCK | BERKELEY ALL BLUES |
| LYNELLE KUGLER | FLANKER | TWIN CITIES AMAZONS |
| JILLION POTTER | FLANKER | GLENDALE RAPTORS |
| SHAINA TURLEY | FLANKER | SAN DIEGO SURFERS |
| SHARON BLANEY | NUMBER 8 | OREGON SPORTS UNION |
| KATE DALEY | NUMBER 8 | CHICAGO NORTH SHORE |
| DEVEN OWSIANY | SCRUMHALF | PENN STATE UNIVERSITY |
| JOCELYN TSENG | SCRUMHALF | BERKELEY ALL BLUES |
| SADIE ANDERSON | FLYHALF | UNATTACHED |
| KIMBERLY ROZIER | FLYHALF | GLENDALE RAPTORS |
| MEYA BIZER | CENTER | PENN STATE UNIVERSITY |
| SYLVIA BRAATEN | CENTER | TWIN CITIES AMAZONS |
| EMILIE BYDWELL | CENTER | SAN DIEGO SURFERS |
| NATHALIE MARCHINO | WING | BERKELEY ALL BLUES |
| VANESHA MCGEE | WING | NEW YORK RC |
| AKALAINI BARAVILALA | FULLBACK | ALIAMANU ALL BLUES |
| HANNAH STOLBA | FULLBACK | GLENDALE RAPTORS |
| | | |
| PETER STEINBERG | HEAD COACH | |

High schoolers through Eagles helped ARPTC to 7s title. (Alex Goff)

The women's 2013 World Cup 7s tournament was held in Moscow June, 29 and 30th. New Zealand beat Canada 29–12 to take the title. The US Women beat Spain in sudden death overtime to place third. U.S. referee Leah Berard officiated the Final.

The 2014 Women's World Cup 15s was held in Marcoussis and Paris, France, August 1-17. England beat Canada in the final 21–9. The U.S. placed sixth, beating Australia 23-20 in a terrific quarter-final, and falling to New Zealand 55-5 in the semi-finals. U.S. referee Leah Berard was among eight referees named to the tournament. The 2014 World Cup was the fourth and last World Cup for Jamie Burke who retired in 2014 with a record of 51 caps.

In 2014, Patty Jervey, became the first woman inducted into the iRB Rugby Hall of Fame. Patty was the first player (man or woman) to play in five Rugby World Cups (1991,1994, 1998, 2002, 2006). Primarily a wing or outside center, Patty made her WNT debut in 1989 and went on to win forty caps. She scored thirty-eight tries in forty international matches. It's important to consider how few international matches the USWNT had during her tenure. Her forty caps—a USA record—stood until 2013 when Jamie Burke surpassed it with fifty-one caps. Jamie's record has since been surpassed by Hope Rogers with fifty-eight caps.

In 2014, former U.S. National Team 7s player and coach, Julie McCoy (New Orleans Half Moons, Little Rock Women's Rugby, Atlantis, West All Stars, and US WNT 7s) and Tania Hahn (New Orleans Half Moons and West All Stars) founded American Rugby Pro Training Center (ARPTC). ARPTC was staffed largely by female coaches and sought to expand pathways for girls

2014 Patty Jervey IRB HOF

Julie Mc Coy

Tania Han

and women looking for elite development, touring opportunities and visibility to national coaches.

"Tania and I did our best to provide Female rugby players 15-30 years of age with an understanding of 'what it takes' to move from recreational to professional rugby, on and off the field. We are certain that the players from ARPTC are not only enjoying the game to its fullest as they now have Olympic 7s, Premier 7s and Overseas Pro leagues to showcase their skills, but are currently growing the type of playing environment they want to see in those places with an understanding of mutual respect for all."

(Dr. Julie McCoy, co-founder, ARPTC)

Left: *2013 U.S. vs. France*

**2016 Olympic Team (Sean Haffey)**

**Alev Kelter with fans**

# 2016 OLYMPIC ROSTER

ALEV KELTER
JILLION POTTER
BUI BARAVILALA
KELLY GRIFFIN (C)
LAUREN DOYLE
KATHRYN JOHNSON
VICTORIA FOLAYAN
CARMEN FARMER
RICHELLE STEPHENS
JOANNE FA'AVESI
RYAN CARLYLE
JESSICA JAVELET

RIC SUGGITT (HEAD COACH)

**Kelly Griffin**

**Phaidra Knight**

2015 The U.S. Women's Touch Rugby Team competes in their first World Cup placing second in the Division 2 Finals.

The first women's Olympic 7s rugby tournament was held in Rio de Janeiro, Brazil, August 6-8. 2016. In a historic match, Australia beat New Zealand 24–17 in the final. The U.S. beat France 19-5 to claim 5th place.

*"People often ask, Oh, did you always dream of playing rugby in the Olympics? I'm like, rugby wasn't even in the Olympics until I'd been playing for five years. To be honest, I just feel like it's a story of women's rugby in America, where I've been fortunate to be in the right place at the right time for these opportunities. There are plenty of women who are even more or equally qualified who didn't have these opportunities."* (Kelly Griffin, interview with PR7's)

In 2017, Phaidra Knight was inducted into the World Rugby Hall of Fame. She was the second U.S. woman to be honored and the first woman of color in the Hall.

**2017 Rugby World Cup**

The 2017 World Cup Women's World Cup was held August 9-22, 2017 in Belfast, Ireland. New Zealand defeated the U.S. 45-12 in the semi-finals. France beat the U.S. 31-23 for third place, leaving the U.S. in 4th place overall. New Zealand went on to beat England 41-32 for the Championship.

# 2017 RUGBY WORLD CUP ROSTER

| | | |
|---|---|---|
| KATY AUGUSTYN | HOOKER | BERKELEY ALL BLUES |
| CATIE BENSON | PROP | WEST GLADIATRIX |
| SYLVIA BRAATEN | CENTER | TWIN CITIES AMAZONS |
| STACEY BRIDGES | LOCK | TWIN CITIES AMAZONS |
| KAYLA CANETT | SCRUMHALF | PENN STATE UNIVERSITY |
| CHETA EMBA | FULLBACK | USA SEVENS |
| TIFFANY FA'AE'E | PROP | NEW YORK RC |
| TESS FEURY | FLYHALF | PENN STATE UNIVERSITY |
| JORDAN GRAY | NUMBER 8 | LIFE WEST GLADIATRIX |
| ABBY GUSTAITIS | FLANKER | NOVA |
| NICOLE HEAVIRLAND | CENTER | USA SEVENS |
| NICK JAMES | PROP | HOUSTON ATHLETIC RUGBY CLUB |
| JESSICA JAVELET | WING | USA SEVENS |
| ALEV KELTER | CENTER | USA SEVENS |
| DEVEN OWSIANY | SCRUMHALF | SAN DIEGO SURFERS |
| SAM PANKEY | HOOKER | SAN DIEGO SURFERS |
| SARA PARSONS | FLANKER | NOVA |
| CHRISTIANE PHEIL | FLANKER | CHICAGO NORTH STARS |
| NAIMA REDDICK | PROP | SEATTLE RUGBY CLUB |
| JAMILA REINHARDT | PROP | SAN DIEGO SURFERS |
| HOPE ROGERS | PROP | SAN DIEGO SURFERS |
| KIMBER ROZIER | FLYHALF | ENGLAND HARLEQUINS |
| KRISTINE SOMMER | LOCK | SEATTLE RUGBY CLUB |
| NAYA TAPPER | WING | USA SEVENS |
| KRIS THOMAS | WING | USA SEVENS |
| ALYCIA WASHINGTON | LOCK | NEW YORK RC |
| JESS WOODEN | FULLBACK | ENGLAND HARLEQUINS |
| KATE ZACKARY | FLANKER | SAN DIEGO SURFERS |
| | | |
| PETER STEINBERG | HEAD COACH | |

**2017 World Cup - Pass**

**2017 Rugby World Cup Team**

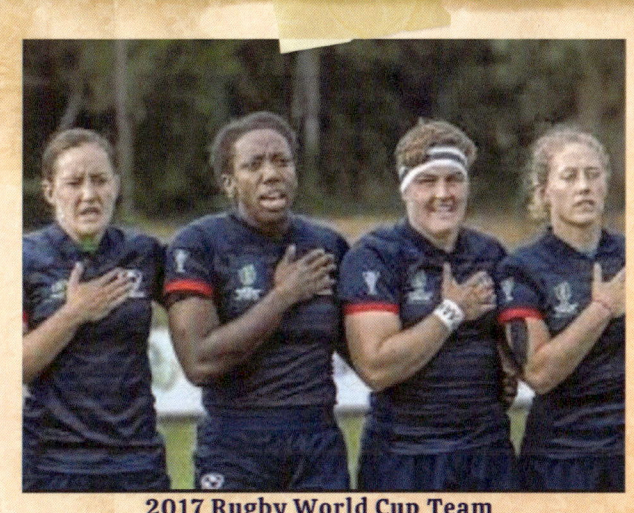

**2017 Rugby World Cup Team**

**2017 Rugby World Cup**

**2017 Rugby World Cup**

**Karameli Fa'ae'e, Captain 2017 World Cup Team**

The U.S. had made it to the semifinals, and I knew our next opponent all too well: the Black Ferns. That moment pulled me back to Paris in 2014. I was in the stands at the World Cup, watching the Black Ferns face the Eagles for fifth place. I was just a fan then, cheering for my friends in the black jerseys. I had no idea that three years later, I would be the U.S. team captain.

As captain, one of my responsibilities was preparing words for our jersey ceremonies. Every ceremony was unique as rosters shifted and oppositions changed. I always used those moments to ground us: to acknowledge where we came from, celebrate where we are, and align where we were going. I remember thinking the Black Ferns are lucky. They get to perform the Haka every time they take the field. I had performed many Hakas and Siva Taus in my life, and I knew the pride, the identity, and the energy that came with them. To me, nothing compares. And I realized—if we wanted to meet the Black Ferns head-on, we couldn't wait for the first whistle. We had to start by taking space at the Haka. I shared my thoughts with our coach, Richie Walker. He suggested we test ourselves. He would perform a Haka, and we'd see how the team responded. So, one day, in a parking lot, Richie stood alone and unleashed a one-man Haka. We faced him shoulder to shoulder, arms linked, fists clenching every time a wave of energy shot through us. The moment he finished; it was silent. Some of us were crying. Others were buzzing, hearts pounding. We shared what we felt: inspiration, motivation, pressure, adrenaline. Every single one of us agreed—we were ready to run through a wall. From that moment, we decided to take the Haka and use it. To mirror our opponents and draw on our ancestors. We used that moment to honor the players who wore the jersey before us. To carry their spirit into battle.

The iRB has a rule that during the Haka, no team can advance past the 10-meter line. So, we made a plan. We would begin five meters back. Then, on my cue, we'd march forward together until we reached the 10- meter line. When the time came, we stepped forward. The crowd roared. People weren't used to seeing a team take space like that. Some thought we were being disrespectful. But this wasn't about disrespect—it was about respect. About answering their challenge. And it worked. At halftime we were trailing 15-7 to the team that became the World Champions. Afterward, a few of my Black Fern friends admitted it shook them. They said they shouted louder, their tongues stretched longer, their eyes burned brighter because of the way we advanced. We had brought something out of them—and that, to me, is respect. Finally, we added one last detail. We wore our jackets over our jerseys. When the Haka ended, we peeled them off, leaving only our armor beneath. We stood together, united, ready for battle.

**(Karameli Fa'ae'e, Captain 2017 World Cup Team)**

**Jessica Watkins - NASA**

In 2017, Jessica Watkins, former U.S. national team player (7s) and Stanford rugby standout was selected as a NASA astronaut. She completed her first spaceflight as a mission specialist on NASA's SpaceX Crew-4 mission (April 27 – Oct. 14, 2022), Jess became only the fifth Black woman ever to travel into space and the first black woman to join a space station expedition.

The **2018** Women's 7s World Cup was held July 20-21 at the AT and T Park in San Francisco. The U.S. lost a close match, 26-21 to New Zealand in the semi-final and lost the bronze medal match to Australia 24-14 to finish 4th overall.

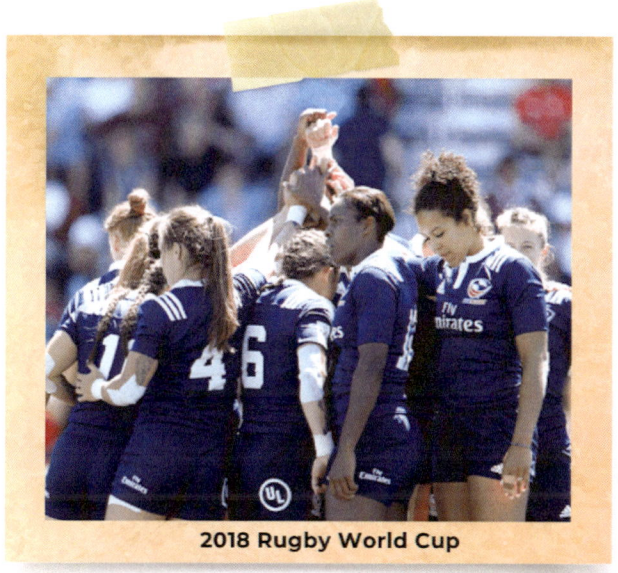

**2018 Rugby World Cup**

**2018 World Cup, General Manager Emilie Bydwell**

RUGBY
**WORLD CUP**™
**SEVENS**
SAN FRANCISCO 2018

⊛ *RUGBY WORLD CUP* ⊛ *2018*

RUGBY
WORLD CUP™
SEVENS
SAN FRANCISCO 2018

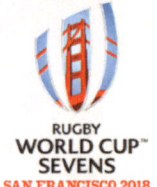

# 2018 RUGBY WORLD CUP ROSTER

CHETA EMBA
RYAN CARLYLE
ABBY GUSTAITIS
NICOLE HEAVIRLAND (C)
KELSI STOCKERT
LAUREN DOYLE
NAYA TAPPER
ILONA MAHER
JOANNE FA'AVESI
KATE ZACKARY
KRISTEN THOMAS
JORDAN GRAY

RICHIE WALKER (HEAD COACH)

## 2018 First WRCRA Conference Panel

In May of 2018 USWRF held a gathering of 50 women leaders in Providence Rhode Island. The two day meeting eventually led to the founding of Women's Rugby Coaches and Referees Association (WRCRA) and the Annual USWRF Women's Rugby Conference.

## SENIOR CLUB

**THE FIRST HALF OF 2010 CHAMPIONSHIPS** were ruled by familiar names, but by 2014 new names began to appear in the Championship finals. The WPL relegation rule meant a few WPL teams moved in and out of the senior club championship as they were relegated out (challenged by a senior club team for the WPL spot).

**2017 Las Vegas Slots**

**2019 Tampa Bay Krewe**

**2018 Chicago Lions**

**2019 Seattle Saracens**

**Left:** *Raleigh Venom v Life University* **Right:** *Austin Valkyries*

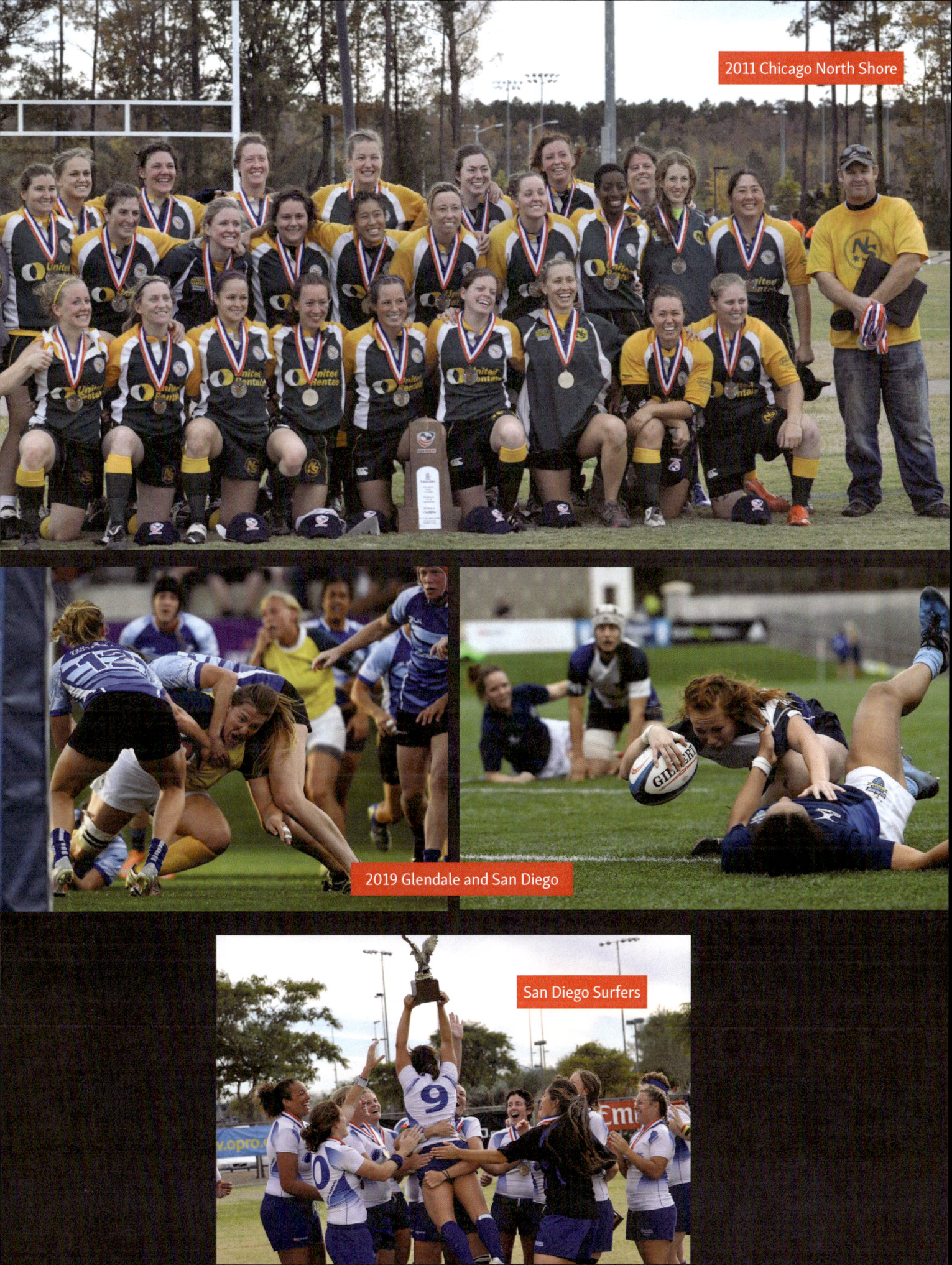

2011 Chicago North Shore

2019 Glendale and San Diego

San Diego Surfers

# USA Club Rugby XVs Champions: DI

| 2010 | 2011 | 2012 | 2013 | 2014 | 2015 | 2016 | 2017 | 2018 | 2019 |
|------|------|------|------|------|------|------|------|------|------|
| San Diego Surfers | Chicago North Shore | Atlanta Harlequins | No Winner* | Oregon Sports Union | Seattle Rugby Club | Seattle Rugby Club | Life West Gladiatrix | Life West Gladiatrix | Northern Virginia Rugby |
| Atlanta Harlequins | Glendale Raptors | Oregon Sports Union | | Chicago North Shore | Beantown RFC | Chicago North Shore | Raleigh Venom | Raleigh Venom | Austin Valkyries |

*No Championship Held Due to Women's League Restructure

## D1 National Champions

2010  San Diego Surfers v Atlanta Harlequins

2011  Chicago North Shore v Glendale Raptors

2012  Atlanta Harlequins v Oregon Sports Union (ORSU)

2013  **No Championship Held Due to Women's League Restructure**

2014  Oregon Sports Union v Chicago North Shore

2015  Seattle Rugby Club V Beantown Rugby

2016  Seattle Rugby Club v Chicago North Shore

2017  Life West Gladiatrix v Raleigh Venom

2018  Life West Gladiatrix v Raleigh Venom

2019  Northern Virginia Rugby v Austin Valkyries

## D2 National Champions

2010 Albany Knickerbockers v Albuquerque Atomic Sisters

2011 Raleigh Venom v Pittsburgh Angels

2012 Pittsburgh Angels v Severn River

2013 **No Championship Held Due to Women's League Restructure**

2014 Pittsburgh Angels v Sacramento Amazons

2015 Wisconsin v Sacramento Amazons

2016 Life West v Wisconsin

2017 Milwaukee Scylla v San Francisco Golden Gate

2018 Charlotte v St Louis Sabres

2019 Sacramento Amazons v Harrisburg

Arguably the biggest leap in the quality of club rugby in this decade was in 7s as pure 7s clubs formed and attracted elite athletes (SCION, ARPTC, the Boston Belles)

**Right:** *2015 Scion*

# USA Club Rugby 7s Champions

| 2011 | 2012 | 2013 | 2014 | 2015 | 2016 | 2017 | 2018 | 2019 |
|------|------|------|------|------|------|------|------|------|
| Berkeley All Blues | San Diego Surfers | Berkeley All Blues | San Diego Surfers | ARPTC | SCION | Seattle Atavus | San Diego Surfers | San Diego Surfers |
| Boston Belles | Seattle | NOVA | Old Blue | Seattle | ARPTC | San Diego Surfers | SCION | Berkeley All Blues |

## National Club 7's Champions

2011   Berkeley All Blues v Boston Belles (first year)

2012   San Diego v Seattle

2013   Berkeley All Blues v NOVA

2014   San Diego Surfers v Old Blue

2015   ARPTC v Seattle

2016   SCION v ARPTC

2017   Seattle Atavus v San Diego Surfers

2018   San Diego Surfers v SCION

2019   San Diego Surfers v Berkeley All Blues

## WOMEN'S PREMIER LEAGUE

**NEW YORK OPENED 2010 BY DEFENDING THEIR** 2009 WPL Championship. The All Blues, under Head Coach Kathy Flores, took the 2011 and 2012 titles. In 2014, the Glendale Raptors won their first WPL Championship. Glendale went on to play in the next six WPL Championships (as the Raptors and Merlins). After a falling out with Glendale over gender/financial equity, Glendale became the Colorado GreyWolves, and went on to win two more championships (2023 and 2024).

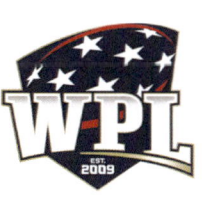

# WPL Champions

| 2010 | 2011 | 2012 | 2013 | 2014 |
|------|------|------|------|------|
| New York Rugby Club | Berkeley All Blues | Berkeley All Blues | Twin Cities Amazons | Glendale Raptors |
| Beantown RFC | Twin Cities Amazons | Glendale Raptors | Berkeley All Blues | Twin Cities Amazons |

| 2015 | 2016 | 2017 | 2018 | 2019 |
|------|------|------|------|------|
| Glendale Raptors | San Diego Surfers | New York Rugby Club | San Diego Surfers | Glendale Merlins |
| Berkeley All Blues | Glendale Raptors | Glendale Merlins | Glendale Merlins | Life West Gladiatrix |

2020 WPL Administrators Ali Gillberg and Kitt Wagner Ruiz

2018 Beantown

2017 New York Rugby Club

2016 Glendale Raptors

2018 Oregon Sports Union (ORSU)

Glendale Merlins 2019 WPL Champions

**Kat Roche Refereeing WPL Game**

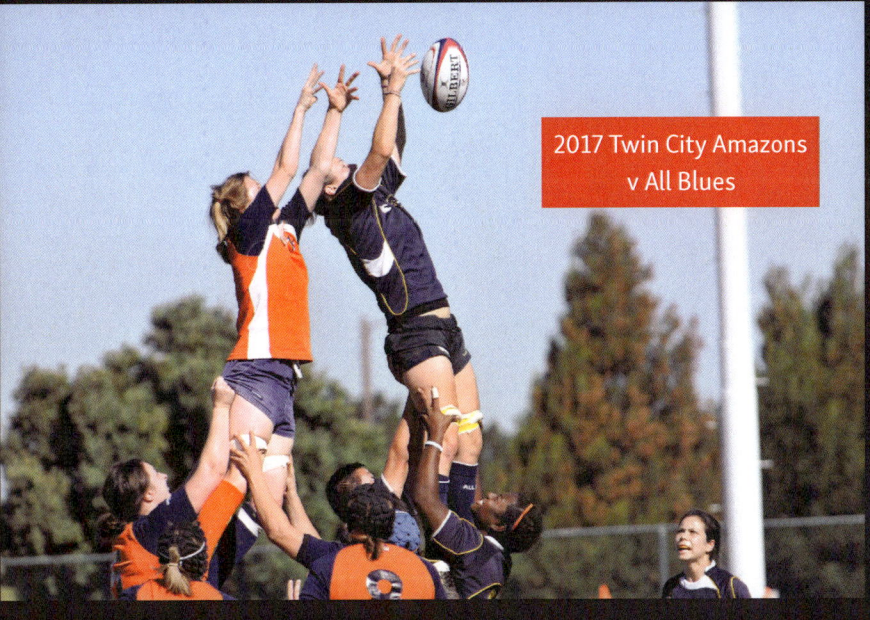

2017 Twin City Amazons v All Blues

## THE COLLEGE GAME (NIRA, NCR, CRAA)

**THE 2010-2019 DECADE SAW COLLEGE RUGBY** move from one governing body (USA Rugby) to three; NIRA (established in 2015), NCR/NSCRO (NSCRO established in 2007 rebranded as NCR in 2020) and USAR. USAR further parsed the championships into 'Elite', D1 (divided into teams that played 15s in the fall and spring—crowning two national champions in one year) and D2. The history of women's college rugby championships is well documented by Jackie Finlan (The Rugby Breakdown, January 2016-15s; The Rugby Breakdown January 2016-7s) and later in 2023 by Alex Goff.

**The Penn State Dynasty:** Penn State played in their first USAR national final in 1995. They won their first National D1 title in 1997. From 1995 to 2017 Penn State played in *twenty-one* D1 National Finals, winning twelve National Championships. From 2010-2017 they were in *every* National final, winning an astounding seven national championships. They won the 2013, 2014 and 2015 National D1 7s Championships. PSU has produced some of the biggest names in the women's game including, Kayla Canett (2016 Olympian), Deven Owsiany, World Cup captains, Kim Magrini, and Kate Daley, Tess Feury, Sadie Anderson, Jenny Lui, Devon O'Crump, Maya Bizer, and the most capped U.S. player of all time, Hope Rogers.

From 2010 to 2015 Penn State played in six, Division 1 National Collegiate Championship finals and won an astounding five titles. But the game of the decade was their 2011 loss to the U.S. Military Academy. Army, led by wing Annie Lee's first half scoring blitz , had to survive a determined Penn State comeback in the second half. Army stood tall during a number of inspiring defensive stands, with less than

Hope Rogers (center with the ball) would go on to be the most capped U.S. player of all time.

a minute left in the match Penn State drove over the line for what would have been the winning try. Annie Lee held the ball up to ensure the Army victory, 33-29.

Penn State rebounded in 2012 to reclaim the national title beating Stanford in the final.

In 2011 Norwich University defeated Boston College in the first USAR Women's Collegiate National 7s Championship. Norwich would go on to win two more championships (2012 and 2013).

In 2014 Wayne State beat South Dakota State University for the first, NSCRO Collegiate 7s Championship. Wayne State would go on to play in the next five championship finals winning five out of six national 7s championships.

The National Intercollegiate Rugby Association (NIRA) was established in 2015, the brainchild of Amy Rusert and Becky Carlson. Conceived as an umbrella

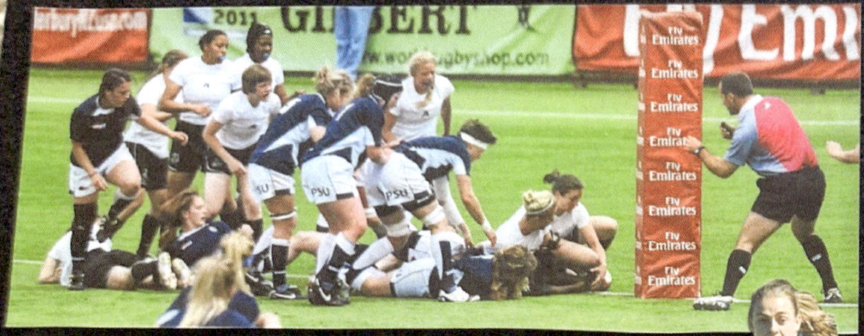
GILBERT
Fly Emirates

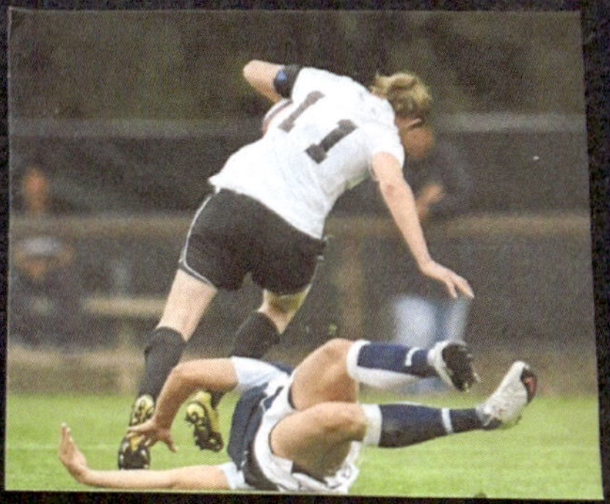

Penn State 29
Army 33

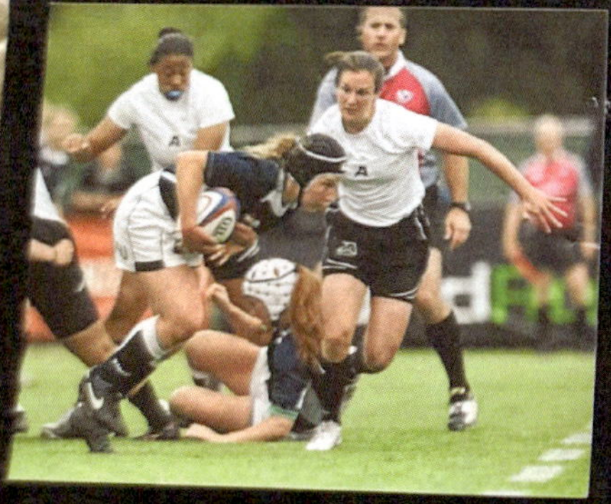

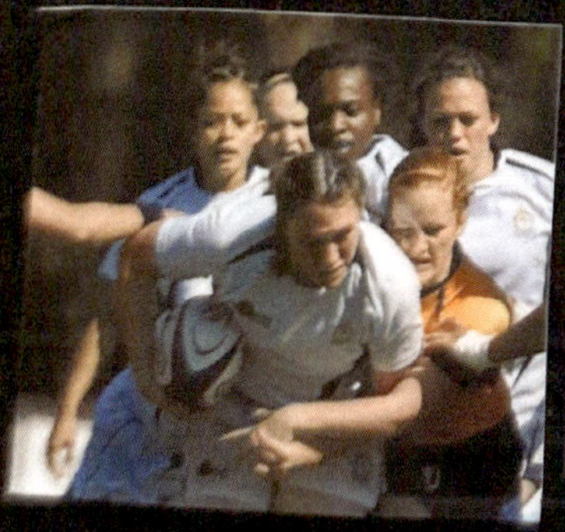

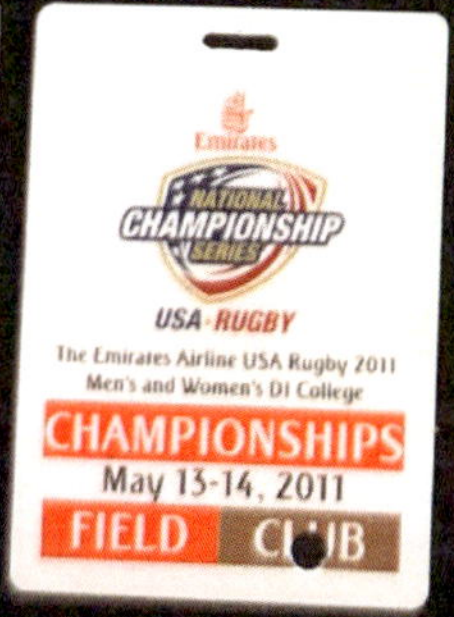
Emirates
NATIONAL CHAMPIONSHIP SERIES
USA-RUGBY
The Emirates Airline USA Rugby 2011
Men's and Women's D1 College
CHAMPIONSHIPS
May 13-14, 2011
FIELD CLUB

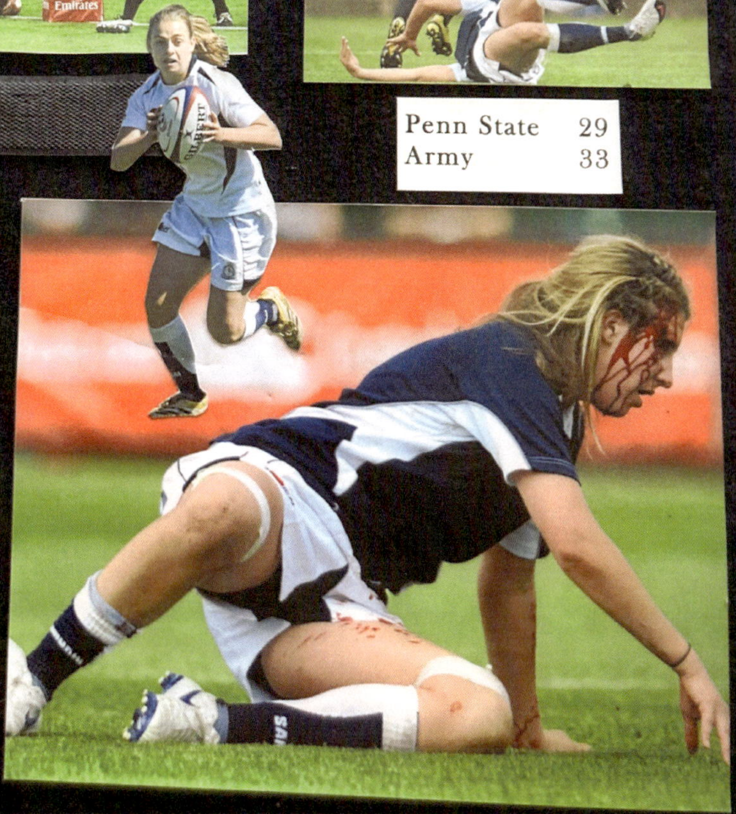

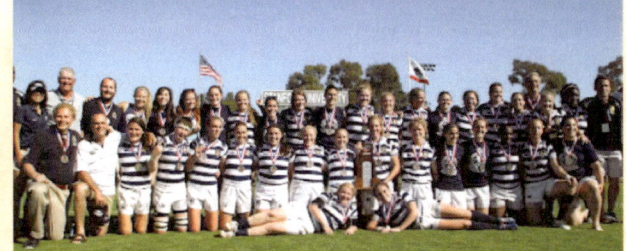

**2012 D1 National Champions: Penn State**

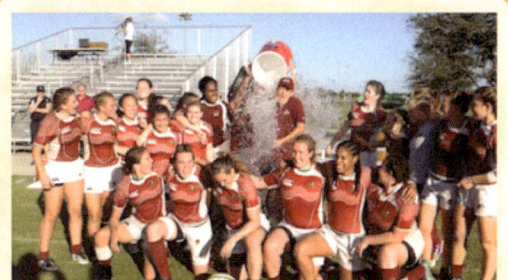

**2011 Norwich University**

**Wayne State University, National Champions**

**Becky Carlson**

organization for collegiate women's rugby teams aspiring to NCAA status, NIRA sought to provide structure, visibility, and legitimacy for the fastest-growing segment of women's rugby.

The inaugural NIRA championship was won by Quinnipiac University, led by head coach Becky Carlson and featuring a young Ilona Mahr at center. Quinnipiac defeated the U.S. Military Academy and went on to claim three consecutive national titles

from 2015 to 2017, cementing themselves as a powerhouse in collegiate women's rugby.

The establishment of NIRA also brought advocacy and visibility to longstanding inequities. In response to Penn Mutual/CRC's mistreatment of women during the 2015 Collegiate Rugby Championship, Becky Carlson launched the #HERRUGBYCOUNTS campaign, which garnered over 10,000 signatures. Top collegiate women's teams faced inadequate field space, lack of media coverage, and denial of locker room access. As Carlson recounted:

*"On Saturday, the women had to share one locker room while the men had three—not having to share with their opponents. On Sunday, the women weren't allowed any locker rooms at all, while the men had all four. This meant our women were unable to shower before our seven-hour bus ride home."*

The campaign highlighted the ongoing struggle for equity in women's rugby and demonstrated how collegiate athletes and administrators had to be vigilant in calling out the casual sexism and inequity that continued in some quarters of the game.

The 2010-2019 decade saw the debut of college players who years later would become the biggest names in the game. Ilona Maher helped propel

**2016 Quinnipiac University NIRA Champions**

Quinnipiac University to three NIRA National Championships; Naya Tapper was picking up the game at UNC, Cheta Emba was honing her skills at Harvard and Hope Rogers was leading Penn State to yet more national titles.

### *NIRA National 15s Championships*

2015 Quinnipiac University v U.S. Military Academy

2016 Quinnipiac University v Central Washington State University

2017 Quinnipiac University v Dartmouth College

2018 Dartmouth College v Harvard University

2019 Tier 1: Harvard University v U.S Military Academy
Tier 2: West Chester University v Brown University
Tier 3: Bowdoin College v University of New England

# NIRA National 15's Championships

## 2018 Life University, first year varsity team

*USAR 'Elite' National 15s Championships*

| 2016 | Penn State University v BYU | 2018 | Lindenwood University v Life University |
| 2017 | Penn State University v Lindenwood University | 2019 | Lindenwood University v Life University |

## USAR 'Elite' National 15's Championships

*2011 Stanford*

Texas State v UTexas

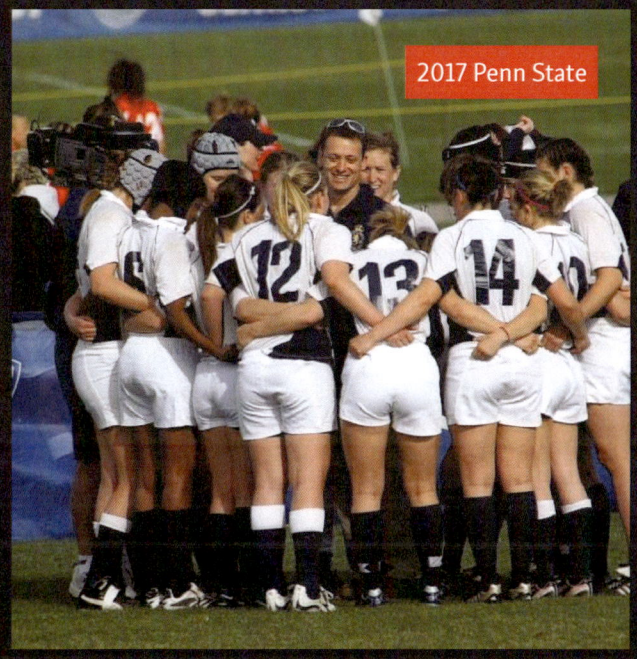

2017 Penn State

2017 Lindenwood vs Life

2016 Jordan Gray, BYU

## USAR D1 National 15's Championships

| 2010 | 2011 | 2012 | 2013 | 2014 | 2015 | 2015 | 2016 | 2016 | 2017 | 2017 | 2018 | 2018 | 2019 | 2019 |
| Penn State | U.S. Military Academy | Penn State | Penn State | Penn State | Penn State | UCONN | UC Davis | Air Force Academy | UC Davis | Davenport College | Chico State University | Air Force Academy | BYU | Air Force Academy |
| Stanford University | Penn State | Stanford University | Norwich College | Stanford University | Central Washington State University (Spring) | Air Force Academy (Fall) | University of Virginia (Spring) | UCONN (Fall) | Notre Dame College (Spring) | Notre Dame University (Fall) | University of Central Florida (Spring) | Davenport University (Fall) | Virginia Tech University (Spring) | U.S. Naval Academy (Fall) |

### USAR D1 National 15's Championships

2010  Penn State v Stanford University

2011  U.S. Military Academy v Penn State

2012  Penn State v Stanford University

2013  Penn State v Norwich College

2014  Penn State v Stanford University

2015  Penn State v Central Washington State University (Spring)

2015  UCONN v Air Force Academy (Fall)

2016  UC Davis v University of Virginia (Spring)

2016  Air Force Academy v UCONN (Fall)

2017  UC Davis v Notre Dame College (Spring)

2017  Davenport College v Notre Dame University (Fall)

2018  Chico State University v University of Central Florida (Spring)

2018  Air Force Academy v Davenport University (Fall)

2019  BYU v Virginia Tech University (Spring)

2019  Air Force Academy v U.S. Naval Academy (Fall)

## 2018 Tulane University D2 National Champions

## USAR D2 National 15's Championships

*USAR D2 National 15's Championships*

2010  Washington State University v Temple University

2011  Radcliffe College v Notre Dame University

2012  Norwich College v Winona State University

2013  Washington State University v Winona State University

2014  Mary Washington University v CSU Northridge

2015  Notre Dame College v UC Riverside

2016  Davenport College v USC

2017  Winona State University v Vassar College

2018  Tulane University v Claremont College (Spring)

2018  Vassar College v Winona State University (Fall)

2019  Fresno State University v Salisbury State University (Spring)

2019  Winona State University v Colorado School of Mines (Fall)

## USAR 7's National Championships

*USAR 7s National Championships*

2011  Norwich College v Boston College

2012  Norwich College v U.S. Naval Academy

2013  Norwich College v James Madison University

2014  *Championship Moved to Spring of 2015*

2015  Penn State v Central Washington University

2016  D1 Life University v Lindenwood University
      D2 Davenport College v Bloomsburg State University

2017  Lindenwood University v Life University

2018  Elite: Lindenwood University v Penn State
      Open: U.S. Air Force Academy v Chico State University

2019  Elite: Lindenwood University v Dartmouth College
      DI: U.S. Air Force Academy v Virginia Tech University
      DII: Bryant University v Fresno State University

## NSCRO/NCR National 15s Championships

### NSCRO/NCR National 15s Championships

2010   Bentley College v Drexel University

2011   Carleton College v Lock Haven University

2012   Wayne State University v Roger Williams University

2013   Wayne State University v Smith College

2014   Roger Williams University v Sacred Heart University

2015   MSU Moorhead v Colgate University

2016   Wayne State University v Colgate University

2017   Wayne State University v Bentley College

2018   Wayne State University v Catholic University

2019   Wayne State University v MSU Moorhead

### NCR Small College 7s National Championships

2014   Wayne State College v South Dakota State

2015   Wayne State College v Mount St. Mary's University

2016   Wayne State College v Mount St. Mary's University

2017   Colgate University v Wayne State College

2018   Wayne State College v Lee University

2019   Wayne State College v University of Rochester

**2019 MSU Moorhead University**

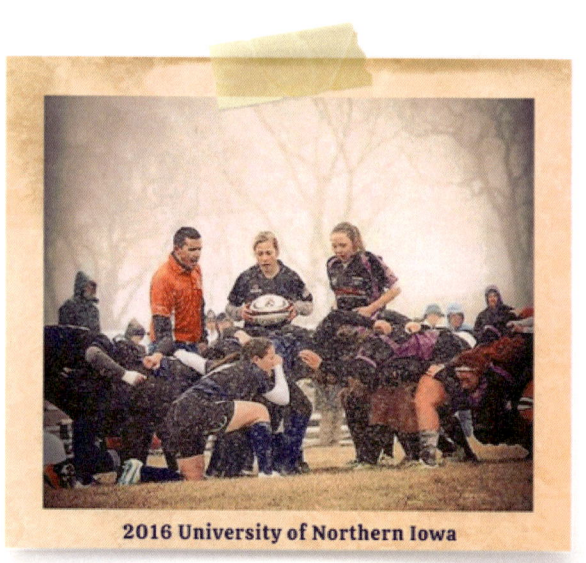

**2016 University of Northern Iowa**

2016 Colagte University

2010 Bentley College

2015 South Dakota State University

2017 University of Alabama

2012 University of Texas

2018 Lee University

*2015 Sacred Heart University*

Jackie Finlan - The Rugby Breakdown

In 2016 Jackie Finlan started *The Rugby Breakdown*.

"*I formed **The Rugby Breakdown** (TRB) in January 2016 because I wanted to focus all of my attention and reportage on girls and women's rugby in the U.S. That's my devotion and object of duty. I strive to produce and circulate original news, covering everything between high school rugby up through the U.S. Women's National Team, for the benefit and enjoyment of women's rugby fans around the country.*"

—Jackie Finlan

## YOUTH & HIGH SCHOOL

**IN 2018, ERIN KENNEDY, JENN HEINRICH AND** Hannah Harper founded Girls Rugby Inc. Starting with three programs Colorado, Oregon/SW Washington and Southern California, Girls Rugby Inc is currently in thirteen locations in eight states and offers leagues and camps for young girls to play flag rugby.

### HIGH SCHOOL AND CLUB NATIONAL CHAMPIONS

Fallbrook Union High School of Fallbrook, California (San Diego, CA), dominated high school rugby with eight trips to the National High School Championship finals and five national titles. Fallbrook's dominance is a tribute to Head Coach Marin Pinnell. Pinnell began coaching Fallbrook in 2007. In 2013 she was recognized as USA Rugby's Female Coach of the Year. Marin, who retired in 2018, was succeeded by her husband Craig.

Girls Rugby Inc.

Girls Rugby Inc.

**2017 Fallbrook High School**

Established in 2007, Fallbrook High School Rugby Club fields up to sixty girls enrolled in three teams (U14, U16, and U19). Fallbrook has produced eight U.S. National Team players; including two Olympians, 2024 Olympic Medalist Kayla Canett and 2016 Olympian, Richelle Stephens.

Throughout the decade, high school rugby underwent tremendous growth. The advent of collegiate varsity programs allowed high school girls an opportunity to showcase their talents and move into more demanding opportunities at the collegiate and U23 levels.

*In 2016, the competition split into single-school and club divisions

## Division 1 High School Champions

| 2010 | 2011 | 2012 | 2013 | 2014 | 2015 | 2016 | 2016 | 2017 | 2017 | 2018 | 2018 | 2019 | 2019 | 2019 |
|---|---|---|---|---|---|---|---|---|---|---|---|---|---|---|
| Sacramento | Fallbrook | Fallbrook | Fallbrook | Fallbrook | Fallbrook | St. Joseph (School) | Sacramento (Club) | DSHA (School) | United (Club | Kahuku (School) | United (Club) | DSHA (SchooL) | South Bay (Club) | South Bay (Club |
| Fallbrook | Sacramento | Lakewood | Kent | Sacramento | Kent | Summit (School) | Fallbrook (Club) | Kahuku (School) | Fallbrook (Club) | Catholic Memorial (School) | North Bay (Club) | Catholic Memorial (School) | Kahuku (Club) | Florida State University |

*Division 1 High School Champions*

2010  Sacramento v Fallbrook
2011  Fallbrook v Sacramento
2012  Fallbrook v Lakewood
2013  Fallbrook v Kent
2014  Fallbrook v Sacramento
2015  Fallbrook v Kent
2016  (school) St. Joseph v Summit
2016  (club) Sacramento v Fallbrook

2017  (school) Divine Savior/Holy Angels v Kahuku
2017  (club) United v Fallbrook
2018  (school) Kahuku v Catholic Memorial
2018  (club) United v North Bay
2019  (school) Divine Savior Holy Angels v Catholic Memorial
2019  (club) South Bay v Kahuku

2017 Girl's Bobcat LVI Team, AZ

**2016 United of Utah Girls HS.**

**Summit CO Girls HS National Champions**

**2016 Sacramento HS National Champs
(Seiller)**

## COACHES, REFEREES, ADMINS

**LEAH BERARD MADE HER FIRST INTERNA-**
tional appearance as an assistant referee for the IRB Men's Sevens Series in South Africa in 2011. Her performance earned her a spot at the first IRB-sanctioned Women's Sevens Challenge Cup in Hong Kong in March 2012, where she refereed the Cup Final between Australia and England in front of over 40,000 spectators. Later that year, Leah was named to the IRB Women's Sevens Panel for the inaugural season of the Women's Sevens World Series.

Reflecting on her career, Leah says: *"My biggest accomplishment thus far has been handling the Women's Sevens Rugby World Cup Final in Russia in June 2013. I also represented the USA as a referee in the Women's Rugby World Cup in August 2014, just four months after reconstructive knee surgery. I was also one of five referees for the one and only season of PRO Rugby in 2016."*

*Leah Berard*

In 2019, Leah transitioned to football officiating, bringing the same discipline and focus to the gridiron. She quickly advanced from varsity high school games to Division I college football, and she currently referees in the Mid-American Conference (MAC), with aspirations to move into the Big Ten and ultimately the NFL. Her journey highlights a remarkable career at the highest levels of sport, both on the rugby field and beyond.

**Bryn Chivers:** Bryn Chivers' rugby career spans over four decades, marked by dedication to coaching, player development, and the growth of women's and collegiate rugby. He began coaching at the University of Michigan in 1982 and led the team to the finals of the first collegiate national championship in 1991, where they fell to the U.S. Air Force Academy.

Shortly thereafter, Bryn organized and coached the first Midwest U23 side and became a tireless advocate for the development of territorial U23 and U20 teams, ultimately contributing to the establishment

*Bryn Chivers*

of national U20 and U23 programs. From 2005 to 2012, he coached the U20 Women's National Teams, helping identify and develop some of the most storied players in U.S. women's rugby.

Bryn also served as the NSCRO Director of Women's Rugby from 2014 to 2020. Over the course of his career, he has won five USA Rugby national championships and one NSCRO national title. While he is widely recognized for his work with collegiate and U20/U23 programs, Bryn was also a highly respected club coach, guiding Chicago North Shore to WPL prominence.

Currently, Bryn serves as the Director of Men's and Women's Rugby at Wayne State University, continuing a career dedicated to cultivating talent, building programs, and advancing the sport at every level.

*Phaidra Knight*

**Phaidra Knight:** Before Ilona Maher, there was Phaidra Knight—the first true superstar of U.S. women's rugby. Phaidra has long been a trailblazer, charismatic leader, and committed community activist. She served on the Board of Directors for USA Rugby and built a legendary international career spanning 1999 to 2017, earning 35 caps and recognition as one of the world's best players at both prop and flanker.

Phaidra competed in three Women's Rugby World Cups (2002, 2006, and 2010) and was named to the All-World Team in 2002 and 2006. She was selected for the World XV Team to play against New Zealand and, in 2010, was honored as USA Rugby Player of the Decade. In 2017, she became the first African-American woman and only the second American to be inducted into the World Rugby Hall of Fame.

At the club level, Phaidra played for the New York Rugby Club for over 15 years, winning three national championships (2006, 2009, 2010) and earning MVP honors at the inaugural Women's Premier League (WPL) Championship in 2009.

Off the field, Phaidra has been a powerful voice in women's sports. She served as President of the Women's Sports Foundation in 2021 and continues to serve on their Board of Trustees. She has also worked extensively in rugby broadcasting, contributing to ESPN, NBC, CBS Sports, FloSports, and USA Rugby TV, making her debut as an analyst during the 2017 Women's Rugby World Cup. She later joined NBC's Olympic broadcasting team for Tokyo 2020 and Paris 2024.

In 2021, Phaidra launched a career in Mixed Martial Arts (MMA) and appeared in Halle Berry's 2020 film Bruised. That same year, she was recognized by Sports Illustrated as one of the 100 Most Influential Black Women in Sports. Her remarkable contributions to rugby and women's sports were honored with a USWRF Lifetime Achievement Award in 2025.

Phaidra Knight's career—on the field, in the boardroom, and in the media—exemplifies the profound impact of a pioneer who has elevated women's rugby and inspired generations of athletes.

*Jillion Potter*

**Jillion Potter:** Jillion Potter began her rugby journey in 2005 at the University of New Mexico, and within a year earned a spot on the U.S. Women's U23 Team. By 2011, she had advanced to the Senior Women's National Team, establishing herself as a force at Number 8 with 21 caps for the USA Eagles 15s from 2007 to 2014. Potter participated in multiple international tours, including the 2007 UK Tour (England), 2008 Nations Cup (England), 2009 Nations Cup (Canada), 2010 CanAm (Canada), and the 2014 Women's Rugby World Cup in France. She also served as captain for two years, leading the team through critical tournaments.

In 2012, Jillion transitioned to rugby sevens, where she would leave an indelible mark on the international stage. Playing prop, she earned roughly 60 caps for the USA Eagles 7s from 2012 to 2016. Her achievements include a bronze medal at the 2013 Rugby World Cup Sevens, competing in the 2013–16 IRB/World Rugby Sevens Series, and, most notably, captaining the USA team at the 2016 Rio Olympics, where rugby sevens made its Olympic debut.

Potter's career is defined not only by skill but by extraordinary resilience. In 2010, she suffered a C4-C5 vertebrae fracture during a test match in Canada, sidelining her from that year's World Cup. After surgery and recovery, she returned to compete at the 2013 Rugby Sevens World Cup. In 2014, just as she was preparing for another World Cup, she was diagnosed with Stage III synovial sarcoma, a rare cancer. After intensive chemotherapy and radiation, she remarkably returned to elite rugby within a year.

Jillion was among the first eight athletes contracted by USA Rugby and captained the 2016 Olympic team, earning recognition as Sevens Player of the Decade in a GRR fan poll. Beyond playing, she has contributed as a coach and referee, serving as an assistant coach at the University of New Mexico, head coach at Marion University, and coaching the Midwest U23 Thunderbirds. She also refereed at the highest level, including five World Cup matches and as an assistant referee at the 2018 Rugby World Cup Sevens in San Francisco.

In 2018, Jillion founded the RAN Leadership Development Scholarship program, designed to accelerate global development of women in rugby and cultivate leadership potential. Her enduring impact was recognized with a USWRF Lifetime Achievement Award in 2024 and induction into the USRF Hall of Fame in 2025.

Jillion Potter's journey—marked by elite performance, leadership, and resilience in the face of adversity—embodies the spirit of U.S. women's rugby and continues to inspire players around the world.

*Peter Steinberg*

**Peter Steinberg**: Pete Steinberg was the coach and architect behind one of the most dominant programs in U.S. women's collegiate rugby. He guided Penn State to 10 Division I National Championships and Temple University to a Division II National Championship. Under his leadership, the Penn State women reached 20 national finals in 30 years, most of them under Pete's guidance, cementing the program as a powerhouse in collegiate rugby.

Pete's influence extended beyond college fields. He coached the U.S. Women's 15s Team in 2011, laying the foundation for the 2014 Women's Rugby World Cup in Paris, and later served as an assistant coach for the Women's Olympic 7s team in 2016. At the 2017 World Cup, he led the U.S. women to the semifinals, showcasing his ability to elevate teams to the highest international level.

Equally important was Pete's commitment to developing the next generation of coaches. Through the Elite Coaching Development Program, he provided opportunities for coaches to shadow and assist at national team camps, creating pathways for women coaches to gain experience and leadership roles at the elite level. Pete's legacy is not only measured in championships but in the coaches and athletes he empowered to advance women's rugby in the U.S.

# 2020s

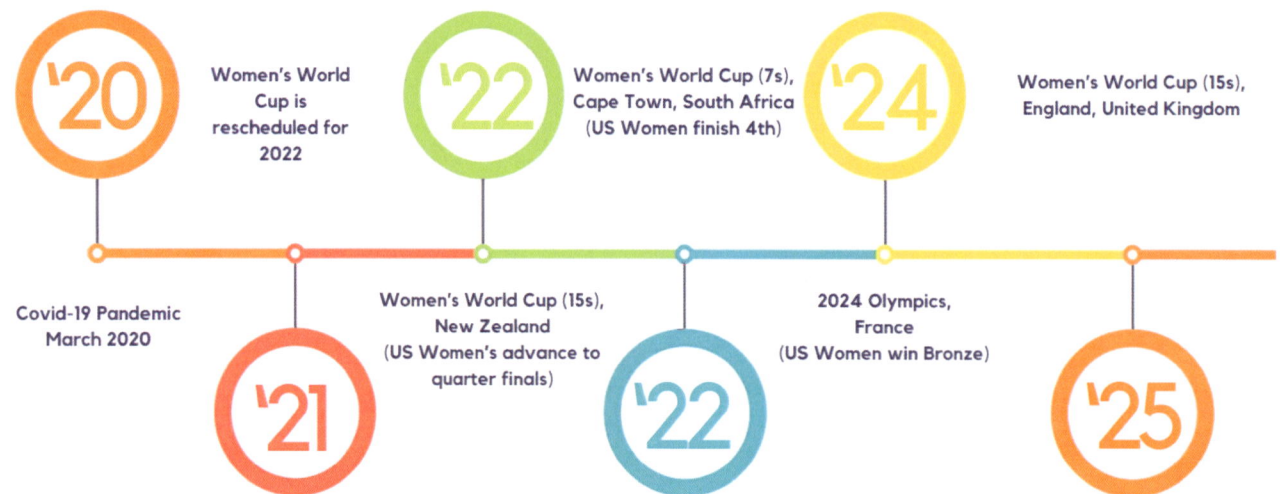

'20 — Women's World Cup is rescheduled for 2022

Covid-19 Pandemic March 2020

'21 — Women's World Cup (15s), New Zealand (US Women's advance to quarter finals)

'22 — Women's World Cup (7s), Cape Town, South Africa (US Women finish 4th)

'22 — 2024 Olympics, France (US Women win Bronze)

'24 — Women's World Cup (15s), England, United Kingdom

'25

## A NEW ERA—2020S

**F**ROM PANDEMIC DISRUPTIONS TO OLYMPIC podiums, women's rugby in the United States entered a dynamic new chapter between 2020 and 2025.

The U.S. Women's Rugby Sevens team competed at both the 2020 Tokyo Olympics (held in 2021) and the 2024 Paris Games, earning a bronze medal, the first-ever Olympic medal for the U.S. women. As impressive as the bronze medal win for the U.S. women, so was the appointment of Kat Roche as head referee for the women's gold medal match.

*Kat Roche refereeing the Spain v Ireland match at 2025 World Cup*

In addition to her Olympic appointment, Kat Roche was a Referee and Assistant Referee (AR) at the 2025 World Cup. Kat was an Assistant Referee at the 2021 World Cup. In 2025 Amelia Luciano served as an Assistant Referee in her first Rugby World Cup selection.

**2024 USA Rugby Olympic Team at Podium**

Hope Rogers – Most Capped Prop of All Time

Kat Roche refereeing the Spain v Ireland
match at 2025 World Cup

2025 World Cup

Professional 15s and USWNT player Hope Rogers, became the most capped U.S. player of all time in 2025 surpassing Jamie Burke with a record 53 caps. In 2024, Rogers earned World Rugby 'Dream Team' honors as the best loosehead prop in the world. In 2025 she was named to her fourth World Cup, becoming only the second USA player to ever compete in four tournaments.

Founded in 2023 by Memphis Inner City Rugby (MICR) and Inner City Education Foundation (ICEF), Urban Rugby America became *the first and only space in American rugby dedicated exclusively for minority students born in under-resourced communities across the country to connect, compete and grow into the bright future we are all building together.*

Programs participating in URA include: ICEF Rugby (Los Angeles), Memphis Inner City Rugby, Chicago Lions Youth Rugby, Play Rugby USA, Washington DC Youth Rugby, Cincinnati, Dallas, North Philly, Nashville, New Orleans, and Patterson (NJ).

In 2020 Alycia Washington and Kristine Sommer founded the XV Foundation to support the U.S.

Urban Rugby America

**Alycia Washington and
Kristine Sommer**

The XV Foundation also partnered with the New England
Freejacks to sponsor the 2023 U23 Team v Canada

**Kathy Flores**

Women's National 15s Team. The XV mission is to *create a financially sustainable platform through diverse, direct, and transparent revenue sources.* In July of 2025, XV raised over $150,000 for the 2025 World Cup team.

The XV Foundation also partnered with the New England Freejacks to sponsor the 2023 U23 Team v Canada (below).

But the 2020 decade was also a time of loss and transition. The U.S. rugby landscape was rocked in 2021 when USA Rugby declared bankruptcy.

In 2022, the American Rugby Pro Training Center (ARPTC) closed its doors after seven years. Founded by Tania Hahn and Julie McCoy, and staffed largely by female coaches, ARPTC was the *first organization* founded to solely support the growth of elite

**2023 - The first USWRF Lifetime Achievement Award Winners from left to right: Julie McCoy, MaryBeth Mathews, KO Onufry, Krista McFarren, Barb Fugate, Martha Daines, Liz Kirk, Nancy Fitz**

women's rugby by expanding pathways and visibility for women.

In 2021, the rugby world lost Kathy Flores, a beloved, trailblazing player and coach. Kathy won multiple national college and club championships and numerous personal awards. She was the first woman to coach *any* national rugby team and the first woman of color to coach a national team. She was the first captain of the U.S. Women's Rugby Team in 1987 and a member of the first 1991 World Cup Team. She was a member of the U.S. Women's National Team from 1987-1994.

From 1994-2010 she embarked on one of the most successful coaching stints of all time, leading the Berkeley All Blues to eleven national senior club championships. She coached the U.S. Women's National Team from 2003 to 2010, and was the head coach of the 2006 and 2010 U.S. Women's World Cup Team. She was one of the founders of the U.S. Women's Rugby Foundation (USWRF) and in 2009, helped establish the Women's Premier League (WPL). In 2014

Kathy became Head Coach at Brown University, one of the first Division I NCAA teams, where she continued coaching until her death in 2021. In 2022, the USWRF established the Kathy Flores Lifetime Achievement Award in her honor. The PR7s Championship Cup is named for Kathy. The WPL 'Heart of a Champion Award' also honors Kathy.

---

## COVID (2020)

THE COVID-19 PANDEMIC AND U.S. WOMEN'S RUGBY (2020–2023)

**THE COVID-19 PANDEMIC BROUGHT RUGBY** activity across the globe to a near standstill. In the United States, major competitions—including the **National Club Championships**, the **Women's Premier League (WPL)** season, and **collegiate rugby across all divisions**—were canceled between 2020 and 2021. The postponement of the **Tokyo Olympics** and the **Women's Rugby World Cup** disrupted elite training cycles and reduced global visibility for the women's game. More tragically, members of the rugby community were lost to COVID-19, and others continue to face the effects of long COVID.

The impact was especially hard on grassroots and collegiate programs. Many college teams faced **budget cuts and roster losses**, while youth and club participation declined amid school closures and public health restrictions. **Varsity programs** largely endured, but community-based play slowed dramatically.

The shutdown also affected **refereeing and coaching development pathways**. With competitions halted, new and emerging referees had limited opportunities to gain experience, and high-performance coaching pipelines were paused or shifted entirely online. National referee camps, coaching clinics, and talent identification programs were either canceled or adapted into virtual formats. While these efforts helped maintain engagement, the lack of live game experience created developmental gaps that took years to rebuild.

Despite these challenges, the rugby community adapted with **virtual clinics**, **modified return-to-play protocols**, and **sevens-focused competitions** to maintain engagement through 2021–2022. By 2023, competition resumed more broadly and participation began to rebound.

The **Women's Premier League (WPL)** responded to the disruption by **restructuring its competition format**—moving to a more flexible, regionalized schedule to reduce travel costs and increase sustainability. It also deepened its governance structure, laying the groundwork to eventually operate independently of USA Rugby.

Similarly, the **National Intercollegiate Rugby Association (NIRA)** leaned on its NCAA-aligned

**Players Wearing Masks**

structure to maintain stability. Through coordinated **virtual compliance meetings**, shared **return-to-play protocols**, and strategic partnerships with athletic departments, NIRA helped programs weather the pandemic with minimal program losses.

**USA Rugby**, facing financial crisis and operational strain, used the COVID years to **reorganize its governance structure** following its 2020 bankruptcy filing. This restructuring created clearer lines of responsibility between USA Rugby, the WPL, NIRA, and community clubs, ultimately granting more autonomy to women's competitions. Virtual governance meetings and strategic planning sessions became standard practice, setting a new tone for post-pandemic operations.

The pandemic also spotlighted **real-world rugby heroes**. U.S. Eagle **Tess Feury** and her mother and longtime coach **KJ Feury** were recognized for their service on the healthcare frontlines, as was **1991 World Cup Champion and U.S. Captain Barb Bond**, an emergency room physician in Oakland, California.

KJ & Tess Feury

## U.S. WOMEN'S NATIONAL TEAM

**THE 2021 RUGBY WORLD CUP WAS THE NINTH** Women's Rugby World Cup, organized by World Rugby. It was held from October 8 to November 12, 2022 in Auckland and Whangārei, New Zealand. It was originally scheduled to be held in 2021, but was postponed by one year due to the COVID-19 pandemic. The 2021 World Cup was the first to not be marketed by World Rugby as the *Women's* Rugby World Cup. World Rugby decided wisely to market both the men's and women's tournaments under the *Rugby World Cup* title with no gender distinction. The window of the tournament was extended and realigned to allow for at least five days rest between matches, as with the men's Rugby World Cup. All matches were scheduled on weekends. Twelve national teams competed. Canada knocked the U.S. out in the Quarter Finals 32-11.

**COVID-19 permanently changed the landscape of U.S. rugby**, accelerating the adoption of **virtual tools**, **hybrid coaching and referee education**, and **more flexible scheduling models**. These innovations strengthened communication networks and increased access to development opportunities—especially for those outside traditional rugby hubs—laying the groundwork for a more resilient and inclusive future for the women's game.

Most importantly, these structural and cultural shifts helped **position U.S. women's rugby for growth** in the lead-up to the **2033 Women's Rugby World Cup** on home soil—a milestone moment expected to elevate the game to unprecedented visibility and participation levels nationwide.

*"I have the opportunity to make a tangible impact on someone's life every day. To me, that's not even work, but what I owe to the world after it's been so good to me."* (Tess Feury)

RUGBY
**WORLD CUP**
NEW ZEALAND 2021
**PLAYING IN 2022**

2021 / 2022 Rugby World Cup

2021 / 2022 Rugby World Cup

 *RUGBY WORLD CUP*    2021 / 2022

# 2021/22 RUGBY WORLD CUP ROSTER

| | | |
|---|---|---|
| ALEV KELTER | FULLBACK | SARACENS |
| BRIDGET KAHELE | SCRUMHALF | BEANTOWN RFC |
| CARLY WATERS | SCRUMHALF | SALE SHARKS |
| CATIE BENSON | PROP | SALE SHARKS |
| CHARLI JACOBY | PROP | EXETER CHIEFS |
| CHARLOTTE CLAPP | WING | SARACENS |
| ELIZABETH CAIRNS | BACKROW | LIFE WEST GLADIATRIX |
| ERICA JARRELL | PROP | BEANTOWN RFC |
| ETI HAUNGATAU | CENTER | LINDENWOOD UNIVERSITY |
| EVELYN ASHENBRUCKER | LOCK | SAN DIEGO SURFERS |
| GABBY CANTORNA | FLYHALF | EXETER CHIEFS |
| GEORGIE PERRIS-REDDING | BACKROW | SALE SHARKS |
| HALLIE TAUFO'OU | LOCK | LOUGHBOROUGH LIGHTNING |
| HOPE ROGERS | PROP | EXETER CHIEFS |
| JENNINE DETIVEAUX | WING | EXETER CHIEFS |
| JENNY KRONISH | LOCK | HARLEQUINS |
| JETT HAYWARD | HOOKER | LIFE WEST GLADIATRIX |
| JOANNA KITLINSKI | HOOKER | SALE SHARKS |
| JORDAN MATYAS | LOCK | USA SEVENS |
| KATANA HOWARD | CENTER | SALE SHARKS |
| KATE ZACKARY (C) | BACKROW | EXETER CHIEFS |
| KATHRYN JOHNSON | BACKROW | TWIN CITIES AMAZONS |
| KATHRYN TREDER | HOOKER | BEANTOWN RFC |
| KRISTINE SOMMER | LOCK | SEATTLE RUGBY CLUB |
| MAYA LEARNED | PROP | GLOUCESTER-HARTPURY RFC |
| MCKENZIE HAWKINS | FLYHALF | LIFE WEST GLADIATRIX |
| MEGAN FOSTER | FLYHALF | EXETER CHIEFS |
| MEYA BIZER | FULLBACK | BEANTOWN RFC |
| NICK JAMES | PROP | SALE SHARKS |
| OLIVIA ORTIZ | SCRUMHALF | COLORADO GRAY WOLVES |
| RACHEL JOHNSON | BACK ROW | EXETER CHIEFS |
| TESS FEURY | FULLBACK | WASPS |
| | | |
| ROB CAIN | HEAD COACH | |

**2021 (Playing in 2022) Rugby World Cup Team**

**Captain Kate Zackary with Hope Rogers (left) for the U.S.**

**2025 Women's World Cup Team**

## 2025 WOMEN'S RUGBY WORLD CUP—ENGLAND

**THE TENTH EDITION OF THE WOMEN'S RUGBY** World Cup took place in England from 22 August to 27 September 2025, a defining moment for the sport's global growth and visibility.

The U.S. Eagles entered the tournament facing one of the most challenging pools in the competition. They opened with a decisive win over Samoa, followed by a hard-fought loss to England, and closed pool play with a dramatic draw against Australia. The tie ultimately kept them from advancing to the quarterfinals—a disappointing finish for a team determined to reassert its place on the world stage.

While the Eagles' campaign ended earlier than hoped, the tournament showcased the depth and character of the squad. A number of emerging players—including Charli Jacoby, Meya Bizer, Katana Howard, Emily Henrich—gained invaluable test-level experience that will shape the next cycle.

Meanwhile, Canada stunned the world with a historic 34–19 semifinal victory over New Zealand, while England powered past France 35–17 to advance to the final. In front of 81,885 fans at Twickenham Stadium—the largest crowd ever for a women's rugby match—England defeated Canada 33–13 to lift the World Cup trophy on home soil. Over the course of the tournament, 444,465 tickets were sold, shattering attendance records and proving the strength of the women's game.

The legacy of the tournament, however, extends far beyond the final whistle. World Rugby's launch of the WXV Global Series will bring structure and opportunity to the women's international calendar, with the top 18 teams competing in more than 100 matches between 2026 and 2028. This new format is designed to drive year-round competition, visibility, and growth ahead of the 2029 Women's Rugby World Cup in Australia.

For the United States, this moment represents a turning point. With renewed investment and a deeper player pool, the pathway from youth to high performance has never been clearer:

- NIRA (National Intercollegiate Rugby Association) continues to expand, providing a varsity platform that feeds directly into the national team.

- The Women's Elite Rugby (WER) remains a potential bridge between collegiate rugby and the international game, offering elite competition.

- A growing network of youth programs, club rugby, and regional high-performance

**Thick Thighs Score Tries
2025 Rugby World Cup**

camps is ensuring that more athletes—and more diverse athletes—have access to the pathway to the Eagles.

- Alignment between USA Rugby, WER, NIRA, CRAA, NCR, Senior Club, and grass-roots programs may create the cohesion and consistency the U.S. has long needed to compete with the world's top sides.

While the 2025 results fell short of expectations, they also illuminated the progress being made at home. The Eagles leave England with hard lessons, rising stars, and a sketch for growth. With a stable international calendar through the WXV Global Series and strengthened domestic structures, the U.S. is positioning itself for success.

**2025 Rugby World Cup Line-Out (Dante Kim)**

U.S. v Samoa

# 2025 RUGBY WORLD CUP ROSTER

**WOMEN'S ENG25**

| CATIE BENSON | PROP | SALE SHARKS / BOSTON BANSHEES, 3RD RWC |
|---|---|---|
| CHARLI JACOBY | PROP | EXETER CHIEFS / QUEENSLAND REDS, 2ND RWC |
| MAYA LEARNED | PROP | DENVER ONYX, 2ND RWC |
| ALIVIA LEATHERMAN | PROP | TRAILFINDERS / TWIN CITIES GEMINI, 1ST RWC |
| HOPE ROGERS | PROP | EXETER CHIEFS, 4TH RWC |
| KEIA MAE SAGAPOLU | PROP | LEICESTER TIGERS / ACT BRUMBIES, 1ST |
| HOPE COOPER | HOOKER | BAY AREA BREAKERS, 1ST RWC |
| PAIGE STATHOPOULOS | HOOKER | EALING TRAILFINDERS / BOSTON BANSHEES, 1ST RWC |
| KATHRYN TREDER | HOOKER | LOUGHBOROUGH LIGHTNING / BAY AREA BREAKERS, 2ND RWC |
| EMERSON ALLEN | LOCK | TWIN CITIES GEMINI, 1ST RWC |
| RACHEL EHRECKE | LOCK | DENVER ONYX, 1ST RWC |
| ERICA JARRELL | LOCK | SEARCY — SALE SHARKS, 2ND RWC |
| HALLIE TAUFOOU | LOCK | LOUGHBOROUGH LIGHTNING / DENVER ONYX, 2ND RWC |
| TAHLIA BRODY | BACK ROW | LEICESTER TIGERS / DENVER ONYX, 1ST RWC |
| RACHEL JOHNSON | BACK ROW | EXETER CHIEFS / DENVER ONYX, 2ND RWC |
| GEORGIE PERRIS-REDDING | BACK ROW | SALE SHARKS, 2ND RWC |
| FREDA TAFUNA | BACK ROW | LINDENWOOD UNIVERSITY, 1ST RWC |
| KATE ZACKARY | BACK ROW | EALING TRAILFINDERS, 3RD RWC |
| CASSIDY BARGELL | SCRUMHALF | BOSTON BANSHEES, 1ST RWC |
| OLIVIA ORTIZ | SCRUMHALF | SALE SHARKS, 2ND RWC |
| KRISTIN BITTER | FLYHALF | DENVER ONYX, 1ST RWC |
| MCKENZIE HAWKINS | FLYHALF | DENVER ONYX, 2ND RWC |
| GABBY CANTORNA | CENTER | EXETER CHIEFS, 2ND RWC |
| NANA FA'AVESI | CENTER | DENVER ONYX, 1ST RWC |
| EMILY HENRICH | CENTER | LEICESTER TIGERS / BOSTON BANSHEES, 1ST RWC |
| ALEV KELTER | CENTER | LOUGHBOROUGH LIGHTNING / BAY AREA BREAKERS, 3RD RWC |
| ILONA MAHER | CENTER | BRISTOL BEARS / USA SEVENS, 1ST RWC |
| ERICA COULIBALY | WING / FULLBACK | DENVER ONYX, 1ST RWC |
| CHETA EMBA | WING / FULLBACK | BOSTON BANSHEES, 2ND RWC |
| SARIAH IBARRA | WING / FULLBACK | USA SEVENS, 1ST |
| BULOU MATAITOGA | WING / FULLBACK | LOUGHBOROUGH LIGHTNING / BAY AREA BREAKERS, 2ND RWC |
| LOTTE SHARP | WING / FULLBACK | SARACENS, 2ND RWC |
| | | |
| SIONE FUKOFUKA | HEAD COACH, ATTACK + BACKS | |
| SARAH CHOBOT | ASSISTANT COACH, DEFENSE | |
| MEL BOSMAM | ASSISTANT COACH, FORWARDS + ATTACK | |

2025 Rugby World Cup (Dante Kim)

2025 Rugby World Cup (Dante Kim)

2025 Rugby World Cup (Dante Kim)

2025 Rugby World Cup (Dante Kim)

2020/21 Olympics in Tunnel (MLEE)

2020/21 Olympics Pregame Huddle (MLEE)

## USA WOMEN'S SEVENS AT THE TOKYO OLYMPICS (2020/2021)

**DELAYED BY THE COVID-19 PANDEMIC, THE** Tokyo **2020** Olympics took place July 29-31, 2021 marking the second Olympic appearance for Rugby Sevens.

USA Rugby named a 15-player squad led by head coach Chris Brown, featuring a blend of veterans and promising new talent. Abby Gustaitis and Kristen Thomas served as co-captains, while Olympians Lauren Doyle and Alev Kelter returned for their second Games.

Ten of the twelve starting players were first-time Olympians, including standout Ariana Ramsey, who had impressed at the 2019 Pan Am Games, where the U.S. won silver.

The U.S. team finished sixth overall losing a tough fifth place match to Australia 17-7.

| ⊛ | OLYMPICS | ⊛ | 2020 / 2021 |

## 2020/21 OLYMPIC ROSTER

KAYLA CANETT-OCA
LAUREN DOYLE
CHETA EMBA
ABBY GUSTAITIS (C)
NICOLE HEAVIRLAND
ALEV KELTER
KRISTI KIRSHE
ILONA MAHER
JORDAN MATYAS
ARIANA RAMSEY
NAYA TAPPER
KRISTEN THOMAS (C)

ROB CAIN (HEAD COACH)

## USA WOMEN'S SEVENS AT THE PARIS OLYMPICS 2024

### THE HEROES WE NEEDED.

At the 2024 Paris Olympics, the U.S. Women's Rugby Sevens team made history by winning their first-ever Olympic medal—bronze—in a thrilling 19–14 victory over Australia.

The team, led by Emilie Bydwell, the first woman to be an Olympic head coach, featured a powerful mix of veteran leaders and first-time Olympians. Returning players like Alev Kelter, Kristen Thomas, Kristie Kirshe and Lauren Doyle provided critical experience, while rising stars such as Ariana Ramsey and Naya Tapper brought energy and explosive scoring ability to the roster. "*Since taking charge of the Eagles in 2021, Bydwell has established herself as a pioneer in rugby sevens and a true tour de force on the training field. In 2023 she was the only woman holding a head coach role on the HSBC SVNS Series.*

"*Ahead of the new HSBC SVNS Series getting underway at the end of 2024 in Dubai, Bydwell is now one of six female head coaches following the appointments of Jocelyn Barrieau (Canada), Crystal Kaua (Brazil), Giselle Mather (Great Britain), Yuka Kanematsu (Japan) and Maria Ribera (Spain), as other nations look to encourage the same success as the USA. 'It is just so special to have had such an influx of female leaders in the game,' she said. 'It's not just special for us but for the players. They may not know how much it means to them, but the fact that they can genuinely see this as a career path for them moving forward and to feel like they have people that understand them and what they've been through is important. It was a monumental moment to kick off with 50 per cent of the World Series coaches being women.' The World Series is competitive, we all want to win with our teams, but it's also a pretty lonely place to be a head coach of a World Series team. 'At the end of the day you're the only one that understands what it is like to be fully accountable. We can be competitive and still try to create that community, because I think if you don't find people like that, it can be pretty hard.'*" (Joe Harvey, RugbyPass 2024)

**Emilie Bydwell**

"*You can only truly create a high performance environment if that is also coupled with this idea of safety, love and care. "I think trying to break down that barrier of trying to cultivate love in the environment, you're trying to cultivate this really strong connection that transcends being on the field.*" (Emilie Bydwell)

 **2024**

**Lauren Doyle**

**Naya Tapper**

**Alena Olsen**

**Alev Kelter**

**Spiff Sedrick**

**Ariana Ramsey**

**Ilona Maher**

**Kayla Canett**

**Kristi Kirshe**

**Sammy Sullivan**

**Sarah Levy**

**Steph Rovetti**

**Kris Thomas**

**Nicole Heavirland**

USA Rugby's Olympic campaign was built on years of rising competitiveness. Before the pandemic, the team had closed out 2019 ranked number two in the world, earning five medals in six tournaments—their strongest World Series performance ever.

The medal win in Paris was more than just a podium finish—it sparked a national surge in interest for women's rugby, especially among high school and youth athletes, many were newly inspired to take up the sport and gave a much needed boost to teams that had been previously depleted by COVID.

Ilona Maher emerged as one of the most recognizable faces in American rugby during the 2020s. A powerhouse on the field and a charismatic force off the field, Maher used her Olympic appearances and viral TikTok fame to blend elite performance with her bold personality. Her advocacy for body positivity, mental health, and visibility for women in contact sports turned her into a 2025 ESPY Award winner and global icon.

**Ilona Maher Celebrates Bronze Medal Victory**

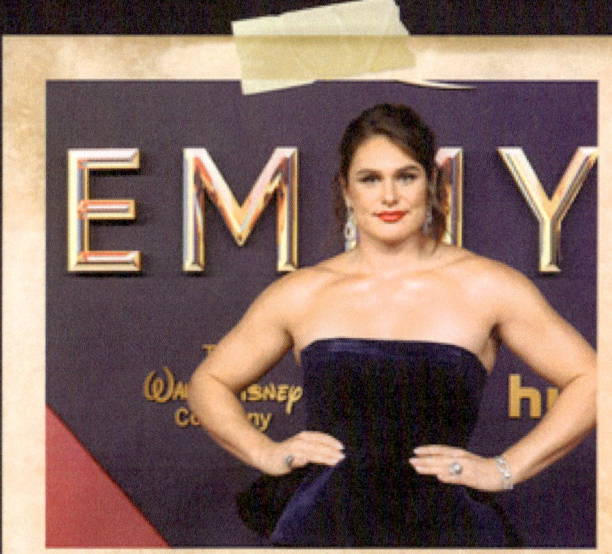

**Ilona Maher on the Red Carpet at the Emmys**

BEAST. *BEAUTY.* BRAINS.

Sports Illustrated

SWIMSUIT

SPECIAL DIGITAL COVER

*Ilona* MAHER

**U.S. Women's National Rugby Team Olympic Bronze Medalist**

PHOTOGRAPHED BY BEN WATTS

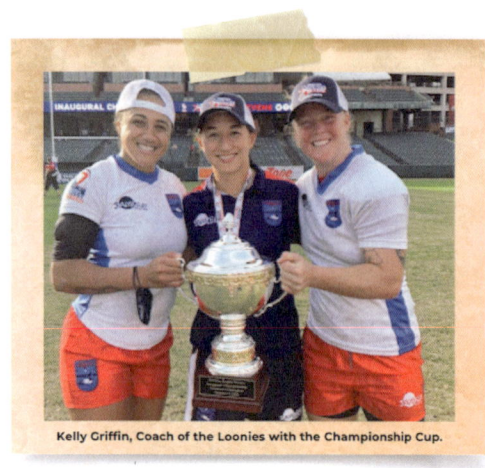

Kelly Griffin, Coach of the Loonies with the Championship Cup.

PR Sevens - Experts

## PREMIER RUGBY SEVENS

**PREMIER RUGBY SEVENS (PR7S) LAUNCHED** on October 9, 2021, debuting as a gender-equitable league with six men's and four women's teams. The Loonies, led by Olympian Kelly Griffin, won the inaugural women's championship.

In 2022, the league expanded to a three-stop circuit, introduced the concept of franchises—each with a men's and women's team—and launched the United Championship. The women's trophy was renamed the Kathy Flores Cup, honoring a legend of the game, and USA stars like Naya Tapper, Alev Kelter, and Abby Gustaitis joined the league.

By 2023, PR7s grew to a five-tournament, two-conference structure, adding the Golden State Retrievers and Pittsburgh Steel Toes, while also welcoming back the Texas Team and New York Locals—now with women's squads. New Zealand's Ruby Tui and other Black Ferns joined the competition, adding global star power.

With the 2024 Olympics shaping the rugby calendar, PR7s shifted its season and hosted a landmark All-Star Weekend on October 22, 2024, featuring the USA Women's and Men's Sevens teams versus PR7s All-Stars. Olympians Kelly Griffin and Sammy Sullivan led the women's All-Star team, closing out a transformative first era for PR7.

PR Sevens - Loonies

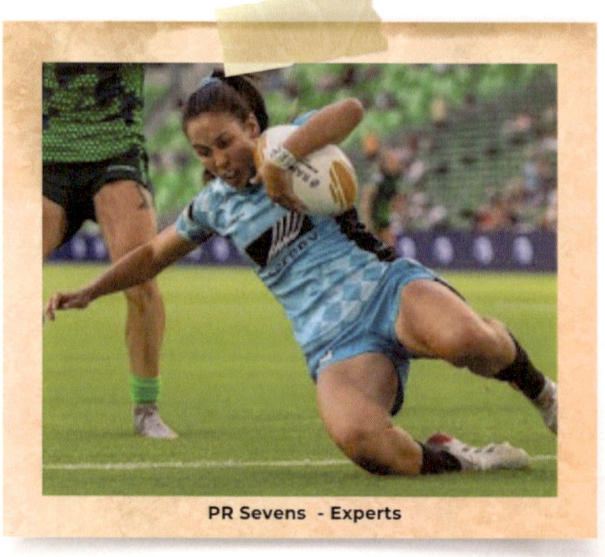

PR Sevens - Experts

## WPL & WER

**FOUNDED IN 2009, THE WOMEN'S PREMIER**
League (WPL), was a national, amateur model that
while producing exceptional talent was financially
difficult to sustain. In 2025 the WPL morphed into
Women's Elite Rugby (WER) the first U.S. women's
professional 15s league.

**Berkeley All Blues vs Twin Cities Amazons - Bill English**

# WPL Champions

| 2020 | 2021 | 2022 | 2023 | 2024 |
|------|------|------|------|------|
| No Winner* | No Winner* | Berkeley All Blues | Colorado Grey Wolves | Colorado Grey Wolves |
| | | Beantown | Berkeley All Blues | Berkeley All Blues |

*No Championship Due to COVID-19

**Oregon Sports Union vs Berkeley All Blues - Bill English**

2023 Colorado GreyWolves

2023 WPL National Championships Runner Ups - Beantown

# WER FOUNDATIONAL FIVE

Led by Jessica Hammond-Graf and Katherine Aversano, WER featured six teams with rosters of up to thirty athletes. The league features general managers, paid coaches, compensation for players' medical and travel expenses, and the aspiration of salaries for players.

## WER FOUNDATIONAL FIVE
### BAY

OLIVIA BERNADEL-HUEY
ELENA EDWARDS
CELINE LIULAMAGA
JADE MCGRATH
ROXELLE THOMAS

**Bay Breakers
(Lodi, CA)**

## WER FOUNDATIONAL FIVE
### DENVER

ERICA COULIBALY
RACHEL EHRECKE
MCKENZIE HAWKINS
MAYA LEARNED
TAHNA WILFLEY

**Denver Onyx
(Glendale, CO)**

## WER FOUNDATIONAL FIVE
### NEW YORK

ADRIANA CASTILLO
MISHA GREEN-YOTTS
MATILDA KOCAJ
CONGETTA OWENS
JENN SALOMON-CLAYTON

**New York Exiles
(Mount Vernon, NY)**

## WER FOUNDATIONAL FIVE
### BOSTON

CASSIDY BARGELL
YEJA DUNN
EMILY HENRICH
AKWELEY OKINE
PAIGE STATHOPOULOS

**Boston Banshees
(Quincy, MA)**

## WER FOUNDATIONAL FIVE
### CHICAGO

ANABEL DIAZ
EMMA FARNAN
CIENNA JORDAN
BETTY NGUYEN
KADIE SANFORD

**Chicago Tempest
(Evanston, IL)**

## WER FOUNDATIONAL FIVE
### TWIN CITIES

EMERSON ALLEN
MARISA HALL
ABBEY JACOBS
KATRINA NUNES
TATYANA REED

**Twin Cities Gemini
(Eagan, MN)**

BRAATEN

COLBRIDGE

CHOBOT

MAQUIEIRA

RUIZ

STOLBA

The Denver Onyx beat the New York Exiles 53-13 to win the inaugural WER Championship. Onyx flanker Talia Brody was named the MVP of the first Championship. Talia, played for the U.S. in the 2025 World Cup (as well as assorted other teams in Spain, New Zealand and England). The loose forward signed with the Loughborough Lightning for the 2025-26 Premier Women's Rugby season.

**Top:** *2025 WER Coaches*
**Right:** *Talia Brody, WER Championship MVP*

*Kitt Ruiz Wagner, Head Coach Boston Banshees*

**Chicago Lions 2023 National 7's Champions**

**2024 D2 Champions Tampa Bay Krewe**

## SENIOR CLUB

**WITH A STRUCTURE UNIQUELY AMERICAN,** senior club rugby remains the cornerstone of women's rugby development and sustainability in the United States. What began in the early 1970s with just a handful of pioneering teams has grown into a nationwide network of more than 1,200 clubs, representing over five decades of continuous growth and community leadership.

Women's rugby clubs can now be found in virtually every major city and countless towns across the country, serving as the primary entry point for adult athletes and a crucial bridge between collegiate, elite, and national team pathways. These clubs are not only competitive entities but also community institutions—recruiting new players, developing future coaches and referees, and sustaining the culture and traditions of the game.

Unlike in many countries where rugby is centralized through provincial or professional structures, the U.S. model is built on local club leadership. Clubs are member-run and often self-funded, reflecting a deeply rooted spirit of volunteerism, community ownership, and player-led growth. This decentralized structure has allowed the women's game to expand rapidly and organically, adapting to the unique geography and demographics of the United States.

Today, the U.S. women's club system spans multiple levels of play—from social and developmental clubs, to highly competitive Division 1 and Division 2 leagues, and the Women's Elite Rugby (WER) and PR7's, which represents the highest level of domestic competition. Many of the country's most accomplished Eagles have emerged from club programs, underscoring the central role clubs continue to play in the national team pipeline.

As the global game becomes more professional and the international calendar expands, the strength, resilience, and reach of the U.S. club structure remains a powerful asset—one that continues to anchor the sport's past, present, and future.

73 year old KO Onufry (far left), one of the founders of Beantown and one of the first U.S. players (1987) continues to play for the Old Girls. Here she confers with her daughter, Skyler (right) at the 2023 Can Am Tournament

**KO Onufry & Skyler**

**2020 Tampa Bay Krewe**

**2021 Seattle Saracens**

**2022 Washington Athletic Club**

**Austin Women's 7's**

**2024 Portland ME**

**2024 NOVA**

## USA Club Rugby XVs Champions: DI

**2020**
No Winner*

**2021**
No Winner*

**2022**
NOVA

**2023**
San Diego Surfers

**2024**
NOVA

*No Championship Due to COVID-19

Colorado Grey Wolves

NOVA

Utah Vipers

**2024 NOVA Women (Jackie Finlan)**

**2024 Scion (Jackie Finlan)**

## USA Club Rugby 7s Champions

**2020**
No Winner*

**2021**
Scion

**2022**
Scion

**2023**
Chicago Lions

**2024**
Scion

Life West

Washington Athletic Club

Camp Pendleton

Chicago Lions

*No Championship Due to COVID-19

## USA Club Rugby XVs Champions: DII

**2020**
No Winner*

**2021**
No Winner*

**2022**
Providence

**2023**
Knoxville Minx

**2024**
Tampa Bay Krewe

*No Championship Due to COVID-19

Knoxville Minx

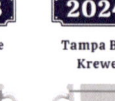
Severn River

Phoenixville White Horse

**Providence Women vs New York**

2023 Knoxville Minx

## YOUTH & HIGH SCHOOL

**USA YOUTH & HIGH SCHOOL RUGBY (USA YHS)** played a central role in the expansion of youth and high school rugby in the United States. In 2024, the organization surpassed 50,000 total registrations, including a 19% increase in female participation from the 2022/23 to 2023/24 season. The US Rugby Foundation supported this momentum through funding and outreach. Ongoing efforts like the "A Ball 4 All" program supplied 2,000 free rugby balls annually to youth and high school teams in need.

USA Youth & High School Rugby (USA YHS)

Doylestown Dragons Youth HS Karen Rosenburg

Catholic Memorial HS (Koenig Photo)

Fallbrook High School
(photo by Jackie Finlan)

Summit High School Girls

St. Francis High School
(photo by Jackie Finlan)

## THE COLLEGE GAME
## (NIRA, NCR, CRAA)

**THE BANKRUPTCY OF USA RUGBY IN 2021 AND** subsequent legal battles, dramatically reshaped the collegiate rugby landscape, ushering in a period of fragmentation and competition among multiple governing bodies. In the absence of a single, centralized structure, three major organizations emerged to stake their claim over collegiate rugby, each with distinct missions, membership bases, and championship pathways.

National Collegiate Rugby (NCR) quickly became the dominant force, absorbing roughly 85% of women's collegiate club programs. Under the leadership of Women's Director Angela Smarto, NCR invested heavily in building a robust competition framework, elevating the standard of play and visibility through well-organized regional and national championships in both 15s and 7s. Their focus on accessibility and strong event management has made NCR the largest and most influential of the three bodies.

Meanwhile, the National Intercollegiate Rugby Association (NIRA)—the only body operating under the NCAA umbrella—represents a smaller number of programs but attracts many of the nation's top-tier athletes. These teams are fully funded varsity programs with professionalized support structures, positioning NIRA as the most elite collegiate competition environment in the country.

The third major organizing body, USA Rugby's College Rugby Association of America (CRAA), retained oversight of a smaller number of D1 universities, particularly concentrated in the Pacific and West regions. CRAA maintains traditional ties to the national governing body and provides competitive opportunities for established collegiate programs with strong rugby traditions.

The resulting structure is both vibrant and fragmented: three governing bodies, multiple competitive pathways, and a crowded calendar of national championships, each crowning their own champion. While this decentralization has spurred innovation and expanded playing opportunities, it has also left players, fans, and stakeholders alike asking the same question: *"Who truly is the best in the nation?"*

National Intercollegiate Rugby Association (NIRA) is the governing body for NCAA women's rugby programs in the United States.

### NIRA National XVs Champions: D1

| 2020 | 2021 | 2022 | 2023 | 2024 | 2025 |
| No Winner* | Dartmouth College | Dartmouth College | Harvard University | Harvard University | Harvard University |
| | U.S. Military Academy | Dartmouth College | Dartmouth College | Dartmouth College | Dartmouth College |

*No Championship Due to COVID-19

### *NIRA National XVs Champions: D1*

| | |
|---|---|
| 2020 | *Canceled Due to COVID* |
| 2021 | Dartmouth College v U.S. Military Academy |
| 2022 | Dartmouth College v Harvard University |
| 2023 | Harvard University v Dartmouth College |
| 2024 | Harvard University v Dartmouth College |
| 2025 | Harvard University v Dartmouth College |

Dartmouth – NIRA D1 Champs 2021

Harvard – NIRA D1 Champs 2024

### NIRA National XVs Champions: D2

| 2021 | American International College v West Chester University |
| 2022 | Davenport University v Lander University |
| 2023 | Queens University v Davenport University |
| 2024 | American International College v Davenport University |
| 2025 | |

### NIRA National XVs Champions: D3

| 2021 | Bowdoin College v University of New England |
| 2022 | Bowdoin College v University of New England |
| 2023 | Bowdoin College v Adrian College |
| 2024 | Bowdoin College v University of New England |
| 2025 | Bowdoin College v University of New England |

## NIRA National XVs Champions: D2

| 2021 | 2022 | 2023 | 2024 | 2025 |
|------|------|------|------|------|
| American International College | Davenport University | Queens University | American International College | |
| West Chester University | Lander University | Davenport University | Davenport University | |

## NIRA National XVs Champions: D3

| 2021 | 2022 | 2023 | 2024 | 2025 |
|------|------|------|------|------|
| Bowdoin College | Bowdoin College | Bowdoin College | Bowdoin College | Bowdoin College |
| University of New England | University of New England | Adrian College | Davenport University | University of New England |

University of Michigan

University of Oregon

National Collegiate Rugby (NCR) is the largest governing body for college rugby in the United States, supporting national championships for various levels of competition, including small colleges, Division II, and Division I men's and women's programs. NCR was previously known as the National Small College Rugby Organization (NSCRO) but changed its name to better reflect its mission of serving all collegiate rugby programs, regardless of size.

### *NCR National XVs Champions: D1*

2020   *Canceled due to COVID*
2021   Life U. Dev. v Northern Iowa
2022   Univ of Michigan v Notre Dame College
2023   Univ of Michigan v Notre Dame College
2024   Wheeling University v Southern Nazarene University
2025

### **NCR National XVs Champions: D1**

| 2020 | 2021 | 2022 | 2023 | 2024 | 2025 |
|------|------|------|------|------|------|
| No Winner* | Life University | University of Michigan | University of Michigan | Wheeling University | |
| | Northern Iowa | Notre Dame College | Notre Dame College | Southern Nazarene | |

*No Championship Due to COVID-19

### NCR National XVs Champions: D2

2020   *Canceled due to COVID*
2021   *Canceled due to COVID*
2022   UW Eau Claire v Marquette University
2023   UW Eau Claire v Vassar College
2024   Vassar College v UW Eau Claire
2025

### NSCRO (Small College) National XVs Champions: D2

2020   South Dakota vs Univ Chicago
2021   Wayne State University vs SUNY Cortland
2022   Endicott College vs Lee
2023   St. Bonaventure vs UW-Platteville
2024
2025

USA Rugby fields the College Rugby Association of America (CRAA) which includes a number of Men's D1A and Women's D1 Elite—along with Men's D1AA, Women's D1 and Women's D2. In summer of 2025 USA Rugby announced they will allow CRAA teams to compete in NCR championships events.

### NCR National XVs Champions: D2

| 2020 | 2021 | 2022 | 2023 | 2024 | 2025 |
|------|------|------|------|------|------|
| No Winner* | No Winner* | UW Eau Claire | UW Eau Claire | Vassar College | |
| | | Marquette University | Vassar College | UW Eau Claire | |

*No Championship Due to COVID-19

### NSCRO (Small College) National XVs Champions: D2

| 2020 | 2021 | 2022 | 2023 | 2024 |
|------|------|------|------|------|
| South Dakota | Wayne State University | Endicott College | St. Bonaventure | |
| University of Chicago | SUNY Cortland | Lee | UW Platteville | |

**UW – EAU CLAIRE – 2022**
**(Jackie Finlan)**

**University of Michigan – 2023**
**(Jackie Finlan)**

2024 Life University (photo Doctor Hawk)

2024 Lindenwood University

2024 UMichigan, Ember Larson

2023 Stanford University

2024 Northeastern University

## CRAA D1A (Elite) National XVs Champions

2020    *Canceled due to COVID*
2021    Lindenwood University
2022    Lindenwood University
2023    Lindenwood University
2024    Life University
2025    Lindenwood University

## CRAA D1 (Elite) National 7s Champions

2020    *Canceled due to COVID*
2021    Lindenwood University
2022    U.S. Naval Academy
2023    Northeastern University (Fall) / Stanford University (Spring)
2024    Harvard University
2025    Dartmouth College

## CRAA DI National XVs Champions

2020    *Canceled due to COVID*
2021    U.S. Naval Academy
2022    U.S. Naval Academy (fall) BYU (spring)
2023    Western Washington State University
2024    Stanford University
2025    Stanford University

## CRAA DII National XVs Champions

2020    *Canceled due to COVID*
2021    Vassar College
2022    Vassar College (fall)/ Claremont College (spring)
2023    Cal Poly San Luis Obispo
2024    Vassar College
2025    Cal Poly San Luis Obispo

**2021** Howard University women's rugby team becomes the first historically black college (HBCU) women's team.

## CRAA D1A (Elite) National XVs Champions

| 2020 | 2021 | 2022 | 2023 | 2024 | 2025 |
|---|---|---|---|---|---|
| No Winner* | Lindenwood University | Lindenwood University | Life University | Lindenwood University | Lindenwood University |
| Life University | Life University | Lindenwood University | Life University | Life University |

*No Championship Due to COVID-19

**2025 DII 15s Champs Vassar College**

**2021 Howard University**

## COACHES, REFEREES, ADMINS

**THE 2020S HAVE FEATURED AN OUTSTANDING** group of women in leadership positions.

**Anne Barry:** In 2025, Anne was appointed as the first woman CEO of the U.S. Rugby Foundation (USRF), marking another milestone in her decades-long leadership within American rugby. A trailblazer both on and off the field, Anne was also the first woman to serve as President and Treasurer of USA Rugby (USAR)—roles in which she guided the organization through one of its most critical periods of transformation. When Anne assumed the role of Treasurer, USA Rugby was operating with minimal infrastructure and burdened by nearly $4 million in debt. Through strategic financial oversight, she stabilized the organization, increased revenues, and built significant financial reserves—funds that would

*Anne Barry*

later help underwrite major international events in the United States. As President of USA Rugby, Anne spearheaded a period of remarkable growth and modernization. Under her leadership, rugby achieved formal acceptance by the U.S. Olympic Committee, laying the groundwork for future Olympic participation. She also championed the launch of a national youth rugby development program and played a key role in the creation of the North American West Indies Rugby Association (NAWIRA), expanding regional collaboration and competition. Anne was also a fierce advocate for the women's game, increasing funding to the USA Women's National Teams and introducing the Club and Individual Participation Program (CIPP)—a groundbreaking registration and insurance system that remains a cornerstone of rugby governance in the U.S.

Widely regarded as one of the most effective leaders in USA Rugby history, Anne's influence extended beyond USAR. She served as General Manager of the USA Women's National Team (2002–2006), President of the Minnesota Rugby Union, a member of the Women's Premier League Governing Council, and a USRF board member prior to becoming CEO. In 2024, Anne received a Lifetime Achievement Award from the USWRF, recognizing her visionary leadership, fiscal stewardship, and unwavering commitment to growing the game for future generations.

**Jamie Burke:** Jamie Burke is widely regarded as one of the greatest tighthead props of her generation and a foundational figure in modern American women's rugby. Over the course of her distinguished international career, she earned 51 caps, represented the U.S. in three Rugby World Cups, and captained the USA Women's National Team (WNT) during the 2010 tournament. Her exceptional skill, leadership, and physicality earned her a place on both World Rugby's (IRB) Dream Team and the World's Greatest

*Jamie Burke*

15s Team, cementing her status as one of the sport's all-time greats. Jamie's excellence on the field has been recognized with some of the highest honors in the game. She was inducted into the U.S. Rugby Hall of Fame in 2020 and received the Kathy Flores Lifetime Achievement Award from the USWRF in 2024—a testament not only to her playing career but also to her lasting influence as a leader, mentor, and coach.

Off the field, Jamie has been a driving force in the development of the women's game. She served as a longtime Assistant Coach with the USA WNT 15s, contributing to the next generation of elite front-row talent. At the grassroots level, she coached the Colorado Girls High School All-State Team, helping grow the sport at its foundation. She also guided the Colorado Gray Wolves Women's and Youth programs, leading the Gray Wolves to back-to-back WPL Championships in 2023 and 2024. In addition to her coaching achievements, Jamie currently serves as the Director of Rugby for the Women's Elite Rugby (WER), where she continues to shape the future of high-performance women's rugby in the United States. Known for her fierce competitiveness, tactical intelligence, and unwavering commitment to excellence, Jamie Burke's legacy is that of a player, leader, and architect of the modern women's game.

**Amanda Cox:** Amanda has been a driving force behind the growth and professionalization of women's refereeing in the United States. A respected leader and tireless advocate, she has served as the Referee Manager for the Women's Premier League (WPL) since 2018, helping to build and strengthen the referee development pipeline at the highest level of domestic competition.

She is a USA Rugby Referee Coach, a World Rugby Referee Educator, and made history as the first woman in the U.S. to earn Level 2 Coach of Match Officials certification. In 2023, she served as the World Rugby Referee Manager for the Pacific Four Series, further solidifying her role as a trusted leader on the international stage.

*Amanda Cox*

Amanda currently works as a Television Match Official (TMO) for Major League Rugby (MLR)—a demanding position that requires hours of game film analysis and split-second decision-making to ensure accuracy and fairness at the professional level. Known for her technical expertise, clarity under pressure, and commitment to excellence, she is a mentor to many referees across the country.

Off the field, Amanda is a founding member of the Raleigh Venom Rugby Club, a powerhouse program and four-time national champion. Her leadership and her willingness to 'be everywhere' both as a referee developer and as a community builder, has helped elevate opportunities for women in officiating and strengthened the foundation of women's rugby in the U.S.

**Emilie Bydwell**: Emilie made history as the first woman to serve as Head Coach of an Olympic Rugby Team, a milestone that reflects her exceptional leadership and deep roots in the game. A two-sport athlete at Brown University, where she excelled in both ice hockey and rugby, Emilie quickly distinguished herself as one of the brightest talents in the college game. In 2009, she was named USA Rugby College Player of the Year after leading Brown to a Final Four finish at the D1 Collegiate Championships. A versatile and powerful player, Emilie represented the U.S. Women's National Team in both 15s and 7s, including at the 2010 Women's Rugby World Cup, as well as the 2013 Rugby World Cup Sevens, where the USA finished third, and the 2014 Women's Rugby World Cup 15s. She was one of the first athletes selected to the 7s residency program, laying the foundation for the professionalization of the women's game in the U.S. After an impressive playing career, Emilie transitioned seamlessly into coaching. She was named USA Rugby Coach of the Year in 2016 and went on to lead three consecutive USA Rugby Club 7s National Championship teams—first with Atavus Academy in 2017, and then with the San Diego Surfers in 2018 and 2019. From 2018 to 2021, Emilie served as USA Rugby's Director of Women's High Performance, playing a critical role in shaping elite player pathways, strengthening the national team program, and expanding opportunities for women at the highest level. Her appointment as Head Coach of the U.S. Olympic Women's Rugby Sevens Team represents not only a personal achievement but also a landmark moment for women in sport leadership.

**Martha Daines:** Martha has been a constant presence in American rugby for nearly four decades. From her first playing days in the 1980s to her current leadership role in the U.S. Women's High Performance Pathway, there hasn't been a single season in 37 years without Martha on the pitch. She began her playing career as a dynamic #8 with the Chicago Women before joining the Minnesota Valkyries, where she became a cornerstone of both the club and the Midwest Select

*Martha Daines*

*Erin Kennedy*

Side, ultimately earning a place with the U.S. Women's National Team. Martha's coaching journey began in 1997 at Macalester College, followed by a highly successful tenure at the University of Minnesota (2000–2007) and with both the Minnesota Valkyries and the Midwest Select Side. Her commitment to coaching excellence and player development soon led to national opportunities. She joined USA Rugby's high-performance programs in 2000 as an assistant coach with the U23 team and remained deeply involved for over a decade. As the program evolved—transitioning from U23s to USA "A" to Collegiate All-Americans—Martha rose to become head coach, playing a central role in identifying and developing future national team talent. From 2015 to 2017, she served as an assistant coach for the Senior Women's National Team, before returning to the pathway as director and head coach of the USA U18s in 2018, further solidifying her legacy as a builder of future Eagles. In 2020, she was appointed manager of USA Rugby's Women's High-Performance Pathway, a role she held through 2025, overseeing

talent identification, coach development, and strategic growth of the women's game.

Beyond her on-field leadership, Martha has been a USA Rugby and World Rugby coach educator and trainer since 1999, mentoring countless coaches and influencing the shape of women's rugby at every level. A USWRF Lifetime Achievement Award winner, Martha's 37-year commitment as a player, coach, and educator stands as one of the most enduring contributions to women's rugby in the United States.

**Erin Kennedy:** Erin is a leading figure in global rugby development and a tireless advocate for growing the women's and youth game. She currently serves as the Chief Executive Officer (CEO) and Co-Founder of Girls Rugby Inc., an organization dedicated to empowering girls through sport and leadership development. She also holds the role of Regional Development Manager for Rugby Americas North (RAN), where she leads strategic initiatives to expand rugby across North America and the Caribbean. Founded in 2018,

Girls Rugby Inc. was built on the belief that rugby can be a powerful platform for personal growth, confidence, and community. Under Erin's leadership, the organization has expanded into dozens of communities across the United States, providing accessible, non-contact rugby programs for girls ages 7–14. Through a focus on leadership development and mentorship, the program has reached thousands of participants, establishing one of the most successful and visible youth girls' rugby initiatives in the country.

Erin's career reflects a deep commitment to grassroots growth and international collaboration. She has held key development and management positions with both USA Rugby and Rugby Canada, where she helped build foundational programs such as Rookie Rugby and Try on Rugby, introducing tens of thousands of new players to the sport. Her international impact expanded through her work with the North American Caribbean Rugby Association, where she focused on youth and women's rugby development in the Caribbean and Mexico, creating sustainable pathways for emerging unions. Erin also worked with the International Olympic Committee (IOC) in Switzerland, coordinating youth engagement initiatives for the Youth Olympic Games and strengthening rugby's role on the Olympic stage. A World Rugby Trainer, Erin has been instrumental in educating and mentoring coaches and administrators around the world. As a player, she competed with multiple teams both in the U.S. and abroad, and as a coach, she has worked extensively at the youth, high school, and adult club levels, using the sport as a vehicle for empowerment and inclusion. Through her leadership, Erin has helped shape the landscape of youth and women's rugby in the Americas and beyond. Her work with Girls Rugby Inc., RAN, and international development bodies has made her one of the most influential development leaders in modern rugby, leaving a lasting impact on future generations of players and leaders.

*Danita Knox*

**Danita Knox:** Danita Knox is a pioneer, visionary, and driving force behind the growth and advancement of women's rugby in the United States. She is the Founder, Board Chair, and President of the U.S. Women's Rugby Foundation (USWRF)—an organization she established in 2005 to provide resources, advocacy, and leadership for the women's game. Nearly two decades later, her strategic vision and unwavering commitment continue to shape the future of rugby for women and girls nationwide.

Danita's rugby journey began in 1985 at Clemson University, where she first picked up a ball at age 18. She quickly developed into a formidable competitor and leader on the pitch. From 1995 to 2005, she played with the Atlanta Harlequins Women's Rugby Football Club, helping transform the team from a strong regional side into a perennial national contender. During this time, she also represented USA Rugby South All-Stars (1998–2004), competing in the prestigious Inter-Territorial Tournaments that helped define the national competitive structure of the era. While her contributions as a player were significant, Danita's greatest legacy is her leadership. She has spent more than two decades advancing the game through governance, strategic development, and advocacy. She served on the USA Rugby Board of Directors from 2004–2013, where she led the TU/LAU Committee, which designed and implemented the Geographic Union structure—a major organizational reform that still shapes the governance of the game today. Her leadership extended deeply into regional and national roles. She served as President of the Georgia Rugby Union (2002–2012), Women's Director and Vice President of USA Rugby South (1999–2013), and has been a trusted advisor to the Women's Rugby Coaches and Referees Association (WRCRA) since 2017.

Through USWRF, Danita has championed investment in women's rugby, funding grants, leadership initiatives, and national programs to support players, coaches, referees, and administrators. Under her leadership, USWRF has become a powerful force for gender equity and opportunity in rugby, elevating the visibility and impact of women in the sport. In 2025, in recognition of her extraordinary impact on the game, Danita Knox was inducted into the USWRF Hall of Fame. Her legacy is one of vision, persistence, and transformation—a testament to how one leader's dedication can build lasting pathways for future generations.

**Ilona Maher:** Ilona has become one of the most recognizable faces in rugby, both on and off the field. In 2024, she became the most followed rugby player on Instagram, captivating fans with her exceptional athleticism, sharp wit, charisma, and outspoken advocacy for body positivity. Following a bronze medal win at the 2024 Olympics, Ilona showcased her versatility beyond sport, competing on *Dancing with the Stars*. With no prior dance experience, she and her

*Ilona Maher*

partner finished second, impressing viewers with her dedication and athleticism. That same year, she was featured in the Sports Illustrated Swimsuit Edition, and in 2025, she won the ESPY Award for Breakout Athlete of the Year. Ilona's rugby journey began at the age of 17 with the South Burlington School Rugby Football Club in Vermont. She went on to play center for Quinnipiac University, helping the team capture three National Intercollegiate Rugby Association (NIRA) championships. A three-time All-American, she was honored in 2017 with the prestigious MA Sorensen Award for outstanding contributions to U.S. women's rugby. Internationally, Ilona made her debut with the USA Rugby Sevens World Cup team in 2018 at a Women's SVNS tournament in Paris. She was selected for the 2020 and 2024 Olympic Games and the 2025 Women's Rugby World Cup 15s Team, cementing her status as one of the top female rugby players in the world. In 2024, she signed with the Bristol Bears in the Premiership Women's Rugby League, expanding her influence to the international club scene.

Today, Ilona is celebrated not only for her elite rugby talent but also as one of the most influential women in sport, inspiring a new generation of athletes through her performance, personality, and advocacy.

**Katherine Roche:** Kat is a trailblazing professional rugby referee whose career has redefined officiating in both 15s and Rugby Sevens. She was the head referee for the 2024 Olympic Women's Gold Medal match and served as a head referee at the 2025 Women's Rugby World Cup, cementing her status as one of the world's top-ranked referees. A member of the Texas Referees Union, Kat's rise has been extraordinary. She began as the youngest referee on the USA Rugby Referee National Panel, later becoming Chairman of the Texas Rugby Referee Association, and has steadily climbed the international ranks. In 2018, she officiated the Rugby Americas North (RAN) U19 Final between Mexico and USA South and, in 2019, worked matches in the Women's Super Series involving Canada, France, New Zealand, and England. That same year, she refereed the Women's Premier League Final and several Men's Premier Club matches. Kat's international experience includes serving as an Assistant Referee at the HSBC World Rugby Sevens Series and the Rugby World Cup Sevens in 2017 and 2018. She joined Major League Rugby (MLR) in 2019 as an assistant referee and, in 2021, became the first female lead referee in MLR history. In 2024, she refereed the opening Six Nations fixture between France and Ireland.

Beyond elite rugby, Kat is deeply committed to grassroots development. From 2018–2020, she coached Rookie Rugby Texas, introducing 3rd–5th graders to flag rugby. She also serves on the boards of the Texas Rugby Union and the Red River Competitions Committee, continuing to shape the future of rugby officiating in the U.S.

**Tamara Sheppard:** In 2023, Tamara Sheppard was appointed General Manager of Men's and Women's High Performance Rugby for USA Rugby. She joined

*Katherine Roche*

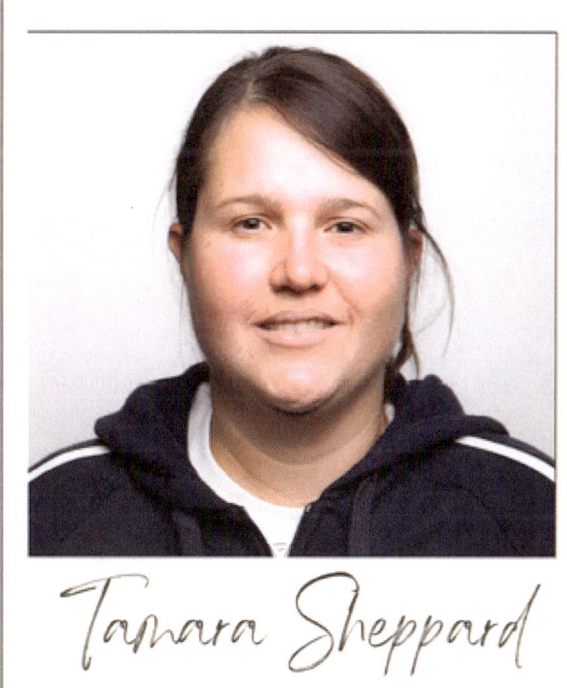

*Tamara Sheppard*

USAR after five years as High Performance Director with Swimming Australia, where she led world-class programs for both men and women. Tamara brought a wealth of experience in developing gold medal-caliber teams, implementing effective human resource practices, and providing strategic consulting for a variety of national sport governing bodies. She played a pivotal role in orchestrating Swimming Australia's most successful Olympic campaigns, culminating in the Tokyo 2021 Games. Her leadership in high-performance strategy proved invaluable to U.S. rugby, as the women's team captured a bronze medal at the 2024 Paris Olympics.

**Angela Smarto:** Smarto served as Women's Rugby Director for National Collegiate Rugby (NCR) and Commissioner of Division I & II rugby, where her leadership transformed the collegiate rugby landscape and established a new standard for national championship pathways. She personally recruited and oversaw approximately 85% of women's collegiate rugby teams, creating opportunities and visibility for players nationwide. Her pioneering work in administration has inspired numerous women administrators to seek her mentorship. In addition to her national level administrative roles, she was the Head Coach

Angela Smarto

at Robert Morris University for 10 years, an Executive officer and Collegiate Coordinator for the Allegheny Rugby Union, the President for the Pittsburgh Forge Rugby Club, and Assistant Coach for Allegheny Women's Select Side Program (2017-2022). Smarto was a standout player for Penn State from 2007-2012 and part of three, D1 National Championship teams with Penn State.

www.ingramcontent.com/pod-product-compliance
Lightning Source LLC
Chambersburg PA
CBRC090825120626
46547CB00008B/611

9 781968 548193